The Rise of the Gothic

THE RISE OF THE
GOTHIC

WILLIAM ANDERSON
Photography by CLIVE HICKS

Salem House

Salem, New Hampshire

The words for Jennifer: from W.A.
The photographs for Colleen: from C.H.

First published in the United States by
Salem House, 1985. A member of the
Merrimack Publishers' Circle, 47 Pelham
Road, Salem, New Hampshire 03079

Text © 1985 by William Anderson
Photographs © 1985 by Clive Hicks

This book was designed and produced by
John Calmann and King Ltd,
71 Gt Russell Street, London WC1B 3BN
Designed by Richard Foenander

ISBN 0–88162–109–9
Library of Congress Catalog Card
Number: 85–50494

Filmset by Fakenham Photosetting Ltd,
Fakenham, Norfolk
Printed in Hong Kong by Mandarin
Offset Ltd

Frontispiece Strasbourg. The presumed
self-portrait of Nicolaus Gerhaerts of
Leyden, a half-length sculpture from the
cathedral choir-stalls of 1467, now in the
Musée de l'oeuvre de Notre-Dame.

Contents

Acknowledgments 6

Introduction 7

Chapter 1   The Beginnings 9

Chapter 2   St-Denis, Sens and Chartres 25

Chapter 3   The Pointed Arch: people, patrons and masons 39

Chapter 4   Technology and the Spirit 55

Chapter 5   A New Image of Man 85

Chapter 6   The World of the Green Man 105

Chapter 7   The Angelic Orders and the Eternal Feminine 125

Chapter 8   The Drama of the Gothic 145

Chapter 9   Gothic Space 163

Chapter 10 The Prentice Pillar 182

Notes 200

Bibliography 204

Index 206

Acknowledgments

I have many debts of gratitude for the help I have received in the course of writing this book. The Trustees of the Nuffield Foundation gave a grant which enabled the Nuffield–Chelsea Curriculum Trust to release me from my work for part of the time in the later stages of the writing of the book and which also contributed substantially towards the cost of travel. I am grateful to Anthony Tomei, Assistant Director of the Nuffield Foundation, Kevin Keohane, Chairman of the Nuffield–Chelsea Curriculum Trust, and Paul Black, now Head of the Centre for Educational Studies, King's College, London, for their interest and support. I also acknowledge assistance from the Arts Council of Great Britain.

I owe much to Mark Cohen who has been godfather to the book and to his colleagues in Century-Hutchinson. Elisabeth Ingles of John Calmann & King has once again been my editor and I am grateful to her and to Jeremy Schonfield for their enthusiasm and hard work. Andrew Spiro read each chapter and gave me much help and useful criticism.

Many friends have given help and advice, among them Alan Caiger-Smith, Catherine Freeman, Pamela Gagliani, Rupert Gladstone, Jonathan Griffin, Anthony and Eliane Grigg, Marie-Claire Malle, Jennifer Moore, and Marina Warner. The Dean of Wells has very kindly allowed me to make use of his paper on the west front of Wells Cathedral.

I am grateful to the following publishers for permission to quote from or use copyright material: Princeton University Press for the passages on pp. 26–7, 28, 30–1, 62 and 131 from Erwin Panofsky, ed., trans., annot., *Abbot Suger: on the Abbey Church of St.-Denis and its Art Treasures*; sec. edn. by Gerda Panofsky-Soergel. Copyright 1946 by Princeton University Press, © renewed 1973, sec. edn. © 1979 by Princeton University Press; to David & Charles for the passage on p. 126 from *Grotesques and Gargoyles: Paganism in the Medieval Church* (1975) by Ronald Sheridan and Anne Ross; to Thames & Hudson for the plans on pages 13, 70, 83, 172 and 180 which are taken from *The Master Builders: Architecture in the Middle Ages*, a (1971) by John Harvey.

Clive Hicks and I are particularly grateful to the clergy and administrators of the numerous cathedrals, churches, and museums in the British Isles and many parts of Europe for permission to photograph and for other help. We would specially like to thank Mlle Nicole Weil of the French Embassy in London for providing us with a letter of introduction.

Our chief expression of thanks appears in our dedication.

W.A.

Introduction

The energy of art derives from emotion under the guidance of the creative imagination. In this book I have attempted to take the source of that energy into account and to describe its immense power in history when directed to positive and fruitful ends. It may therefore be read as a contribution to the study of civilization. Though it concentrates on the phenomenon of the rise of the Gothic style in a short period of the twelfth century, it also ranges over certain themes in the art and architectural features of the style that acted as constants, inspiring the creation of masterpieces up to the sixteenth century. When we look at a movement such as Gothic civilization which extends over several centuries, we find that certain of these constants are present as recurring images—as though they are abiding symbols directing currents of feeling and thought within the flow of time but themselves free of time. Therefore I have taken certain of these symbols such as the new image of man, the Green Man, the Eternal Feminine and tried to show not only how they were the means of reconciling conflicting elements in society and in the religious past of Europe but also how they are related to the greatest wonder of the Gothic churches—their spatial effects and their radiant spirituality.

The heritage of buildings left us by the Gothic Masters arouses love in us as much as wonder. The great cathedrals and churches are among the most visited and most cherished of all the past works of Western man. It has been said of them that they were the first vast monuments in all history to be built by free labour.[1] We recognize that spirit of freedom which was expressed in an architecture unexampled in its dynamism. It is a spirit that helped to form the western sense of individuality and is therefore mirrored in our present selves. As the supreme achievements of the technology of their time the great cathedrals exemplify man's new-found freedom to master and make more beautiful his environment. In their sculptures and other works of art they unveil the force within the creative imagination that is liberated when archetypal images within the dream life of humanity are brought to consciousness and undergo transformation through the practice of art. In their depictions of vegetation and the natural world they reveal a new freedom for the eye to observe and enjoy. In their multiplied spaces they reflect man's hard-won freedom to speculate and think, and in the exuberance of their decorations and in the smiles of their virgins and angels they express, not only the right to be happy, but the freedom and lightness of spirit that make happiness itself. The Gothic Masters taught Europe new ways in which to be happy. If there is one central thought to be taken from these pages it is the importance of the freedom of the creative imagination whether on the scale of the individual or of society, the freedom to experience and express 'the intercommunion between the inner being of things and the inner being of the human self'.[2]

CHAPTER 1

The Beginnings

The source of every civilization that has enriched the course of history is in the spirit of Man. The means by which each civilization has flourished and left its mark have depended on certain men and women turning in their need to the springs of consciousness and creation which they share at the deepest levels with all humanity. They are the interpreters of the dreams of their fellow men, the clear-sighted namers of the ruling symbols, the archetypes of power, whose raw energies must be purified and directed by the prayers and contemplations of the saint, by the courage and expressive capacities of the poet and the artist, and the rationality and speculative genius of the philosopher and the scientist.

The purpose of civilization is to conquer barbarism, which is the condition of living in a state of fear. A great civilization provides, on the scale of nations, the expression of love, a basis of security, the sharing of experience, and hope for this life and the next. It allows the development of talents that would languish in small enclosed societies preoccupied solely with self-preservation. Cicero's name for the higher pursuits of civilization was *humanitas*, a term that was familiar to the scholars of the Middle Ages[1] and one that centres all studies and skills on the fully developed nature of man.

Civilization may be seen as the application of conscious will to the amorphous energies of the human psyche, diverting those energies away from their dissipation in fear and war into peaceful and fruitful ends. The technology of a civilization has always been employed to develop methods of attack and defence for the preservation of society, in other words to provide security from physical fear, but true civilization deals with fear at the deeper levels of the mind. Technology, seen in this way, is, in the first place, a matter of the spirit.[2] Behind the social, political, and economic forces that dictate the life of humankind are the infinitely more powerful archetypal powers of the psyche, and it is by drawing these powers into the light of consciousness and giving them direction that the artist, the thinker, and the man of religion free us from the superstition, the fear, and the prejudices by which our lives are otherwise ruled.

The story of the rise of the Gothic starts at the transition point from one stage of civilization in the history of Western Christianity to another when, in the twelfth century, the first signs of the Gothic style appeared in the region surrounding Paris and began over the next hundred years to supersede the earlier Romanesque civilization in all parts of Catholic Europe. The monks and the architects who created Romanesque civilization in about AD 1000 had to cope with generations of terror caused both by the upheavals, migrations and invasions of the Dark Ages and by the psychic shock inflicted by the imposition of Christianity on the old religious beliefs of Northern Europe. Drawing on Roman models of the classical and early Christian periods (from which the name of the style derives) and on influences from Byzantium, they built massive stone churches which were castles of the spirit, as opposed to the stone castles of the new feudal

2   Amiens. The Gothic cathedral as the work of many generations: a view of the west front begun by Robert de Luzarches and finished up to the gallery between 1220 and 1236. The south tower and gallery were built by Pierre Largent after 1366 and the north tower was finished by Colart Brisset *c.* 1430.

overlords. The spirit of tenderness in which they often built and the desire to provide a refuge for the wounded soul are beautifully conveyed in these words from the Book of the Foundation of St Bartholomew the Great, a later Romanesque church begun in London by Henry I's jester Rahere in 1123.

> This spiritual house Almighty God shall inhabit and hallow it and glorify it; and His eyes shall be open and His ears intending on this house night and day; that the asker in it shall receive, the seeker shall find, and the ringer or knocker shall enter. Truly every soul converted, penitent of his sin, and in this place praying, in heaven graciously shall be heard; the seeker with perfect heart, for whatsoever tribulation, without doubt he shall find help; to them that with faithful desire knock at the door of the Spouse, assistant angels shall open the gates of heaven, receiving and offering to God the prayer and vows of faithful people.[3]

Such reassurance and comfort were given by thousands of churches, great and small, as the dwindled and indigent populations of Western Europe undertook the regeneration of their society in the course of the eleventh century. With their success in developing fallow and virgin lands, they created the surplus necessary for trade and civilization. Better communications and increase in trade led to the revival of city life on a scale unknown since Roman times. In its roots, the word civilization means the style of life of the *civitas*, the city; aided by the concentration of wealth in flourishing cities a fresh style was required that would signify the confidence of North-Western Europe in its new identity, free of the Mediterranean origins of the Romanesque, and that would make its own statement of the meaning of Christianity.

The achievement of the monks and architects who created Romanesque civilization is nothing short of heroic; it was in many ways greater than that of their successors in the Gothic style because they had to reinvent or rediscover so many techniques that had been lost. The range of possibilities within its architectural and sculptural styles was, however, too limited for the explosion of new thoughts and new feelings that erupted in the twelfth century, with the birth of scholastic philosophy and the rediscovery of the Eternal Feminine that was manifested in various forms such as Mariolatry and the lyrics of the troubadours. The sculptors of the Romanesque had also released the latent archetypal powers of the ancient gods and a new indigenous style was necessary to contain and reconcile these powers. This style was the Gothic, and one of the ways in which we shall delineate the history of Gothic civilization is through the dualisms between Christianity and the pagan past to which it brought unity and reconciliation. Yet another way is through the effect of great and abiding ideas that continued to give inspiration to the masters of the Gothic style over a period of four hundred years.

One of the signs of a new intellectual and aesthetic movement is an interest in the processes of creation, both on the scale of nature and of individual man. This may be seen in one of the many works that mark the transition from the Romanesque to the Gothic: the Tapestry of Creation, made in about 1100 and now displayed in the museum of the cathedral of Gerona in Catalonia (fig. 3).

The Tapestry of Creation, a large embroidered panel, depicts, in a roundel at the centre, God the Creator as a wise solemn young man with eyes of great authority, His hand raised in the blessing that begins the process of creation. Radiating from Him are the six days of creation in segments of unequal size, from the separation of the firmament to the

3 Gerona. The Tapestry of Creation, c. 1100, now in the cathedral sacristy.

making of Eve. The roundel of creation is set within a rectangle embroidered with a lively meander pattern; at the corners are winged angels seated on inflated goatskins from which the winds blow to the borders of the tapestry, where the labours of the months, the seasons of the year, and the works of time appear. The tapestry is embroidered in the dominant tones of earth colours and various greens so that it seems an evocation of the Catalan countryside, with the warm browns of its soil out of which rise the upright needles of the umbrella pines, bright green after the Tramontana has blown, and the darker hues of the lentisk and the cypresses.

The tapestry is a diagram of the Divine Imagination. It shows the entry of the divine creative power through mediating worlds of the spirit to the physical world of men and women. In its four major divisions it portrays, according to Neoplatonic philosophy, God, the eternally existing, the One, from whom radiates the whole of creation in essence, here shown as the six days of creation, not as a progression in time, but eternally present in the Nous or Divine Mind. The angels of the winds depict the action of the spirit, the *anima mundi* or soul of the world, beating down with its enlivening breath on the world of time in the outermost borders of physical life. These ideas were common ground to the meeting of Islam, Judaism, and Christianity in Spain and they are fundamental to the rise of Gothic civilization. Basing their studies on the Bible and writings of the Fathers and of later Christian authors, and on only a few surviving fragments of classical texts, including part of Plato's *Timaeus*, and the development of the Neoplatonic tradition in the writings of Dionysius the Areopagite and John Scotus Eriugena, the cathedral schools of Chartres and of Laon and the monks of the Abbey of St-Denis had for years been laying an essential basis for the new civilization.[4]

Since the early eleventh century the building of stone churches in the

4   Gerona. Guillem Boffill's nave vault, begun in 1416. This is the widest span encompassed by ribbed vaulting in the Middle Ages.

Romanesque style had become common to much of Western Europe. The transmission of Islamic architectural features such as the pointed arch from North Africa through Sicily, and events such as the capture of many Moslem craftsmen among the thousands of prisoners taken in 1064 at the siege of Barbastro (some 200 miles inland from Gerona), added greatly to the range of possibilities in Western Christian architecture.[5] It was when the creators of the philosophical foundation of the new civilization met architects and artists capable of appreciating the artistic significance of these ideas that Gothic civilization was born at St-Denis, Chartres, and Sens.

The architects who created the Gothic style were men of exceptional boldness and originality and they achieved something extraordinary. They were to form an international organization that for four hundred years, from about 1140 to 1540, trained through succeeding generations artists of genius who could maintain the standards of their art and at the same time develop it to suit the fashions and the requirements of their particular epoch. In this period they were the supreme masters of the applied sciences and technology, and because of the range of skills so many of them had at their command I have chosen to call them in general throughout the book the Gothic Masters, an honorific to which they would have been accustomed.

Another example from Gerona, the nave of the cathedral (fig. 4), provides an outstanding example of the continuity of their tradition. Here the choir, consisting of a chancel and two aisles, had been built in 1316. A hundred years later the architect Guillem Boffill was commissioned to rebuild the cathedral westwards; he wanted to construct a nave where the vaulting would be supported entirely by the exterior walls and their buttresses. As the vaulting would be 73 ft (23 m) across, the widest space vaulted in the Middle Ages without the interior support of piers, eleven other architects were consulted, seven of whom were against the project and four of whom were enthusiastically in favour. Guillem Boffill was upheld in his arguments by the cathedral canons and the nave stands faultlessly today to his credit and our pleasure. In his sworn deposition Boffill had said that the open single nave would have the advantage of more light and the canons, in accepting his proposal, picked up this point, saying it would 'refulge with greater clarity which is happier and more joyful'.[6] This might seem odd to a visitor accustomed to the great windows of northern Gothic churches because the windows of the nave are very high up and comparatively small in proportion to its size. What Boffill and the canons are both, in fact, describing is the quality of spiritual light that would be diffused about the vast uncluttered space, and here they show themselves part of a tradition that goes back to Abbot Suger and the rebuilding of St-Denis, the desire to create in stone and glass an interior expressing the Neoplatonic idea that our visible and corporeal light derives from a higher and incorporeal light. Climbing up the ninety steps to the cathedral's Baroque entrance in the sunlight, the visitor enters the grey stone interior, lit by rose windows above the choir aisles and the high nave windows, and is taken up in spirit into the height of the nave as though its centre of gravity is not in the stone but pitched high above his head, just below the vaulting at a point where the light-beams meeting from the windows may awake in him the felicity of expanded consciousness.

The Gothic tradition in which Boffill was working began in France at the three centres of St-Denis, Chartres and Sens. It is remarkable that the chief elements of the style, together with a philosophy behind it, all appear in the space of about twenty years, between 1130 and 1150. There were naturally, as has already been said where the study of Neoplatonic ideas is concerned, precursors and initiating developments, social and religious as well as artistic, on which the first Gothic architects could draw. What is new is the fresh conception of man, expressed both in the earliest figure sculpture of the young style and in the psychological effect and symbolism of the buildings. Soon we shall consider some of the buildings that were precursors, such as Cluny and Durham, but first we must establish the grandeur of the scale on which we have to think.

All the studies of artistic and scientific creativity tend to confirm that the primary inspiration for a work of art or an insight into the physical world comes in a flash of time,[7] an instant to be measured in microseconds rather than minutes or hours. In a twinkling the mind of the artist is ordered in a new way, working with preternatural efficiency. William Blake says:

> Every Time less than a pulsation of the artery
> Is equal in its period & value to Six Thousand Years
> For in this Period the Poet's Work is done and all the great
> Events of Time start forth & are conciev'd in such a Period
> Within a Moment, a Pulsation of an Artery.[8]

The period of preparation for such an inspiration may have been long in terms of learning a craft, or of study and investigation, but the moment of synthesis of past impressions and contributory thoughts, when they are merged by a higher faculty of mental order into something new, is, by

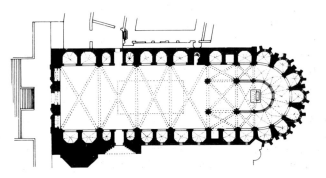

Plan of Gerona Cathedral.

5   Chartres. The west front showing (*right*) the south-west tower, begun 1142, the Royal Portal and lancets, *c.* 1150, the rose window, after 1194, the north-west tower in its lower stages, 1134 and its spire by Jean de Beauce, 1507–13.

comparison, a mere breath. By extension, we can think of the start of a civilization in terms of inspiration that comes to a few men as to the apostles at Pentecost, or to one man as to St Francis on his knees before the crucifix in San Damiano, creating in a few minutes causes that may affect mankind for centuries.

The earliest—and practically the only—writer I know of to comment on the way in which new civilizing influences appear in sudden bursts is Velleius Paterculus, the Roman historian writing in the time of Tiberius. 'Who can marvel sufficiently,' he says, 'that the most distinguished minds in each branch of human achievement have happened to adopt the same form of effort, and to have fallen within the same narrow space of time?'[9] He points to the single epoch that 'gave lustre to tragedy through three men of divine inspiration, Aeschylus, Sophocles, and Euripides', and to the creation of the Old Comedy. 'The great philosophers too, who received their

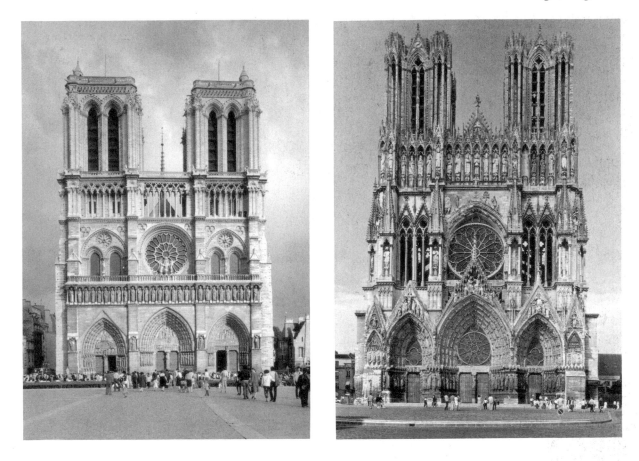

6 *Above* Notre-Dame, Paris. The west front, begun in 1200 and completed in 1250. The sculptures, severely damaged during the French Revolution, were restored or replaced under the guidance of Viollet-le-Duc in the last century.

7 *Above right* Rheims. The west front, begun by Jean d'Orbais after 1210 and completed to the stage of the gallery by 1311. The upper parts of the towers (fifteenth century) were meant to be crowned with spires. The tympana of the portals are replaced by stained glass, the rose windows are incorporated within pointed arches and the effect of the whole is made sculptural by the open arcades, tabernacles, and windows.

inspiration from the lips of Socrates . . . how long did they flourish after the death of Plato and Aristotle?'[10] A comparison of dates shows that 'the same thing holds true of the grammarians, the workers in clay, the painters, the sculptors, and that pre-eminence in each phase of art is confined within the narrowest limits of time.'[11] He states honestly that though he has searched often for the reasons for the flowering of particular talents within a short period, he can never find any of which he is certain—though he tends to think that genius is fostered by emulation, and that what is cultivated with supreme zeal reaches the highest perfection. From the attainment of perfection there is always a decline and the talented are forced to seek some new field of achievement.

The sudden manifestation of civilizations is complementary to the nature of inspiration, which is sudden and imperative in its appearances. Thus in a very short time there must have come to a small group of trained architects, masons and sculptors the realization that the three elements of the future Gothic style, the pointed arch, the ribbed vault and, in incipient form, the flying buttress, were the means of expressing a new conception of man and his relationship to the divine world, a new sense of light, and a soaring, aspiring, hungering desire for the unity they had already conceived in their own souls. They were lucky, as well as gifted, for they found highly placed patrons in Abbot Suger and in the bishops and canons of Chartres, men who, working from a different direction, had come to similar conclusions about the need for a new form of artistic expression that could enhance their spiritual experience and satisfy them with symbolic representations of ideas for which the magic of art was necessary to preserve their miraculous power. With such patrons and with the later backing of the Capetian monarchs of France, who saw in the style a means of increasing their prestige and consolidating their authority in conquered territories, the Gothic, which began in so small an area around Paris in the cathedrals and abbeys of the Ile-de-France, spread in a hundred years to the furthest reaches of Europe and as far as the Holy Land.

How could Gothic civilization achieve this? It achieved it because it was popular in the sense that it provided agreed and unifying channels for thought and feeling, wider in scope than the Romanesque culture it superseded, answering the needs of all classes of society, and because it possessed the true character of civilization in drawing together in harmony the religion, the science and technology, the philosophy and the art of the period.[12] The philosophers of the school of Chartres and the sculptors working there were quite conscious of this character, because the theme of the Royal Portal is the unity of knowledge depicted in the seven liberal arts, all looking towards the source of all knowledge, Christ in glory, who sits above the agents of revelation, the prophets, kings and queens of the statue columns below. How does the Gothic compare with other civilizations in this?

Paul Frankl says that if we ask what is the root of Gothic culture, taking into account scholasticism, mysticism, liturgy, the crusades, the cult of relics, asceticism, poetry, and all the other components,

> the answer has to be that the root of all roots is Jesus from Nazareth . . . The ideal of following his teaching generated different blossoms; they are alike Christian, only in different degrees and according to other interpretation. Gothic culture seems to be the purest and most intensive realization of the spirit contained in the New Testament.[13]

Frankl's last sentence is like a text for this book, to which we will frequently return. All civilizations within the Christian framework are developments of different aspects of the new ideas, emotional understanding, and attitudes to men and to nature given out by Christ in the three years of His ministry— a time span that would have been of interest to His contemporary Velleius Paterculus. Creativity, as the effect of direct participation in the truth, is the message of Christ's words:

> Believest thou not that I am in the Father and the Father in me? The words that I speak are not of myself: but the Father that dwelleth in me, he doeth the works.[14]

The promise of direct participation is extended to others in the same passage of St John's Gospel:

> I will pray the Father, and he shall give you another Comforter, that he may abide with you for ever: even the Spirit of truth; whom the world cannot receive, because it seeth him not, neither knoweth him: but ye know him; for he dwelleth with you, and shall be in you.[15]

One of the achievements of the Gothic artists was to bring to the portrayal of the drama of Christ's life an immediacy and a realism unparalleled in earlier Christian cultures; this was partly owed to the attention they paid to another part of the Gospel message, hitherto barely realized in the visual arts, which was the stress on the worth of the individual soul. For the celebration of the Christian liturgy they created new effects in the disposition of space; these effects owe much to the influence of the mysticism implicit in the works of Plato and his later followers, known as the Neoplatonists. Neoplatonic philosophy had been incorporated into Christian thought in the writings of St Augustine and, more important for our present subject, by a Syrian monk of the fifth century who put out his works under the name of the much earlier Dionysius the Areopagite, converted to Christianity by St Paul during his visit to Athens. His works have an infective enthusiasm that was to inspire Abbot Suger at St-Denis and the artists working with him. We can imagine the effect on a master worker in stained glass of Suger translating for him a passage from Dionysius such as this. Dionysius explains why the Word of God, in describing angels,

> prefers the sacred symbol of fire almost above all others . . . it is used not only under the figure of fiery wheels, but also of living creatures of fire, and of men flashing like lightning who heap live coals of fire about the Heavenly Beings, and of irresistibly rushing rivers of flame. Also it says that the Thrones are of fire, and it shows from their name that the most exalted Seraphim themselves are burning with fire . . . Therefore I think that this image of fire signifies the perfect conformity to God of the Celestial Intelligences . . . It is irresistible and invisible, having absolute rule over all things, bringing under its own power all things in which it subsists. It has transforming power, and imparts itself in some measure to everything near it. It revives all things by its revivifying heat, and illuminates them all with its resplendent brightness. It is insuperable and pure, possessing separative power, but is changeless, uplifting, penetrative, high, not held back by any servile baseness, ever-moving, self-moved, moving other things. . . . When not thought of, it seems not to exist, but suddenly enkindles its light to do so, uncontrollably flying upwards without diminishing its blessed self-giving.[16]

Even more important to future mystics and artists than the authority Dionysius gave to the depiction of divine matters and angelic beings was the way to God he taught, known as the *via negativa*, the realization of the might and unity of the Godhead by the denial and the transcendence of all epithets and all attributes. This, again, as we shall see in Chapter 9, was a profound influence on the inner vision that led to the conception of the soaring vaults and towers of the Gothic.

Christian mysticism developed amongst the first monks in the Egyptian desert, led by St Anthony of whom St John Cassian reported:

> That holy man uttered these superhuman and celestial words concerning prayer: 'There can be no perfect prayer if the religious is himself aware that he is praying.'[17]

This description of complete unity in contemplation is mirrored in the symbolism, the practice, and the desire for immersion of their personalities in their craft and work of the Gothic artists. 'A man cannot paint a face unless he *is* it first,'[18] says Dante, and the artists we are concerned with found a way of carving themselves into the stone to express a higher conception of individuality. The practices and beliefs of the Egyptian monks were to reach Ireland, newly converted to Christianity in the fifth century, and then to spread through France, Switzerland, and Italy through the work of Irish saints and missionaries. Contemporaneously St Benedict of Nursia founded the most important religious order of Western Christianity at his monastery in Monte Cassino. Here he brought about a revolution in the attitude to labour of the educated classes. Since the Greek influence on Roman culture, the ruling classes had regarded physical labour and crafts as the business of slaves. By insisting that his monks should work with their hands as part of their spiritual discipline, St Benedict not only ensured that the monasteries modelled on his foundation of Monte Cassino and following his rule of prayer and work should be self-sufficient communities, but also restored dignity to the act of physical labour.[19] The sanctification of work is a theme the Gothic sculptors took up in their many carvings of the labours of the year (fig. 28).

How vital it was for the survival of civilization that the monasteries should be self-sufficient became clear as the Dark Ages fell upon Europe, leaving the monks virtually the sole inheritors of the learning and the technical knowledge of the classical ages. The monasteries multiplied in number so that, however terrible the havoc wrought by the waves of invaders, the Norsemen, the Magyars, and the Saracens, enough survived to transmit the essential traditions, skills, and learning to another generation. Often hidden in obscure places or on mountains difficult to attack like San Pere de Roda, the monasteries sometimes became great centres of civilization. The most important of these was Cluny, whose later buildings were among the grandest precursors of the Gothic.

Cluny was founded in a sequestered Burgundian valley in 910 when William, Count of Auvergne, gave his hunting-lodge there to the Abbot of Baume in the Jura mountains. The founding charter threatened with a curse thirty lines long anyone, including the Pope, who should dare to interfere with the abbey's complete independence. This became a place where the

8   Cluny. Romanesque height: a view up into the barrel vault (100 ft, 30 m, high) and dome of the south transept (c. 1100) of the third abbey church, once the largest church in Christendom.

abbots and the monks thought and worked on a huge scale. The distinctive feature of the religious life of the Cluniac order was the time the monks spent on their offices and services and the splendour with which they celebrated the liturgy. They made music night and day; they needed great churches to resound with their singing; they needed artefacts of gold, silver, and ivory, the vessels of the mass, candlesticks, glowing vestments, fans for cooling the celebrants during the long services, and programmes of sculpture that in the capitals of the columns about them recorded the tones of the music they sang, the virtues they aspired to and the vices from which they fled. The object of the splendid services of Cluny and her dependencies was the welding of a body of monks into the unity of a team through the ceaseless practice of monodic plainsong. These monks, who were nearly always of noble birth, had sacrificed the warlike ways and the riotous love-making of their brothers and cousins for another kind of life, one in which they were made into a family of the spirit close to the worlds of the dead and the angels. In the eyes of the outside world their chief function was to pray for the dead: in their own eyes they were following a way closed to other men, the only way to perfection, a way that depended on obedience, faith, and song. Their

9   Beauvais. Gothic height: the choir, built between 1247 and 1272, at 158 ft (50 m) the highest vaults ever built. The vaults collapsed in 1284, and were rebuilt with additional piers in each bay.

patrons, aware of their future need for such intercession, deeply appreciated their prayers for the dead and made generous gifts.

This was one of the ways in which the Cluniacs gained land and influence, enabling them to act on a greater scale in another field, that of international politics. A century after their foundation they controlled over a thousand square miles. They intervened constantly in society with the aim of peace, devising the Truce of God which applied to times when no one could fight, under pain of excommunication. In the place of invasion and attack, they promoted a milder form of travel and circulation in the great pilgrimages in whose routes they took a special interest, thereby increasing the communication of ideas and cultural contacts. When they returned from their many missions, of peacemaking, of controlling the pilgrim routes to Compostela, of advising popes, emperors and kings, what they must most have wanted was to be reabsorbed into the corpus of perpetual song.

By the time the First Crusade was proclaimed in 1098, under their most notable abbot St Hugh of Cluny, the third great abbey church of Cluny was already being built. Here, again, the scale on which the Cluniacs conducted their affairs was seen in the largest church ever built in Christendom before the reconstruction of St Peter's, Rome. The new choir of Cluny was begun in 1088; the design of the church included two sets of transepts, a nave so wide it required double aisles and a narthex or antechamber to the nave. It was well over 500 ft (154 m) long with high barrel vaults. Largely destroyed during the French Revolution and after, the abbey church now consists only of the south transept, known as the *Tour de l'eau bénite* (fig. 8), and a few lesser parts. Most of the sculpture was also destroyed.

To enter the south transept now and to look up is to receive an architectural shock comparable to one's first entrance into the later cathedral of Beauvais (fig. 9). The eye is sped up tall pilaster columns, superhuman in their height, 100 ft (30 m) into the vault that once was the sounding-board for the psalms of Gregorian plainchant and where the echo of song seems to draw up our amazement. Here we see the verticality of Gothic achieved without Gothic means, features, or spirit. We experience something of what the world might have been if the monasteries had remained the chief harbourers of civilization, but we also feel the same spirit of mystery which the priests and monks aimed to convey as they impressed on the unruly outside world that with them resided the ultimate power, the last sanction on where the souls of men and women would proceed on death.

This long and massive church brought together the masons and artists who founded the school of Burgundian Romanesque, which continued in buildings such as Autun (fig. 29) and Vézelay (fig. 30) into the period contemporary with the first Gothic. It also set a model both for the scale on which the Gothic architects were to build and for the intricate and abundant iconographic schemes with which they were to decorate their cathedrals and churches.

Fortunately the Romanesque church that combines the main technical elements which the Gothic style was to develop still survives. It is the cathedral of Durham. The choir and nave were built between 1093 and 1133. The choir was begun by the second Norman bishop of Durham, William of St Carileph, and work on this part and on the nave continued under his successor Ranulf Flambard. What impresses us in the nave of Durham is the evidence of the scale of mind of the anonymous architects who conceived this design. Here we find, though every detail up to the vaulting is purely Romanesque, the first note of the authority and magisterial conception that were soon to characterize the Gothic. Here, too, the architects brought together for the first time the three technical elements that, united, enabled the construction of the high stone Gothic vaults: these are the ribbed vault, the pointed arch (in the main arches rising from the piers of the nave and dividing the vaulting bays), and the flying buttress (though these are concealed in the roofs of the aisles). The style of the Durham architects had no followers on the continent: the masons who worked there went north to build Dunfermline Abbey for St Margaret of Scotland and the cathedral of St Magnus on Orkney for Earl Rognvald. At a time, however, when news travelled fast in the French-speaking world of which England had become part, the news of the technical achievement would have been brought quickly to the architects who were soon to work at St-Denis and Chartres.

Durham also displays another gift of the Romanesque to the early Gothic in the alternation of piers and columns: the columns answer one another across the nave with designs of chevrons, lozenges, flutings and spirals and the chevron pattern is taken up in the mouldings of the triforium arches, the clerestory windows, and the vaulting ribs themselves (fig. 35). Originally painted black and red,[20] these might be considered a bold but simple way of covering big spaces with geometrical designs that had no particular meaning in themselves, except that to anyone familiar with much older art forms, they immediately recall carvings of the Megalithic period. The ornament of Romanesque art has been traced to Mesopotamia, the Steppes of Russia, ancient Sumer, Coptic Egypt, Armenia, Georgia and Syria as well as drawing on Norse and Celtic styles and symbols. The patterns at Durham go back much further, to the spiral and chevron carvings on the great stone slabs of the Megalithic site of New Grange which are dated to c. 3300 BC and to the grooved pottery that was characteristic of the important religious sites of the Neolithic and Bronze ages.[21] These patterns are thought to be sacred to the threefold Great Goddess—the bride, the mother, and the hag—of prehistoric times, and it is strange to see her symbols in a building to which women were barely admitted. There is a mark at the west end on the nave floor beyond which women might not pass. What is also strange about these designs used in the context of the nave of Durham is that they convey an atmosphere of great certainty and tranquillity, unlike so much of Romanesque art which, with its monstrous and hybrid beasts, its concentration on nightmare forests of tendrils and branches come alive to trap unhappy man, seems very often like an exorcism of all the fears and troubles of the Dark Ages.

It is not difficult to surmise where the Durham architect found these ancient symbols.[22] As they were woven by country people into corn-dollies at harvest-time well into this century, how much more would they have been available in all the rites, pastimes, and seasonal celebrations of pagan origin whose vigour and indelibility are revealed by the Church's need to denounce them so frequently. The transformation of pagan symbols in this way relates very closely to the presence of ancient Celtic and Nordic themes in Romanesque art and to the way that the Gothic, when exported beyond Northern France, so rapidly developed national styles and drew on native traditions—in the way, for example, that the figure of the Green Man (see Chapter 6) recurs in Gothic sculpture (figs. 80–2, 85–6, 88, 97, 132, 148) or the heroines of the *Nibelungenlied* stare out from the north portal of Worms cathedral to the scene of their quarrel.[23] For though the elements of Gothic came from far away, the pointed arch perhaps from Armenia and the ribbed vault from Islam, the style itself and the whole culture connected with it are the creation of North-Western Europe. It arose in the inspirations of Northern European architects, artists, and mystics and it was greeted quickly in some areas, more slowly in others as the style of every church of stone. The strong and characteristic Gothic line soon migrated from the churches to the design of palaces and communal buildings and entered into the form of every object in ordinary use, down to the jugs that carried the wine from the cellar or the cupboards that stood by the best bed.

Where does such a revolution in thought, feeling and taste come from? Elsewhere, drawing on numerous examples of descriptions of the creative process, I have suggested that true inspiration is the action of a state of higher consciousness in bringing together the two sides of the brain, allowing the most rapid interpretation by the speech-dominated side of the powerful and emotion-laden symbols and rhythms of the tacit side of our natures.[24] Inspiration can come only to the individual or to a few individuals with minds tuned to one another, not to the crowd, but the history of science and of art demonstrates time and again the synchronicity of discovery, the similitude of theme and treatment, in people who know nothing of one another. Should such people meet and find a common aim, a common interpretation of their experiences, and furthermore be given the time, the funds, the encouragement they need to express their ideas in a new form of the religious life, of art, of philosophy, or science, would this not produce an energy controlled by a force of will that is insuperable because of the efficiency with which their mental and emotional powers are used? And would not the energy they could unleash upon the world be of a magnitude to stir the hopes of ambitious rulers? Could not that energy be channelled so that the earth puts on 'a white cloak of churches'[25] or released to make an explosion 'brighter than a thousand suns'?[26] The Capetian monarchs did in fact take up the Gothic style as a means of increasing their prestige, but the blessing of its presence departed like an affronted angel to other lands in the decline of the dynasty after the death of St Louis in 1270. During the preceding period of agreement between the Capetians and the makers of the Gothic, however, an average of one-third of the resources of France each year were devoted to the building of churches. Taking into account Romanesque building as well in the three centuries from 1050 to 1350, eighty cathedrals, five hundred large churches and many thousands of parish churches were constructed or rebuilt,[27] a diversion of resources to civilizing and spiritual ends of permanent value that would otherwise have been dissipated in ever greater wars and civil strife.

This was the effect of men working together in a common spirit in which their religion, their art, their philosophy, and their science and technology were in harmony. For the opposite effect in the present century one can point to the achievements of the international body of physicists, who, freed from an outworn religion, careless of art, taking from philosophy its intellectual and logical rigour but not its speculative and moral purpose, made of their science and its applications so powerful a weapon for investigating and changing the natural world that their knowledge became desirable to governments and administrators. Lacking the support of all the other higher forms of knowledge and of inspiration which they had rejected as superstitious or irrelevant, knowing no moral imperative except the furtherance of their science, they sold themselves in exchange for government support to the forces of barbarism. In the determinist philosophy guiding the paradigm of modern science there is no sanction for the working of conscience.[28]

Gothic art is an art based on the proper working of conscience. When an artist receives an inspiration, he has the choice of interpreting it in a personal and limited way or of surrendering his personal will and of making the inspiration serve the universal purpose of its origins. The early Gothic artists released a new sense of joy in Europe with their soaring vaults and spires, their young happy Virgins, and their delight in the animals, flowers and leaves of nature. They transformed the horrific monsters of the Romanesque into an art of praise—an attitude summed up in the epitaph of Hugues de Doignies, a lay brother and goldsmith in a monastery near Namur in about 1300:

> *Ore canunt alii Christum; canit arte fabrili Hugo.*
> Let others sing Christ with their mouths; Hugues sings with his goldsmith's work.[29]

The necessity of creating an atmosphere of happiness is a constant throughout the period of Gothic art; thus the canons of Gerona accepted Guillem Boffill's bold design for the nave of their cathedral because it would be *laetius et jucundius*, happier and more joyful.

Again, one of the characteristic emotions associated with descriptions of individual artistic and scientific inspiration is impersonal joy. If one were to try to answer the question on which this book is based, 'Where does civilization come from?' in terms of the Neoplatonic school of Chartres, the reply would be that it comes from the eternal world of the Nous or Divine Mind through the medium of the *anima mundi* or soul of the world to be manifested in the physical world. One of the finest works associated with the school of Chartres is the *Cosmographia* by Bernardus Sylvester, who dedicated it to the chancellor of the school, Thierry of Chartres. It is a portrayal of creativity in the universe, of how order is brought to the primal chaos from the eternal essences. 'Time,' he says, 'may be seen to be rooted in eternity, and eternity to be expressed in time. All that is moved is subject to time, but it is from eternity that all contained in the vastness of time is born,

10 *Below* Chartres. The north transept and portal, *c.* 1210. The main themes of the sculptures are the creation of the world and the precursors of Christ.

11 *Below right* Chartres. A view into the portal of the south transept. Different in architectural and sculptural styles from the north portal, its theme is the Christian Church on earth.

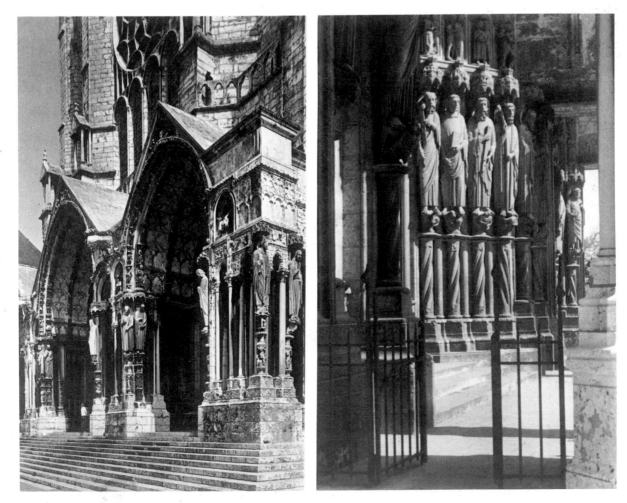

and into eternity that it is to be resolved.'[30] The moment of inspiration can be seen as the intersection of the line of time by eternity through which the artist is instructed by the everlasting archetypes. The short and sudden period in which civilizations arise can be seen as windows in history in which men are made more widely aware of the need and the means of enlightenment. The ground-plan of the Gothic cathedral can be seen as a symbol of the intersection of time by eternity: with its transepts it is based on the shape of the cross. The cross-bar of the transepts signifies the line of time; at Chartres the sculpture of the north transept porch tells the story of creation and of the precursors of Christ in the Old Testament (fig. 10). The south porch sculptures are concerned with the coming of Christ and His apostles and martyrs (fig. 11). They are divided by the eternal world of the upright of the cross that starts with the sculptures of the end of time in the Last Judgment in the west front, and continues up the nave which is based on divine number, weight, and measure to the high altar where daily the angels and archangels are invoked in the preface to the sacrifice of the mass.

The presence of eternity was also felt in the services in the cathedral churches and abbeys. With their music they were seen as a reflection on earth of the unending celestial chorus of praise. With the change from Romanesque architecture to the Gothic, the music changed from the monodic plainsong of the monks to the beginnings of polyphony in the school of Notre-Dame under its early choir-masters and organists Leoninus and Perotinus. The great churches were conceived as the sounding-boards of gigantic musical instruments with elaborate sets of choir-stalls, hooded and spired, in which the canons and monks stood, like the saints in their niches on the exteriors of the buildings, to chant their praises. One such set of choir-stalls was built and decorated in Strasbourg cathedral by the sculptor Nicolaus Gerhaerts of Leyden in 1467. These choir-stalls are now demolished, but in the Museum of the Works of the Cathedral one can see the half-length statue of a sculptor which is presumed to be the self-portrait of Nicolaus Gerhaerts (frontispiece). He has portrayed himself having laid down his mallet, which rests in one of his hands on the ledge before him. His other hand supports his chin and with eyes closed and a gentle smile he listens. He listens to what? Obviously in one way, like a charming compliment to the task on which he was engaged, he carved himself as listening to the succeeding generations of the choir of Strasbourg beneath him, perpetually caught in a moment of rest from his labours. In a further sense, he listens to other harmonies, more powerful because they are closer to the primordial sources of art, instinct with rhythms on the edge of silence that are so far from definition that they could be compared to a figure hidden in a block of stone or the expression on the faces of a choir about to sing. He listens for the instructions of a will other than his own, the will of the tradition of the masters to which he belonged, and in his repose, as though resting on behalf of all his predecessors, we can also sense the continuing peace of those contemplations in the first Gothic artists as an effect of which we still feel the exhilaration and the soaring inspiration of the RISE OF THE GOTHIC.

CHAPTER 2

St-Denis, Sens and Chartres

Abbot Suger of St-Denis, the foremost patron of the Gothic style, was born of a peasant family in 1081.[1] He went to school close to the ancient royal abbey of St-Denis north of Paris. At school he was befriended by a boy who was to become King of France as Louis VI (known also as Le Gros because of his corpulence). Suger entered the monastery of St-Denis as a monk in his youth and from his earliest days he desired to rebuild the abbey church in a way that would honour the martyrs buried there and the royal connexions which went back to the Merovingian founder, King Dagobert. Its chief relics were the remains of St Denis and his fellow martyrs St Rusticus and St Eleutherius. Here the kings of France were buried, and the decline of the abbey under Suger's predecessor as abbot was a reflection of the decline of the French monarchy at Paris in the same period. The area around Paris over which the kings exercised effective control was small in itself, and was hemmed in by the counties and duchies of often richer and independent lords who acknowledged the king's overlordship only in name.

The most troublesome of these neighbours were the dukes of Normandy who, by this time, as kings of England by conquest, had acquired wealth and prestige that dwarfed their brothers of France in both respects. Suger got to know many of the Norman leaders, including Henry I of England, when he was sent as a young monk to administer one of his abbey's properties in Normandy. His reputation as an administrator and diplomat grew as, after his coronation in 1108, Louis VI used him on many missions, including several to Rome. In 1122 he became abbot of his monastery, introducing gentle reforms and improvements which drew the approval of St Bernard of Clairvaux, the leader of the Cistercians. St Bernard had at first conducted a campaign against him but relented, writing to him in 1127 and offering an olive-branch of friendship. On the death of Louis VI in 1137, Suger withdrew from court and was able to give his energies to the rebuilding of his church. In 1147 he was made Regent of France while Louis VII was on crusade. By the time of his death in 1151, comforted by a message and the gift of a handkerchief from St Bernard, through a policy of reconciliation he had done much to restore the position and the prestige of the French throne and he had also given the first artists of the Gothic the chance they needed to change the forms of civilization in Europe.

Suger was a delightful man, a good conversationalist, finding power given into his hands because of a universal acknowledgement of his abilities, not because he actively sought it. Above all, where the pleasure of future generations is concerned, he was an aesthete, a patron, and a passionate collector, whose consuming love was for precious stones, gold, vestments, fine buildings, and the subtle intermingling of colours in stained glass. His work at St-Denis survives only in part, in the west front (fig. 12) and narthex (fig. 20) and in the choir (fig. 37) and crypt, because the major portions of the church, the nave, transepts, and upper region of the choir, were remodelled in the thirteenth century on the orders of St Louis. Enough can be seen there, however, to understand the originality of the scheme he

12   St-Denis. The west front of the abbey church, begun under the direction of Abbot Suger in 1137. It includes the first rose window. Formerly two towers rose above the parapet, but the north-west tower was destroyed in the last century.

and his architects and craftsmen introduced.

The grant of the revenues of a famous local fair, the Lendit, had greatly increased the revenues of the abbey. The crowds that attended the fair wanted to see the relics of the martyrs and the relics of the Passion which were displayed to them, and better provision had to be made for these worshippers. In 1137 work began on the construction of a new west front which owed much in its form to Norman architecture, including the use of the round arch, and in its sculptural scheme something to Burgundy (fig. 12). Here great gilded doors inscribed with Suger's verses invited the pilgrim to enter and to marvel:

> Whoever thou art, if thou seekest to extol the glory of these doors,
> Marvel not at the gold and the expense but at the craftsmanship of the
>   work.

Bright is the noble work; but, being nobly bright, the work
Should brighten the minds so that they may travel, through the true
    lights,
To the True Light where Christ is the true door . . .
The dull mind rises to truth, through that which is material
And in seeing this light, is resurrected from its former submersion.[2]

The gilded doors are now replaced by wooden ones and much of the sculpture is either destroyed, scattered, or completely restored. One thing that we can be sure of, though, is that it represented a new mood of calm and invitation. The same subject as that employed in Burgundian Romanesque, the Last Judgment, was chosen but, instead of an emphasis on terror and damnation, the intention and effect was to console and reassure. The west front had been raised to the height of its parapet when, before the towers were begun, Suger turned to the east end of the church. It is not known exactly why he did this but it may be that he had come across a new architect, someone who shared his longing to create in the church the feeling of a

13   St-Denis. A view of the crypt beneath the choir, begun by Suger in 1140. The capital of the central column reflects a greater fidelity to classical models than had been usual in Romanesque art.

spiritual luminosity that had been kindled in his mind by his reading of Dionysius the Areopagite.

Quite erroneously he thought that St Denis, the Apostle of the Gaul whose relics were buried in the ancient crypt in his care, was the same man as Dionysius the Areopagite whom St Paul converted. The error was doubly compounded by the fact that his favourite reading, the works ascribed to Dionysius the Areopagite, were not by him at all, but are, as we have noted, much later compositions of the fifth century (see page 16). The errors were not his alone but sanctified by ancient tradition; the prickly Peter Abelard, who cast doubt on these accepted facts, fled the abbey for his own safety. The writings of the Pseudo-Dionysius (as he is often called) gained immensely in authority because they were thought to contain some of the secrets revealed to St Paul when, 'whether in the body, or whether out of the body', he was taken up in ecstasy to the Third Heaven and shown unspeakable wonders; St Paul was thought to have talked of these matters to the original Dionysius and therefore the books ascribed to him on the Celestial Hierarchies of angels, on the Divine Names, on the Mystical Theology, and on the Ecclesiastical Hierarchy came to have, by association, an apostolic authority. The Emperor Louis the Pious, who was one of the most important earlier patrons of the abbey of St-Denis, sent to the Emperor Michael the Stammerer of Byzantium for copies of these works: they were translated at St-Denis by the great Irish scholar of the ninth century, John Scotus Eriugena, who also wrote an authoritative commentary on them. To Suger they were utterly authentic; his abbey possessed the relics of their author and the writings themselves; it only lacked fitting expression of their exalted ideas in art and architecture. If his belief was based on a series of misconceptions in one way, it was also based on a higher truth; this truth lies in the community of experience that links the ecstasy of St Paul with the mystical knowledge of the later Dionysius, the profound thought of Eriugena and the reaches of feeling into which Suger was carried by the intensity of his aesthetic delight. Thus he wrote of the effect on him of gazing in transport on precious stones:

> When—out of my delight in the beauty of the house of God—the loveliness of the many-coloured gems has called me away from external cares, and worthy meditation has induced me to reflect, transferring that which is material to that which is immaterial, on the diversity of the sacred virtues: then it seems to me that I see myself dwelling, as it were in some strange region of the universe which neither exists entirely in the slime of the earth nor entirely in the purity of Heaven; and that by the grace of God, I can be transported from this inferior to that higher world in an anagogical manner.[3]

For the building of his choir between 1140 and 1144 (fig. 37) Suger had found in his new architect someone who could translate the Dionysian ideas into architecture. Though we do not know the architect's name, he almost certainly had been trained in or near Paris. We know this because he insisted on the use of thin walling, an archaic practice going back to Carolingian times, and still preferred in Paris to the currently fashionable thick walls used, for example, by the Anglo-Norman architects. It was the synthesis of the archaic thin walls with the most up-to-date techniques in rib vaulting that produced the technical origins of Gothic architecture.[4] Keeping the walls thin meant that, if the architects were to vault in stone, they had to depend more on buttresses. It was the overall desire for spaciousness and lightness of construction, in order to image the Dionysian ideas, that brought about the revolutionary change.

The choir is surrounded by the ambulatory raised on an apsidal extension of the old crypt, formed by twelve columns which Suger compares to the twelve apostles surmounted by Christ the Keystone.[5] Within the ambulatory are another series of twelve columns, symbolizing the prophets who foretold Christ and marking off the nine chapels of the apse which may signify in their number the nine ranks of the angelic hierarchies. The design has a precursor in the Cluniac church of St Martin-des-Champs[6] in Paris (built 1130–1142), where the example of a continuous zone of windows around the chapels of the apse facing in on the first double ambulatory was taken up by Suger at St-Denis and improved so that there is no interruption of the light by the columns.

Not only are the columns of Suger's choir slim and graceful but they are aligned on axes radiating from the centre of the choir so that they permit the coloured light from the surrounding chapel windows to pour in with no let

14   Ely. An example of the massive style of Anglo-Norman architecture against which Suger's architects were to react in favour of lightness of construction: the nave, early twelfth century.

or hindrance. This was an achievement as startling in its simplicity as in its originality, and it created the model for the luminous interior of the Gothic church. The use of round columns, instead of the heavy compound piers generally favoured in Romanesque architecture, also gave life to another archaic usage. Round columns were probably chosen because they would harmonize with those of the old Carolingian nave, but they also added greatly to the sense of spaciousness and in fact determined the style for Gothic architecture up to the end of the century. Some of Suger's windows remain in the choir, rich creations designed to express another Dionysian idea. As Otto von Simson says:

> These translucent panels 'vested' as he put it with sacred symbols are to him like veils at once shrouding and revealing the ineffable . . . the entire cosmos appeared like a veil illuminated by the divine light.[7]

In a panel of glass depicting the Annunciation Suger is shown prostrate at the feet of the Virgin. Suger's feeling for the medium and the subject with which he chose especially to associate himself are both recalled in a much later English religious lyric:

> As the sun that shines through glass
> So Jesus in His mother was.

Many of the designs Suger chose and had executed set a model for the iconographic schemes of later sequences of stained glass, one of the most influential being the Tree of Jesse window in which the genealogy of Christ is set out in the form of a tree.

The overall effect of the stained glass would have been much darker in Suger's time than now—much more like the interior of Chartres. This was partly because, however much it might have been desired to use more white glass, this was the most difficult kind to make and the greater use of white glass in succeeding generations depended on increasing technical skill.[8] More than that, though, it was the mystical light, not pure daylight, after which Suger and his artists hankered, conveyed most of all in the strange blue of twelfth-century glass which seems to filter to our souls the essence of other skies in other worlds (fig. 87).

When the choir was completed, Suger, having thus rebuilt the west end and the east end of the church, was now faced with the problem of the old Carolingian nave. The problem was that, according to legend, Christ Himself had appeared at the consecration of this nave, and Suger decided to keep those parts which had been touched by Christ's hands. This probably meant that he preserved the round columns of the nave arcade while intending to incorporate them in a scheme with double aisles that was never completed.[9] The scheme nevertheless probably provided the prototype for Notre-Dame of Paris, begun twenty years later. He expressed his resolution to rebuild in a poem:

> Once the new rear part is joined to the part in front
> The church shines with its middle part brightened.
> For bright is that which is brightly coupled with the bright
> And bright is the noble edifice which is pervaded by the new light.[10]

In 1144, in the presence of King Louis VII and his Queen, Eleanor of Aquitaine, the new church was consecrated. Nineteen archbishops and bishops took part in the ceremonies. Suger exclaims with wonder at:

> . . . how so great a chorus of such great pontiffs, decorous in white vestments, splendidly arranged in pontifical mitres and precious

orphreys embellished by circular ornaments, held the croziers in their hands, walked round and round the vessel [of holy water] and invoked the name of God by way of exorcism; how so glorious and admirable men celebrated the wedding of the Eternal Bridegroom so piously that the King and the attending nobility believed themselves to behold a chorus celestial rather than terrestrial, a ceremony divine rather than human.[11]

Suger, in writing his accounts of the rebuilding and conservation of St-Denis, was partly defending his position against St Bernard and the Cistercians. St Bernard had launched a scarifying attack on the luxury and the ornamentation of the Cluniac churches.[12] He demanded in the churches of his own order the exclusion of all carvings and ornamentation except wooden crucifixes and, though he allowed more elaborate decoration in churches used by the laity, he thought it scandalous that monks, themselves devoted to a life of poverty, should take the offerings of the poor for the adornment of edifices. His influence is also to be seen on our next example of one of the first Gothic buildings, the cathedral of Sens (fig. 15).

The Archbishop of Sens, Henri le Sanglier, was faced in 1128 with rebuilding his cathedral because fire had destroyed the old one. If St-Denis gave the future the model of the Gothic choir and Chartres (to which we come next) the model of the Gothic west front and spired tower, then Sens provides the model of the unified Gothic interior. St Bernard had condemned the great height and vacuous spaces of Cluniac churches but he had also paid great attention to the proportions, based on the musical scale, of Cistercian abbey churches such as Fontenay. This sobering influence came to Sens first of all through Bernard's attack on the Archbishop for his worldly life. Henri le Sanglier repented and put himself under the guidance of St Bernard, who wrote for him a treatise on how a bishop should conduct himself.

Only part of the apse, in a severe Romanesque style, had been completed when Henri died in 1142. The main part of the cathedral was started in about 1145, probably by an architect who had worked in St-Denis and who aimed to maintain the same note of sobriety. The nave is not of great height, following the dictates of St Bernard, but it has a quiet and unifying rhythm that, seeming to start from the ribs of the sexpartite vaults, is carried down from the shafts to the colonnettes of the great piers (or *piles fortes*) to their very bases. This vertical rhythm is countered in the horizontal rhythm of the alternating great piers and the lesser piers (*piles faibles*) formed of coupled columns. As we see it now, there are two major changes to the interior since it was first built: the clerestory stage was altered in the thirteenth century to allow larger windows to give more light and transepts were cut out to make a crossing in the fifteenth century.

The interior of Sens is nevertheless complete enough to give a good sense of its original design and also to arouse a sense of wonder at a building planned from the outset to make its skeleton the chief element of its design in ribs, arches and piers. Where the Romanesque builders made their churches stand by the piling on of masses, the Gothic works by the opposition of forces. Here at Sens one sees very clearly the opportunities that would be given by this light and elegant new style in opening up the wall spaces, which are in fact infilling, to greater and greater expanses of glass. Underlying the unity of Sens is the simple musical proportion of the octave, 1:2, for the aisles are half the width of the nave. The use of a tripartite elevation in the nave, instead of the four stages common in many great churches of the time, also allowed the same proportions to be applied to the

15 Sens. A view across the mid-twelfth-century nave showing the double columns of the *piliers faibles* and the pairs of arches in the triforium. The clerestory windows, originally in pairs, were altered in the thirteenth century.

relative heights of the aisles and nave. The number 2 also played an important part in the design of the original elevation when in each bay there were two clerestory windows, two openings in the triforium, and two columns in each *pilier faible*. This combined with the octave proportions makes one suspect there was a deliberate play with numbers, 2 having the positive symbolism of the relationship of God to man as well as the more obvious one of division.

Turning now to Chartres, we consider the creation of the Gothic exterior, the first manifestation of the spired and towered profile that was to give expression to the forceful energy of Europe in the twelfth and thirteenth centuries. The moment you first see the twin towers of Chartres rising above the farmlands of the Beauce, you know the world about you has changed for the better (fig. 5). Once you are before the cathedral, you realize you could spend days looking solely at the exterior, at the mysterious and unnameable figures of the Royal Portal, at the sculpture, depicting the Old Testament in the porch of the north transept and their echoing fellows of the New Testament in the south porch, not only to savour their moods and beauty, but to prepare yourself, as by an exquisite procrastination of certain future pleasure, for the moment when you enter the cathedral. Then you would find yourself in the architectural night of the interior, into which light is transmitted only through the medium of the predominantly blue and red windows. There you have to accustom your eyes and your body until you can walk about as entranced as though you had discovered some secret chamber of the mind, where you could never be disturbed, which was palpable with stillness and with pure emotions, but with the added delight that you know you are not dreaming, that you can lay your hand on stone to reassure yourself of your waking state, and that the secret chamber is not only within you but also extends to the vaulted and columned spaces about you.

Then you will find the little door in the north transept that leads you by spiralled stairways up past the galleries and the clerestory out into the open air again. You are on a parapet, with the eaves of the copper-plated roof of the nave on your left and on the other side the rounded tumbling flying buttresses that carry, as an easy burden, the weight of the vaulting and the clerestory down to the earth (fig. 140). Dragon visages and the faces of men

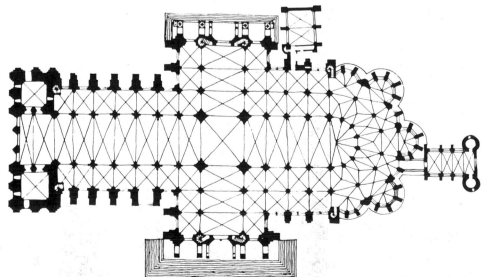

Plan of Chartres Cathedral: the west front *c.* 1140 onwards; the rest after 1194.

sprout from the buttresses, staring at worlds invisible to us, thinking thoughts beyond our conjecture. The walk along the parapet takes you direct to the north tower which, built in 1134, is the earliest tower of Gothic design. In 1507, right at the end of our period, Jean de Beauce built the splendid upper stages and spire that surmount it. You come to an ancillary tower built into the side of the spire up which, by a winding staircase, you ascend to a gallery; from there, you can look down at the old roofs of the town clustered about the cathedral or see, eastwards, the angel of Chartres flashing with gold in the sun above the choir or, best of all, enjoy the proximity of the gabled spire of the south tower (fig. 16).

In looking at this south tower you are gazing at one of the greatest surviving achievements of the earliest Gothic art. You are looking at the beginning of a civilization. This spired tower, seeming, at first, so bare of ornament and so widowed compared to the florid and exuberant superstructure from which you regard it, was begun in 1142 at the time when Abbot Suger was completing his choir at St-Denis. While Suger at St-Denis, as we have seen, was creating the model of the light-filled interior of the Gothic church, here at Chartres they were making the model of the Gothic exterior with its spired profile that, through the thousands of great and small spires deriving from it, was to give a new beauty and poignancy to the landscapes of so much of Northern Europe. As your eye starts to take in the patterns of the scalloped stone tiles that make the spire appear as though coated in a sleek lizard-skin, and as the gabled tabernacles of the centres and corners start to work their heart-piercing magic on you, you begin to realize that all the wonders you have already seen in the cathedral are the consequences and effects of what was achieved in the making of this tower. It has the subtlety and the simplicity of primal creation, drawing, for its effect on us, on the highest level of inspiration, which is not the inspiration of one individual but of revelation among a group of men.

It arouses strange feelings in you, this south tower. It may be partly the effect of the physical elevation after the stretching and varied experiences of seeing the lower parts of the cathedral that induces a mental and emotional elevation, but it is also something in the tower itself. It is alive; it sings to the watcher of a profound joy drawn from the earth round its foundations, and you feel in your balconied eyrie under Jean de Beauce's spire an affinity with the unnamed masters of the earlier tower, a knowledge and a kinship with that joy that inspired its making.

The towers were built in front of the Romanesque cathedral, erected by Bishop Fulbert in about 1020. Shortly after the completion of the towers, they were linked by the Royal Portal with its famous statues and joined to the main body of the old church by what is called a narthex or extended antechamber. The uppermost stages between them, with the rose window, were part of the rebuilding of the nave, brought westwards after the fire of 1194. The reason why the north tower beneath you is regarded as the first Gothic tower is the design of the buttresses, which emphasize the vertical drive of the building in a truly Gothic manner as opposed to the horizontal effect of Romanesque buttresses, which carefully delineate and mark off the stages of the towers they support. What helps to give the south tower its originality is the way the builders solved the problem of raising the octagonal spire from its square base, masking the join by a gentle modulation in the disposition of the gables so that the transition from one form to another is as natural and as graceful to the eye as the extension of branches from a beech-tree or the harmony of parts in the chambered nautilus.

It is the organic and natural quality of the south tower that evokes the feeling in you that it is alive. Ernst Levy, who devoted thirty years to the study of its proportions, came to the conclusion that its design is based upon the octagon, the width of the tower being a side of an octagon whose centre is placed midway on the height of the tower.[13] He has also demonstrated that, in constructing the spire on the north tower 350 years later, Jean de Beauce used the same principle of expanding and contracting figures to make a companion to the earlier tower that, though higher, expresses in the fashion of a later age the same harmonious beauty. But why the octagon?

At the time these towers were built the School of Chartres was the most important institution of learning in Western Europe. It was particularly devoted to the study and exposition of Neoplatonic ideas, developed through the teaching of the seven liberal arts—those arts which received their first depiction in stone in the carvings of the Royal Portal. Among these arts were music and mathematics. In their studies of the natural world they had biblical authority for believing that God disposed all things in number, weight, and measure. Therefore any work of man, if it were to fulfil in execution the divine message conveyed in its inspiration, should be constructed according to the proportions and the number symbolism that best accorded with its purpose and meaning. Amongst the meanings of the number eight in the octagon are those of regeneration and the new life, eight

17   Senlis. The south-west tower and spire, c. 1160 and later, one of the spires influenced by that of Chartres.

18   Chartres. Pythagoras with his tintinnabulum. He symbolizes music as one of the representations of the liberal arts on the Royal Portal, *c.* 1150.

being the number of the octave and therefore symbolizing a fresh beginning.

Here we have, in the building of this south tower at Chartres, a collaboration between the most learned philosophers of the period on the one hand and a great architect instructed in the same mathematical and symbolical tradition with his skilled craftsmen on the other. Here at Chartres they consciously chose to erect, as a belfry designed with the meaning of a new life incorporated in its proportions and structure, a building that with its contemporary constructions at St-Denis and Sens was to change the architectural face of Europe. The building of this tower provoked an outburst of popular enthusiasm known as the 'cult of the carts'. The Archbishop of Rouen wrote to the Bishop of Amiens in about 1145 that at Chartres men in their humility were yoking themselves to the carts carrying materials for its building and that miracles were reported associated with their devotion. A Norman abbot describes how this cult began at Chartres and spread to Normandy:

Whoever saw, whoever heard, in all the generations past, that kings, princes, mighty men of the world puffed up with honours and riches, men and women of noble birth, should bind bridles upon their proud and swollen necks and submit themselves to wagons which, after the fashion of brute beasts, they dragged with their loads of wine, corn, oil, lime, stones, beams, and other things necessary to sustain life or to build churches.[14]

The abbot of Mont St-Michel records in his annals for 1145 the same extraordinary happenings at Chartres, of men dragging carts with stones, wood, and provisions 'needed for the new church, whose towers were being built at this time.'[15]

It is not surprising that this should have happened at Chartres because it was the chief centre of devotion to the Virgin Mary in Western Europe. Furthermore, it was a site of veneration long before the Christian period. It was certainly a centre of Druid worship and may well have been the chief centre of Druidism in Gaul; the holy well still to be seen in the crypt was probably the sacred spring always associated with the groves in which the Druids practised their cult. The well became a well of Christian martyrs and an image of the Virgin, one of the ancient series of Black Virgins, was venerated in the crypt. (The one to be seen there now is a copy, because the original was destroyed in the French Revolution.) Charles the Bald in about 876 had presented to the cathedral its most sacred relic, the silk tunic worn by the Virgin when giving birth to Christ. The presumed loss of the relic in the fire of 1194, which left only the west front untouched, caused as much despair as the destruction of the cathedral, and after its miraculous discovery unharmed in the crypt, it was said that the fire was sent by grace of the Virgin because she desired an even more beautiful church to be built in her honour.

Among the works to survive the fire are the beautiful early windows of the west front underneath the rose, one of them a Jesse window deriving directly from St-Denis (fig. 87). Another work was the part of a window known as *Notre-Dame de la Belle Verrière*, depicting the Virgin and Child. This masterpiece of early stained-glass art was so highly regarded that, in the rebuilding of the cathedral, the panels of which it is composed were inserted in a window of the south choir aisle and surrounded by figures of adoring angels. The Virgin, crowned as Queen of Heaven, sits with the Christ Child upright on her lap. Jesus, with His right hand raised in blessing, has His head in its halo centred on His Mother's heart. He gazes directly out into the world while His Mother gently inclines her head and looks down at the devotee, which every visitor must become before art of such magnitude. Though much restored and defying photography on account of stains and dark patches, Mother and Child express such tenderness, such intelligence, such individuality, that one is drawn, however much else there is to see in the cathedral, back again and again to look upon the evidence of a higher consciousness, a higher conscience, that their eyes proclaim. They are civilization made manifest.

19 Chartres. The well of the martyrs in the Romanesque crypt, *c.* 1020.

CHAPTER 3

The Pointed Arch: people, patrons and masons

The pointed arch is the dominant feature of the Gothic style, both as a means of recognition and for its symbolism. Why was it to replace the rounded arch in most church and secular architecture for the next four hundred years? What deep hunger in the soul of Western man was assuaged by its adoption? What lack in the soul did it restitute? What new aspiration did its sharpened profile signify? The practical reasons for its introduction on so wide a scale are easy to rehearse: the pointed arch is stronger than the rounded arch because it works by the opposition of forces and exerts less thrust; where bays have to be of unequal width, the pointed arch can still rise to the same height as its fellows; used in conjunction with the closely related ribbed vault and flying buttress it permits the raising of buildings to heights rarely, if ever, attained in Romanesque times; and it tends always to the abolition of the solid wall, with its replacement by the traceried and glazed window.

If it brings with it all these advantages, why had it not been used earlier, by, for example, those masters of constructional technology, the Romans? The Romans did not need it in its form as the pointed and ribbed vault because of their exceptional skill in the use of mortar to cover the interiors of great public buildings; they did not need it for capturing light because they were more concerned to exclude light, and as an expression of their attitude to the world they did not need it because they had created their own great cosmological symbol in the dome of the Pantheon, a form that was to be adopted, with changes in its method of construction, by the Eastern Empire in St Sophia and its numerous copies.

The introduction of the pointed arch must be seen, therefore, as an expression of the nature and the needs of North-Western Europe, no longer the home of wandering and barbarous tribes hemmed in by forests and river swamps, no longer the further provinces of a distant Empire centred on the Mediterranean, no longer the prey of hordes from the East and the North but now, in the earlier twelfth century, the most important region of the planet, for its vitality, its inventiveness, and its desire to expand, not merely territorially, but into regions of the mind and the spirit. Introduced from Islamic culture, which had already made great advances in all the sciences then practised, the pointed arch, in migrating to Christian Europe, became the symbol of Western domination in science and technology; its lancet form is the cross-section of the space-rocket of today. As all great symbols contain in themselves the past and the future, so in its clustered ribs, its overarching forms, and the spatial effects of the recession of vistas, it represents the triumph of Western man over the primeval forest of his ancestral environments, its gods and goddesses, its darknesses and fears. It was the felling of those forests that revealed the fertile soils yielding the wealth which built the cathedrals and churches that display the form of the arch in every aspect. Though the pointed arch went into desuetude during the

20 St-Denis. The pointed arch is seen in many forms in this view from the narthex, *c.* 1137, built by Abbot Suger, through to his choir, dedicated in 1144. The nave, transepts, and upper stages of the choir were rebuilt, perhaps by Pierre de Montereau, from 1231 onwards in the *rayonnant* style, the court style of St Louis.

21   Autun. The pointed arch in Burgundian Romanesque architecture, a view of the nave, 1120–1130. The flat sides of the arches show clearly their Islamic origin.

Renaissance, it was revived, both in the religious architecture and the engineering constructions accompanying the Industrial Revolution.

When introduced into Burgundian Romanesque architecture, as at Autun (fig. 21), the pointed arch kept the plain straight-sided form of its Saracen relatives.[1] From its first use in the true Gothic buildings it would taper inwards from the wall in which it formed an aperture, in a series of mouldings that allied it to the infolded and ribbed forms of the columns and vaults, so that each aperture is not one but a sequence of pointed arches adding to the form's intensity of expression. We may also see in it, as well as the historical and prophetic significance, the urge to question and to experiment which makes it so much more expressive a form than the regular accepting bows of the round arch. In this it recalls the contemporaneous rebirth of intellectual life in the schools of Chartres, Laon, and Paris, the very centres of the birth of the Gothic style when men discovered the infinite possibilities of their reasoning faculties. One of the greatest gifts of the Gothic style was its immeasurable extension of the possibilities of emotional as well as intellectual expression. Thus above and including all these meanings is the ultimate mystical one: the piercing towards heaven which echoes the Dionysian thrust of the soul towards its Maker.

The pointed arch refers us, therefore, to that state of higher awareness in which the mind and the heart find union. It is always rewarding, in one of the great cathedrals such as Amiens (fig. 22), where there is so much to marvel at, to concentrate on one arch of one bay and, ignoring everything else for a time, to let its piercing shape, simple and clear within its repeated mouldings, work its spell upon our minds. Sometimes it is in the furthest outposts of the Gothic that I have come across a pointed arch or window, often perfectly carved, that in its simplicity has struck me with all the force of a realized archetype. I think of the dark chapel of the Krak des Chevaliers, covered in green mould but with its apse windows looking southwards to an unseen Jerusalem and opening onto the milky mists of the Anti-Lebanon mountains, through which the voice of the muezzin arose. I think of the pure beauty of the triple lancets of Killaloe, with the gleam of the fast-running Shannon reflected through them as pencils of light (fig. 25). I think of the exquisite fineness of the mouldings of the west door (fig. 24) and the nave arcades of Dunblane, erected at the orders of a Dominican bishop in about 1235, the door itself rutted by centuries of Highland gales and rain, the nave finely preserved though it stood roofless for three hundred years. In such places we can feel, all the more intensely because of their loneliness and quietness, through the pointed arch's symbolic form, the seal and the sanction of a higher and immanent world, the invisible source from which true civilization draws its life.

22 *Below* Amiens. The pointed arch in High Gothic architecture, a view in the nave of one of the grandest of all Gothic interiors, begun in 1220 by Robert de Luzarches.

23 *Below right* Le Mans. Looking up into the clerestory windows of the choir.

24   Dunblane. The pointed arch seen in multiple form in the west door, *c.* 1235, overlooking the river Allan on the edge of the Highlands.

25 *Below*   Killaloe. The pointed arch in the two side lancets of the eastern end, *c.* 1225, of this small Irish cathedral, seen across the Shannon.

Through what means did the success of the Gothic style come about? Let us try and formulate an answer through the people for whom it was devised, the peasants, townspeople and ruling classes, the patrons who realized its possibilities, the bishops, abbots and monarchs, and the actual creators of the style, the artists, architects and masons.

First, the peasants, from whose labours came the surplus wealth that allowed the rebirth of town life and created the Age of the Cathedrals. The rich alluvial soils of Northern France had never been fully exploited in the long period of Roman domination.[2] The general adoption of the heavy plough at some time in the Dark Ages meant that the soil could be ploughed deep enough to release its hidden energies in greater and more varied crop-yields. The great expense of acquiring and maintaining heavy ploughs with their teams of oxen meant that they were often jointly owned by groups of peasants, each of whom possessed a different part of the equipment. Joint ownership had led to farming families living more closely together: this is the phenomenon known as 'balling', by which living in villages replaced living in scattered settlements, something to which both fear of marauding Norsemen and the rise of feudalism had also contributed. These villages, with their churches and chapels, were the basis of the parish system, with each priest answerable to the bishop of the region who was in turn answerable to the archbishop of the province.

Greater productivity of the land had led to a population explosion in the eleventh century, not only of humans but of domesticated animals which needed winter feed. This had led in turn to extensive works of clearing forest and wildland in order to bring them into use as arable or pastureland. The extent to which the land north of Paris was cleared by the 1130s is illustrated in a story told by Suger. Exasperated by his carpenters, who informed him that no trees of great enough size could be found for the next stage in the rebuilding of St-Denis, he made them ride with him for miles into the country until suddenly they came across twelve trees which answered perfectly to their need.[3]

How deep Christianity had penetrated into the peasant culture of Northern France is a fascinating matter for conjecture. The local saints and angelic forces had taken the place of local deities as the invisible protectors of each region, but there survived numerous pagan festivals, rites and practices associated with the cycle of the farming year, with love, and with healing, some of which the Church could absorb and some of which her priests tried in vain to ban—if they were not practising them themselves. The extraordinary extent to which pagan beliefs survived in Romanesque and Gothic sculpture is discussed further in the next four chapters. But here is one example: just as we have seen the symbols of the Great Mother carved on the drum columns of Durham in Northern England, so we can see, in the miracle-working Black Virgins which were venerated all over France at this period, the survival of the most ancient known religion given a Christian garb in these numinous wooden madonnas (fig. 26).[4] The reassertion of the Ideal Feminine through the increasing glorification of the Virgin Mary was to be one of the greatest triumphs of the Gothic, an achievement which its artists owed to the presence in society of a deep feeling for the feminine which the church with its male hierarchies had tried to repress.

The contribution of the peasant to the cathedrals is acknowledged time and again in a series of sculptures devoted to the Labours of the Year (fig. 28). The cathedral where one most feels this acknowledgement is Laon (fig. 46), whose town is built on a high steep hogsback of limestone rising out of the Northern French plain. The site of the cathedral was occupied in Celtic times by the shrine of the god Loucetios,[5] the guard of the Great Mother:

various Christian churches were built over the shrine, notably in the Carolingian period. When the stone for the Romanesque cathedral was being dragged up the steep slopes of the hill one of the oxen foundered in its traces from exhaustion, but miraculously another ox suddenly appeared to take its place, returning day after day until the task was accomplished. This miracle was later celebrated in the construction of the west towers of the present Gothic cathedral, when sixteen gigantic oxen were carved and set high in the towers to stare down on the city with the slow curiosity of their kind (fig. 27). Just as all representations of beasts and birds in medieval art have a symbolic reference to the kaleidoscopic variety of human nature, so these oxen reflect not only their contribution to the new wealth of North-Western Europe but also the patient resignation to a life of toil shown by their companions in labour, the peasants.

Though the usual state of the peasant in society was that of serfdom to ecclesiastical or secular overlords, it is remarkable how many born to a life on the soil managed to escape. One way for the young and fit was through soldiering: other ways were provided by the growing need for trained craftsmen in a variety of skills. International trade by the turn of the eleventh century was reviving through the establishment of a series of great fairs where the main commodity for sale was the fine cloth now being produced in the towns of Northern France and Flanders. This meant a greater circulation of the money vital for building works. Much of the funding for Suger's works at St-Denis came as we have seen from his control of the fair outside the Abbey known as the Lendit, which was held in conjunction with the chief pilgrimage to the relics of St Denis and other saints.

The rise of the Gothic style, the rebirth of the towns, and the develop-

26 *Above left*   The Black Virgin: one of the many twelfth-century versions of this much revered type, seen here in the church of Notre-Dame de Dijon.

27 *Above*   Laon. The oxen who look down from the two towers of the west front (*c.* 1200), commemorating the miracle of the ox which helped in the building of the earlier Romanesque cathedral.

ment and exploitation of new advances in technology are inextricably linked. The building and furnishing of a new cathedral requires workers in stone, wood, glass, ceramics, and metals of many kinds, as well as textiles. The provision of all these skills over the generation or two it could take to construct a major portion of a cathedral enriched not only the diversity of skills available within the town where it was built but also the neighbouring countryside. The fame of a new cathedral would draw pilgrims and travellers who would increase the trade of the town, and the guilds of the various crafts and trades were often proud to present windows or series of statues devoted to their patron saints to adorn the aisles and side chapels of the great buildings in whose shadows they lived and worked. Metallurgy provides one example of a technological advance essential to the development of the Gothic style. The monk Gervase, in noting the differences between the construction of the old crypt and choir and of the new works at Canterbury, remarked on the way William of Sens's sculptors carved the capitals with chisels instead of axes.[6] He was watching the results of a great advance in the making of strong reliable metal tools that could take the force of hammer blows without shattering or spoiling the stone. The provision of such tools allowed the deep undercutting that permitted the marvellously accurate depiction of vegetation and of drapery, and, above all, the precise delineation of human expression.

The rebirth of town life increased the wealth and the responsibilities of the bishops and the higher clergy. They were the patrons in a sense that is hardly known today. We do not now have patrons who are concerned to direct our souls to salvation in the afterlife through the right practice and execution of art. We have directors of galleries of modern art who want to educate us to an awareness of what is vital or fashionable in art today. We have art-dealers whose living depends on their responses to the desires of

28   Amiens. Examples of the Labours of the Months seen beneath their associated zodiacal signs (l. to r.): harvesting under Leo, threshing under Virgo, and fruit-picking under Libra, c. 1220.

31 *Above* Rheims. The coronation of the Virgin over the central portal of the west front; a scene of apotheosis demonstrating the exaltation of the Virgin in Gothic art. This group is a copy of the original sculptures, *c.* 1240, whose battered remains are in the cathedral museum.

29 *Above left* Autun. The tympanum of the Last Judgment signed by the sculptor Gislebertus, *c.* 1130. On the right of the colossal figure of Christ are the saved; on the left are the damned.

30 *Left* Vézelay. The tympanum, *c.* 1140, the theme of which is the spreading of the gospel message by Christ through the apostles to the nations of the earth.

private and public patrons. We have many artists and sculptors, often moved and inspired by the deepest religious feelings, but few even of these would claim that the power of their art could change the direction of men's lives today to the degree that was expected of art in the Middle Ages. Though this applies today in Western society, there are also in our century many examples of attempts to direct artists to the glorification of a nation, as under Hitler or Mussolini, or of a revolutionary theory as in Soviet Russia and her satellites, and these examples have left us with a horror of associating art with a philosophy or a political purpose.

Such considerations should not blind us to the fruitful achievements by patrons of imagination and taste such as St Hugh of Cluny and Abbot Suger. Our society today is happier and richer in experience because of the roles they undertook. A patron who thinks on the scale of a continent as did St Hugh, or of a rising nation as did Suger, and can divert great resources of men and money to his aims, is a benefactor of humanity. Though he would rarely have the time or the expertise to practise even one of the arts whose exponents he directs, he must be an artist in men, a maker of opportunities for great dreams to become great realities. A man in such a position with responsibility for the souls of thousands of men and women can become a portal for the issuing into general awareness of new images, new symbols, new ideas and interpretations of doctrine. To his people he stands in the place of Christ who said 'I am the door', and it is of the deepest meaning, when we consider the role of art in drawing out the lacks and imbalances of society, that many of the profoundest changes can be traced in the series of portal and tympanum sculpture that virtually begins with the tympana of Cluny in the 1080s and continues to the west façade of Rheims, with its depiction of the coronation of the Virgin. Each one of these portals, from Moissac, Autun (fig. 29), and Vézelay (fig. 30)—to take earlier

Romanesque examples—to St-Denis, Chartres (fig. 5), Notre-Dame at Paris (fig. 6), up to Amiens and Rheims itself, were the expression not just of the artists, mediators though they were of great psychic forces, but of bodies of learned clerics, canons, and bishops, many of whom, especially at cathedrals closely associated with schools of learning as at Laon, Chartres, and Paris, would have been among the most advanced thinkers of their day. In this connexion it must be remembered that on a great many points of doctrine the teaching of the Church was nothing like as evolved or definite as it later became; in working at the iconographic schemes of the cathedrals the clerics associated with the building programmes would have been, in many cases, defining as much for themselves as for ordinary people the new directions the faith should take.

One particular feature of the development of west front sculpture from the early Gothic period is that the Virgin Mary, who is almost excluded from Romanesque tympana, grows in importance with the passing of time. At Chartres, in 1145, she is placed on the right-hand portal. At Senlis, by 1194, she is over the central portal. At Rheims by the middle thirteenth century she is raised above all the doors, in front of the western rose, equal in status to her Son who crowns her (fig. 31).

In this development of doctrine through art Georges Duby sees the work of the Gothic architects and sculptors as entirely subservient to the aims of the Church in establishing true doctrine and crushing heresy.[7] Against this view I would maintain the role of the artists in effectually transforming the interpretation of doctrine through their art. The Church may have wanted the central doctrine of the Incarnation emphasized in sculpture in order to counteract the effect of heresies, such as Albigensianism, which denied its importance. The expression of that doctrine in writings by influential churchmen such as Anselm in his *Cur Deus Homo*, for example, is one of gloom at the wickedness of man. Similarly, a popular theme of the twelfth- and early-thirteenth-century churchmen with a literary bent was *de contemptu mundi*: they vied with one another in depicting the horrors of this world, the terrors of damnation, and the distant joys of paradise which were reserved for remarkably few. Churchmen such as Suger, with his discovery of Dionysian mysticism, and the members of the School of Chartres, with their development of Christian Neoplatonic thought, were rare in their appreciation of the beauties and wonders of creation. It is significant that they were the patrons of the early Gothic, and that is why they were dependent on the artist for the full manifestation of the ideas that inspired them.

The schools of Paris, Laon, and Chartres created free space for the mind to speculate and explore its own nature and its capacities for analysing the world. The Gothic artists created a free space for man to discover his higher intellectual and emotional capacities. How and why were they able to create this free space?

C. G. Jung says that every period

> has its bias, its particular prejudice, and its psychic ailment. An epoch is like an individual, it has its own limitations of conscious outlook, and therefore requires a compensatory adjustment. This is effected by the collective unconscious in that a poet, a seer, or a leader allows himself to be guided by the unexpressed desire of his times and shows the way by word or deed, to the attainment of that which everyone blindly craves and expects—whether this attainment results in good or evil, the healing of an epoch or its destruction.[8]

Jung's theory of balance applies very well to Romanesque art and

32   Chartres. A view of the double ambulatory of the choir showing the radiating chapels with their stained glass.

architecture and to many of the movements of the time, such as a new expression of the feminine ideal both through the troubadour poets and through devotion to the Virgin Mary, which arises to balance the overemphasis on a masculine deity whose rites were limited to male priests. With its emphasis on the collective unconscious, however, Jung's theory carries the implication that civilizing movements are inevitable. If we were to apply it wholeheartedly to the rise of the Gothic, we could explain it entirely as the expression of unconscious desires in the population of the time. That would be to mistake the energy, the psychic power or potential, for its manifestation and development.

For a phenomenon in civilization such as the Gothic we need a theory of collective consciousness rather than the collective unconscious. To explain what I mean more clearly, let me take an example that may be in many people's experience. You are in a small museum with articles of quality from many periods and civilizations: the smallness of the museum causes you inevitably to make comparisons and there may be pieces from certain countries or epochs that give you a totally different impression from the rest. You come upon an Egyptian stone figure of a scribe, a Greek bronze head or marble fragment of the Praxitelean period, a Chinese Lohan in glazed terracotta, an Indian temple sculpture, or a Gothic leaf capital, and you say involuntarily to yourself: the makers of these knew what they were doing. The other artefacts may have charm, vitality, decorative qualities or even numinosity, but they are entirely of their period and culture.

These other works, though from such scattered cultures, possess a quality of awareness that wakes you up. They exhibit a command over the inner vision, over the skills of execution, and over the effect they are meant to have on the onlooker, which indicates the presence of a conscious inspiration. They also, in conveying this sense of awareness, transcend their particular periods and express the light of the Perennial Philosophy. In the case of Gothic works of art, this quality is the achievement of the architects and sculptors, not of the patrons and churchmen who believed they were directing them, nor of the kings, barons, townspeople and peasants whose various labours and funds paid for them.

Though Suger's omission of the name of his architects may seem odd, there is enough evidence from long before his time to show in what esteem the architects or master masons were held. The master masons of Lombardy may have been the descendants of Roman craft organizations and, therefore, the only lay profession to have maintained continuity from the fall of the Empire. Later evidence shows that they prided themselves on their ancient constitutions, their status as freemen, and their honourable calling. That we know few names from Suger's period in France is probably owed to the accidents of history, such as the loss of records or the obliteration of inscriptions in the course of later building, rather than their suffering from a lack of esteem. When we see, for example, in Notre-Dame, the huge inscription on the south transept commemorating Jean de Chelles, its first architect, we have no doubts about the prestige he commanded. The inscriptions recorded from the now lost mazes of Rheims and Amiens giving the names of the architects reveal that they were held in the highest honour

33 Strasbourg. The inscription, now in the Musée de l'oeuvre de Notre-Dame, commemorating Master Erwin, the architect responsible for the work on the west front of the cathedral from 1276 to 1318.

34 Salisbury. A view from the north-east showing the superb exterior of the choir and Lady chapel, choir transept and main transept built by Nicholas of Ely, 1220 to 1258, and the spire built by Robert Mason and Richard Farleigh between 1320 and 1380.

35 *Overleaf left* Durham. The nave with its vaulting, completed in 1133. The pointed arch appears in the transverse arches of the vaulting; the ribbed vaulting forms a sexpartite pattern within each bay of alternating composite piers and round columns; the flying buttresses are hidden behind the composite piers at the triforium stage.

36 *Overleaf right* Salisbury. The nave interior looking westwards, built by Nicholas of Ely from 1220 onwards.

for their genius and their accomplishments.

Their high position was owed to their monopoly of skills which they guarded jealously. They transmitted them only to those who had undergone the correct sequence of early education in a church or monastery school and then of an apprenticeship lasting from five to seven years in learning carpentry or how to carve stone, as well as studying the geometrical knowledge necessary for design. Progression to the higher grades was through examinations, ceremonies, and evidence of the ability to produce master work. There was strict supervision through the craft organizations. John Harvey suggests that the craft was revitalized by influences from Moslem Spain and the Near East around 1100 and that the craft organizations became fixed in France and England with frequent contacts between the countries in the course of the twelfth century.[9] The organizations were later carried into Germany and Spain. The Strasbourg masons under their Master Erwin founded their lodge in 1275 and the lodge was described as one 'of freed masonry according to the English fashion', the phrase 'freed masonry' meaning that they had their own jurisdiction.[10] This lodge soon became the master lodge of the Holy Roman Empire and its English links may help to account for the strong influence of English Gothic on German architecture in the fourteenth century.

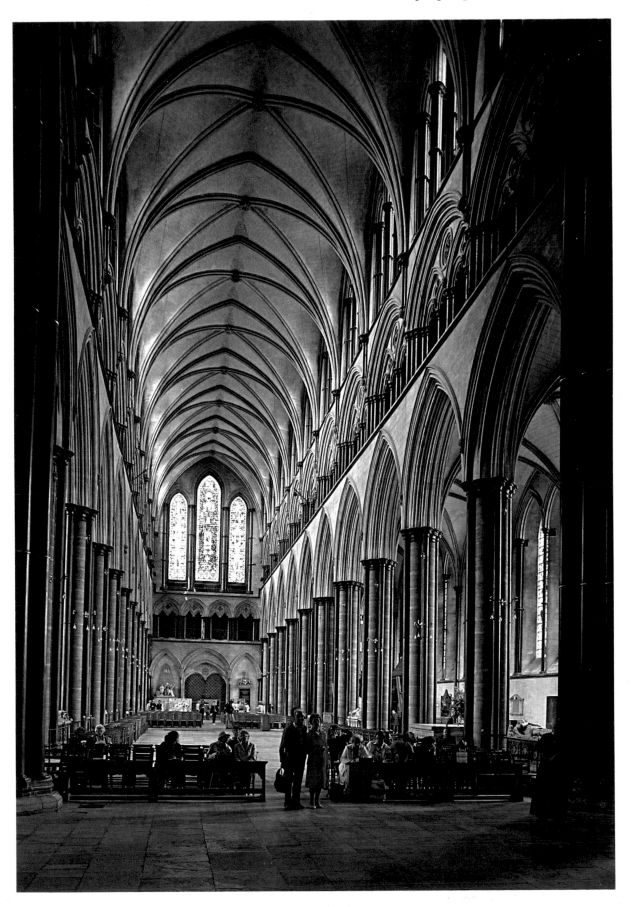

They had to collaborate with their patrons over the essentials of the building and its iconography, but once it came to the actual design and its implementation they were free to play with light and shade in the enclosing and opening out of space. They kept complete control over the templates from which the mouldings were cut, and all papers essential to the design and elevation. Nicholas of Ely, the architect of Salisbury, had a gifted clerical colleague in a canon of the cathedral, Elias of Dereham, but when it came to transforming the raw materials—the 50,000 tons of Chilmark stone, the 15,000 tons of Purbeck marble, the 3,500 tons of oak, not to mention 400 tons of lead—into a unified architectural masterpiece, it was the skills of Nicholas of Ely and his successors as architect that were paramount and that no one lacking their background and training could supply (fig. 34).

For all their eminence and high social standing, the Gothic masters appear little in the gossip of the chronicles of the time. For the later period it is not unusual for portrait sculptures of them to be placed in their own churches and it may be that, among the numberless heads of twelfth- and thirteenth-century buildings, there are many depictions of the masons and their families, whose identification is lost beyond recall. If there is any benefit to be gained from the survival of a name beyond the grave, they are fortunate because the record of their personalities is in the stone they carved and the spaces they enclosed.

What we know about them is the best of their natures—the transcendent free spaces of Laon and Notre-Dame de Paris with their ample galleries, the soaring definition of Amiens, the warm huge-minded charm of Chartres. All these began as visions—emotional visions in the minds of men who were capable of transmitting their visions not only to those in the immediate circle of their craft with whom they worked, but also to succeeding generations. To study them through their works is to come to a realization that in true art the artist is only a medium for the transcendent, that his personality is as much a part of the raw material of art to be transformed into a style as are the words, the stones, the pigments with which he works, and that when, as in their case, there is an agreed meeting of geniuses, where there is indeed an abasement of individual genius to a greater cause, we have to speak of a collective consciousness.

CHAPTER 4

Technology and the Spirit

The makers of the Gothic style enriched and enlarged the imagination of Europe, guiding the minds and hearts of future generations to think universal thoughts on a grander scale and to feel deeper and more magnanimous emotions. Long before Dante had created modern literature by the device of individual characters who reveal their natures in their own words, they had devised a means of conveying the visual conception of individuality.[1] Decades before St Francis composed his Canticle of all Creatures, they had freed their imaginative perception of nature from the Romanesque connexion between animal and plant life and the depiction of sin, and, instead, had begun to portray birds, beasts, and vegetation with a naturalness and a delight that proclaimed the goodness of creation.[2] A century before the time when, through Arab influence, the science of optics was developing in the west under Grosseteste and his followers at Oxford,[3] they had succeeded in creating new ways of enclosing space and of making light stream through windows of stained glass, past arcades of columns and from transepts and apses, so that its effects seemed a portrayal of the heavenly light from which our visible light derives.

They achieved this through their ability to manipulate stone. They built mostly with limestone, rock formed of the deposits of ocean creatures millions of years ago, frequently in sandstone, another sedimentary rock, and rarely, as at Mont St-Michel and Aberdeen, in granite. In their hands heavy stone was made to soar to heights undreamed of by earlier generations and invested with a new lightness as they carved it into crocketed finials and fretted spires. They took dense stone and made it form the skeleton or the envelope of the largest interior spaces ever to be enclosed until the works of the engineers of the last century. They took lifeless stone and made it express the history of mankind and all living creatures from the creation to the Last Judgment. They took formless stone and made it their medium for the most accurate delineation of the natural forms of leaf and branch ever depicted to their date, and out of its blank and mindless blocks they carved their piercingly exact portrayals of human beings of every kind from saints in ecstasy to souls in torment. Beyond all this, they made blind, glum, heartless stone the vehicle for a new vision of luminosity and a new sense of happiness in art, and through their work they established, quite as much as their contemporary philosophers and mathematicians, the beginnings of western supremacy in science and technology.

This supremacy must be owed in the first place to a new attitude to matter. The manipulation of matter on the smallest scale, which is one of the achievements of our modern science, can be said to derive from the ability of the Gothic masters to manipulate on the macroscale. The great cathedrals demonstrated how man could transform the raw materials that surround him both by quarrying and shaping stone and by smelting, refining, or mixing earths, minerals and metals to create acres of stained glass and square miles of lead or tiled roofing. We change matter according to our imaginative perception of nature. The worlds of molecules, atoms and

subatomic particles are in one sense constructs of our imaginations and in another sense can be said to have an objective reality because, on the basis of theory which is also a product of imagination, their combinations can be changed, their qualities altered and their very natures transformed into something else. Before science could achieve such command over the resources of nature, it was necessary that the imaginations of men in relation to nature should be enlarged by the construction of huge permanent reminders of their actual and potential power over matter.

This new power over matter shows further how Christianity freed the men and women of Western Europe from being slaves of their environment and the puppets of the gods and spirits of forest, river, field and sky.[4] The building of the great cathedrals was an act of liberation from the forest-bound mentality of Northern Man, transforming the prison of the woods into temples of stone trees. That the iconography of the cathedrals, from the west front of Chartres to that of Rheims, reveals an ever-increasing emphasis on the Doctrine of the Incarnation has been interpreted as showing the desire of the clergy to defend that doctrine against the attacks of heretics such as the Albigensians, who slighted or disbelieved it. It has, however, a deeper significance in terms of our subject: as God became Man in Christ so He sanctified all the elements of which men and women are made and, as Christ in death descended into Hell, He changed the stony bowels of the Earth from being the fastness of the damned to the very material from which the art of His praise should be fashioned in the great Gothic cathedrals and churches.

The quarrying of stone was the biggest mining industry of medieval Europe. Jean Gimpel, in making this point, says that in France from the eleventh to the later thirteenth centuries more stone was quarried than in the whole history of ancient Egypt.[5] Paris today stands upon rock burrowed with 300 kilometres of underground galleries from which the stone of the medieval city was cut. Though much of the output of stone was devoted to the building of castles and defensive works, the skills that enabled the construction of secular and military works were largely devised for, and perfected in, ecclesiastical buildings. It was a spiritual need, the need for stone churches, which provided the impetus for mining a resource that only in Roman times had ever been drawn on to the same extent.

If we consider the symbolic nature of stone, the sense of permanence, of fixity, of unalterability it conveys, then we get an idea of the boldness of the early Romanesque quarry-workers and builders who began the large-scale exploitation of its resources. They were out to change the unchangeable. Although they intended to give stone a sacred character through using it to build churches, at a primordial level they were committing sacrilege by delving into their mother earth. The awe they felt for their material is evident in the massive nature of their constructions. It is a feature that continues throughout the Romanesque period: the western walls of Speyer Cathedral, begun in 1030, are 20 ft (6 m) thick and it is usual in Anglo-Norman churches of a century later to find walls at least seven ft (2 m) thick. Though they conveyed this sense of awe, the Romanesque builders were also aware of a higher duty, to transform stone into an image of perfect man—so that we find an eleventh-century abbey church, that of St Trond, near Liége, being described in terms of the human body: the chancel and the sanctuary are the head and neck, the choir with its stalls the chest, the transepts the hands and arms, the crossing the belly, and the north and south aisles the thighs and shins.[6]

The Gothic masters freed themselves of this stylistic dependence on weight and mass. To give one instance, the clerestory walls of Notre-Dame

37   St-Denis. The ambulatory of Suger's choir, built 1140–44.

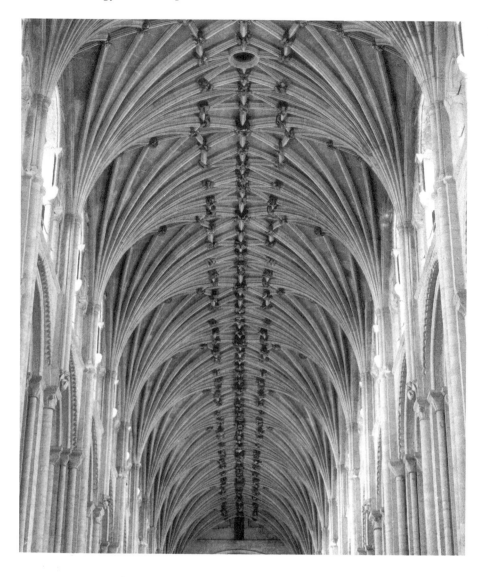

38 Norwich. The vault bosses of the nave, which tell the history of the world from creation to the Last Judgment, rising with their vault, constructed after a fire in 1463, from the Norman walls. From the open hole in the vaulting an angel would be suspended at Whitsun (see Chapter 8).

are a mere two ft (60 cm) thick. They still thought of their materials in symbolic terms. A contemporary verse description of Lincoln Cathedral, as rebuilt in the Gothic style, says that by the hewn white stone should be understood the chaste and wise: 'whiteness is decency and its shaping, doctrine',[7] a statement that reveals much about how stone was humanized and thought of as matter that could undergo regeneration.

This process of regeneration began in the quarries only after the clerical patrons, the bishop and his canons, the abbot and his monks, had chosen and briefed the architect. They would have had to convince him that they had the initial funds for their schemes just as much as he would have had to impress on them his talents and capability, and to get their general agreement to his design. With agreement on both sides, the architect would visit the local quarries and if the stone was not suitable, he would make arrangements further afield. One of the greatest expenses of medieval building was transport; overland carriage was by ox- and horse-drawn cart. It was often cheaper to bring the stone by water. Throughout the Middle Ages, for instance, Caen stone was transported across the Channel and far up the east coast of England to sites such as Norwich. To save transport costs, as much cutting of the stone as possible would be done at the quarries. Using the templates drawn by the architect which were accurate guides to the moulding of column bases and shafts, the voussoirs of arches, and tracery for the arcades and windows, the masons would start carving the stone and marking each piece for its position.

After the bases of the columns were set and the first courses of the walls had been laid, there was a need for scaffolds and cranes and other machines for hoisting. Water-power could be used for sawing logs and hammering iron, examples of the new technology of which it has been remarked that in the twelfth century more machines were at the beck of men than ever before in the history of the world.[8] Once the stone had been brought by the oxen and draught-horses, all the further stages depended on human muscle-power, using block-and-tackle pulleys, and cranes and hoists worked by treadmills. Examples of these treadmills still survive at Beverley and Freiburg-im-Breisgau. Every open section of the church, its arches, its windows with their tracery, the flying buttresses, the stone vaulting, had to be constructed round the wooden framework known as centering (fig. 39). The accuracy with which each opening was built depended on the carpenters who made the centering. It is probable that it was the carpenters of the Normans, skilful in shipbuilding, in military works such as the wooden prefabricated castles they brought across the Channel at the Conquest, and in domestic buildings, who developed the techniques that greatly aided the development of the Gothic. It is equally probable that it was the influence of Islamic masonry techniques that brought about the marked improvement in the accuracy of jointing stone that is noticeable after 1100.

As the walls reached their destined height, the carpenters would construct the wooden roof. On this the plumbers would unroll their sheets of lead, ridging them in patterns that counteracted the tendency of the soft metal to slip. Or else the roof would be coated in tiles—plain red tiles like the roof of Sens Cathedral or, following a later fashion, brilliantly coloured glazed tiles like those on the great hall at Sens next to the cathedral. Under cover of the roof the vaults could be built in stone. Suger tells a dramatic story of the great storm on 19 January 1143 which bore down on the choir, whose arches had been completed but which had not yet received the webs of its vaulting. The skeletal choir stood under a wooden roof; during the storm Geoffroy de Lèves, the Bishop of Chartres, celebrated mass for the

39   Modern centering in use in the recent restoration of the cloisters at Canterbury, built *c*. 1400 by Henry Yeveley and Stephen Lote.

40 *Overleaf left*   Holy Cross, Schwäbisch-Gmünd, begun 1351. The elaborate pattern of ribs in the choir vaulting, built by Aberlin Jörg and Hans von Urach in the early sixteenth century.

41 *Overleaf right*   Cologne. The clerestory and apse of the choir, the work of the architect Gerhard, begun in 1248 and completed by others in 1322.

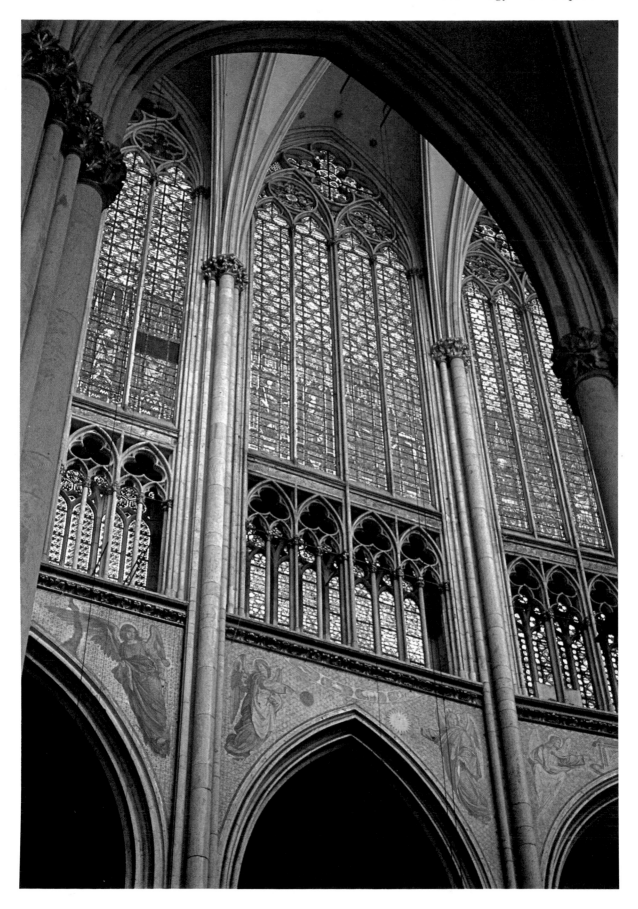

soul of King Dagobert. The arches vibrated and trembled in the force of the gale and the bishop, alarmed by the thought that the construction might collapse, frequently made the sign of the cross and held out a reliquary containing the arm of St Simeon in the direction of most danger. As Suger remarks of the tempest, while it brought calamitous ruin in many places to buildings thought to be firm, it 'was unable to damage these isolated and newly made arches, tottering in mid-air, because it was repulsed by the power of God'.[9] It would not have occurred to him that the divine power had saved the arches because it had worked through the creative power of the architect who had devised a new and stronger method of construction as much through the prayers of the bishop and the virtue of St Simeon's arm.

The construction of the vaults must have been work involving great physical danger and constant strain (see p. 70 for William of Sens' accident). First the wooden centering would be mounted on a scaffold. The centering would conform to the shape of the desired vaulting. Then earth would be poured on the frame and moulded into the form of the vault. Each section of the ribs would be hoisted up and set in the earth and linked to the bosses or keystones. The bosses are often several feet in diameter. When, as at Norwich—where there are 225 bosses in the nave vault telling the whole history of the world—they formed an elaborate iconographical scheme (fig. 38), the slightest damage in hauling one of these up could have set back the building programme by weeks while a new boss was carved. The interstices of the cage formed by the ribs and bosses would be filled with thin stonework and the earth and some of the centering would be taken away to allow the painters to decorate the bosses, ribs and webs of the vaulting. When a bay was completed, there would be a celebration and the scaffolding and centering would be re-erected for the vaulting of the next bay. From the later thirteenth century the design of vaults became more and more intricate; the masons developed the patterns formed by subsidiary ribs, known as tiercerons, as in the high vaults of Exeter (fig. 143), or in the magnificent later German vaults as at Schwäbisch-Gmünd which are like the criss-cross of scimitars in a sword-dance (fig. 40).

While the main building work was in progress, the canons or monks would have to conduct their services in any part that was least disturbed. When each section was finished, there was still work for other craftsmen, the painters, metalworkers, tilers, and glaziers, to carry out their embellishments. At last there would come a day when a cathedral was considered complete enough for its consecration. Then the bishop would lead a procession to the west front. One of his clergy was not in the procession because he symbolized the devil and lurked inside the church. The bishop would knock three times on the door and the procession would sing 'Lift up your heads, O ye gates, and be ye lifted up, ye everlasting doors, and the King of Glory shall come in.' This was followed by silence and then a voice from inside asked 'Who is the King of Glory?' To which the procession replied: 'The Lord of Hosts, he is the King of Glory!' The doors would open and the cleric playing the devil slipped out into the crowd as the bishop entered to consecrate his new cathedral.[10]

At the consecration of the choir of Cologne Cathedral on 26 September 1357 the mystic Johannes Tauler preached on the true consecration of churches, saying that this was a rite to be celebrated within the man who turns inward. 'Churches make no man holy but men make churches holy.'[11] Tauler was a follower of Meister Eckhart and a prime influence on the mysticism of Rhineland art in the later Middle Ages. Other saints, mystics, and leaders of religious movements had earlier profoundly affected the development of the Gothic style. Chief among these were the Cistercians.

In their rejection of what they regarded as the luxury and over-ornamentation of Cluny and in their return to a more primitive Christianity and a greater fidelity to the Rule of St Benedict, the Cistercians, at the turn of the eleventh century, sought out wild forested valleys where, largely aided by the numbers of *conversi* or lay brothers who gave their labour where they could not read, write, or sing, they brought large tracts of land into cultivation. To keep their growing communities healthy and fed, they had to make each foundation self-dependent and, in doing so, had to draw on nearly everything that was most up-to-date in the technological expertise of the time. They trained their rivers into leets that gave them power to mill their corn, to full their cloth, to work bellows and hammers for their smithies, and to sweep away the waste of their bodies. Their earliest churches, being under the influence of Burgundian Romanesque, soon adopted the pointed arch, as may be seen at Fontenay, and among the first

42 Pontigny. Severe Burgundian Cistercian architecture in the ambulatory, *c.* 1185, of this remarkable abbey church.

examples of the pointed arch in England are those at the Cistercian abbeys of Kirkstall and Fountains in Yorkshire.[12] Though St Bernard forbade his monks towers, figural stained windows, and many of the other features that gave opportunity to the invention of the sculptor and the painter, his own interest in music and proportion inspired his followers to devise or commission interiors that accentuated the abstract and spatial qualities of the Gothic. Thus the interior of Pontigny (fig. 42), built 1151–85, is one of the most harmoniously severe and heart-uplifting creations of the early Gothic period.[13] The Cistercians were driven inevitably to give their authority to the new style, partly because it gave a visual impression of newness and difference to their works but also because their need for the new technology forced them to think in the ways of the masters of that technology, who were the architect-masons of the great cathedrals.

In speaking of technology in this period we have to reverse our modern attitudes: today inventions and styles, originating as responses to the needs of industry, communication, administration, and business, are adapted to the buildings that ought to serve a higher purpose, so that modern churches, theatres, concert halls and university buildings nearly always have the air of shabby but eccentric imitations of parts of factories, warehouses, airports or the enclaves of civil servants. The effect of the building of the great cathedrals and churches was quite otherwise: not only did they make the greatest demands on the technology of the time, requiring the transport of stone by sea and river often over great distances, the collaboration of numbers of craftsmen with specialized skills, and the most expert management of the shifting and placing of great weights into permanent place, all this for the purpose of praising God: they also set the style for all great secular buildings. Just as the roof bosses, drawing up the eye to the high vaulting of a great church, make one often feel that the inspiration of the building began in the architect's mind from the top, and that the digging of the foundations and the crafting of the walls and windows were all subsidiary to that first inner sight of the vault, so the effect of the Gothic style spread from the spiritual heights downwards. It changed and made more beautiful the halls and castles of kings and barons, granting a fuller expression to civic pride in the town halls, hospitals, fountains and public works of the cities, and left its mark on industrial buildings such as the shipyards of Barcelona or engineering works such as the aqueduct of Spoleto. Elements of the style were adapted for military purposes: the wooden floors of castle keeps were replaced by vaulted stone. In the great thirteenth-century round keeps or towers, such as the tower of Constance at Aigues Mortes or the now destroyed keep of Coucy (diagram left), the vaults sprang from buttresses round the interior circumference. This meant that the weight was more evenly distributed and that, even if part of the wall was destroyed by mining or battering rams, the arches would sustain the rest of the building.[14] The pointed arch was adapted to form the earliest form of machicolation—the provision of projecting galleries to eliminate blind ground where the enemy could attack the wall bases with impunity. Richard the Lion-Heart used this machicolation at Château Gaillard and it may also be seen at the Palace of the Popes at Avignon (fig. 44).

After the successful establishment of the Gothic style at St-Denis, Sens and Chartres by 1150, the next notable developments were through three separate schools. The influence of Sens was furthest spread, reaching Jerusalem before 1149 when the Church of the Holy Sepulchre, probably rebuilt by masons from Sens, was reconsecrated. Nearer home Sens set the style for new building in Champagne, as at the abbey of St-Rémi in Rheims, and the regions south of the Ile-de-France. Another school, based on Paris,

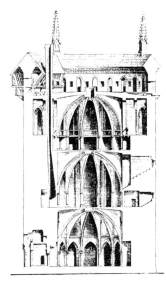

Coucy. A cross-section by Viollet-le-Duc of the thirteenth-century donjon built for his castle by Enguerrand III de Coucy. It was so strong that Richelieu's engineers were unable to blow it up, a task accomplished by German troops in the First World War. It rose to 150 ft (50 m) in height.

43 Notre-Dame, Paris. Looking from the nave towards the choir (begun in 1163): the first Gothic interior to demonstrate the possibilities of the style in building on a huge scale.

was responsible for such churches as Mantes, Senlis (fig. 17), and Melun. The third school, based on the northern trade routes, was deeply influenced by the four-storey elevation of the Anglo-Norman architects, and to this school we owe the marvellous interiors of Noyon (from 1150 onwards) (fig. 45), Laon (1155 onwards) (fig. 46), and the surviving south transept of Soissons (fig. 47). There was an independent development of the possibilities implicit in the use of rib vaulting and the pointed arch in the Angevin lands ruled by the young Henry II of England. Here at Le Mans, Angers, Angoulême, and Poitiers, the domical vault was employed. Though it remained a regional style, it was its synthesis at Poitiers with the style of church known as the hall church, in which all the aisles are of equal height, that was to be of wider and important influence.

It was the rebuilding of Notre-Dame, the cathedral of Paris, under its energetic bishop, Maurice de Sully, from 1163 onwards that set the model for the great Gothic church. Its high vaulting reaches 108 ft (35 m), 30 ft (10 m) higher than that of Laon. In scale, height, and the grandeur of its dispositions, Notre-Dame represented an advance into a new order of magnitude on the part of patrons and architects. It was under construction at a period when Paris was the intellectual centre of Europe. Forced to leave England for France in the year Notre-Dame was begun, John of Salisbury said of Paris, 'happy the exile to whom such a place is given',[15] and other writers compared the city to Athens. The new cathedral towered over the roofs of the halls and houses of the thinkers and their students who were continuing the intellectual revolution of scholastic thought begun there a few decades earlier. Notre-Dame is the architectural counterpart of the *studium* or university of Paris but, as an all-embracing symbol of the age, it encompasses infinitely more than all the treatises on God, Man and Nature written within sight of its flying buttresses and towers (figs. 6 and 43).

On account of its height and vast scale it was the first of the great Gothic

44   Avignon. A view of the Palace of the Popes, begun 1334–42, showing the use of the pointed arch for defensive purposes in reinforcing walls and providing machicolation.

45 *Above* Noyon. A view down the nave towards the choir of this harmoniously proportioned cathedral built between 1150 and 1180, showing the four-stage interior elevation with the tribune gallery.

46 *Above right* Laon. The nave, *c.* 1160, looking towards the eastern rose of the choir: another example of the four-stage elevation. The tribune gallery runs nearly all round the interior. Unusually for France the choir has a square eastern termination: this was built after 1205 when the earlier chevet showed signs of collapse.

cathedrals to exemplify the soul of a city, by uniting the strands of its past and providing a dominating presence for the future. Its size was soon to inspire emulation in other cities, notably Bourges and Chartres and, after them, Rheims, Amiens, and Beauvais. Though to us gigantic size is no recommendation in itself, to contemporaries unused to such vastness it must have seemed one of the most striking features that the new architecture presented and, equally, evidence of the power over matter that had been put into the hands of man.

Though we do not have certain attributions for the first architects of Notre-Dame, their achievement is enough to make us reflect once more on the exceptional position they and their fellow masters held in medieval society. Through their community of interest in this world and the next, kings, aristocrats and churchmen could agree on the diversion of vast resources to the building of great churches. In their desire for new and more beautiful churches they became dependent on the artist, the architect, the sculptor, who were the spokesmen of the archetypes of the age.

The artists drew on some of the greatest movements of the twelfth century. They expressed man's discovery of his own intellect, then currently making itself known through the beginnings of scholasticism in Chartres and Paris. They mirrored in their works the mysticism of their patrons such as Suger and St Bernard. Through their participation in exalting the Virgin Mary in the iconography and practices of the Church, they were making their own contribution to the reassertion of the Ideal Feminine which had already appeared in the lyrics and songs of the troubadours of the heretical South. Furthermore, they were party to one of the most extraordinary features of twelfth-century history: the rediscovery and transformation of pagan myth. Joseph Campbell has described this period as one when myth

47   Notre-Dame, Paris. A view from the south-west tower of the flying buttresses of the nave and the south transept.

changed its function from maintaining society in unaltered ways to a revolutionary and radical force.[16]

The revival of the Arthurian legends and their translation into terms of Christian chivalry had powerful political and social effects. Though the Arthurian legends appear as incidental adornments in Gothic art and sculpture, it is to other aspects of Celtic and Nordic religion and mythology that I will be drawing attention, particularly the depiction of flowers and vegetation and the mysterious figure of the Green Man. From the evidence presented in the next three chapters it could be suggested that there was a deliberate attempt on the part of the Gothic masters to draw on the still vital pagan past, both of the classical and Mediterranean kind and of the Northern kinds, and to synthesize their influences in the new style— thereby carrying out a redemption of the past that their Romanesque predecessors could only pose as a problem to be solved.

The synthesis of experience and influences is one of the most fascinating aspects of artistic creation. What is it in the individual artist that brings about this synthesis? I believe it is the action of states of higher consciousness working on the deeper dream levels of the mind and bringing a new emotional understanding to the symbols and figures that are revealed. If we apply the same theory to the collective spirit of a group of men devoted by contemplative practice, such as we have seen at Cluny, to the voiding of their minds and hearts of personal desires and preconceptions, then taking into account the greater energy contained within a body of people with a common aim, we may get an inkling of the powers the Gothic masters drew on and controlled, the powers of the collective unconscious yoked to the purpose of a greater power, that of consciousness itself, in creating the new civilization of the Gothic. The difference between the monks of Cluny and the Gothic masters is this. The prime purpose of the Cluniac community was the transformation of the individual awareness of each monk into a greater collective consciousness—a transformation achieved through music and the liturgy. All their social, religious, and artistic influences were side-effects of this inner transformation. In the case of the Gothic masters it is possible that it was the practice of their art—the devotion of their powers of attention in sculpting and carving and in the application of geometry to the service of a new vision of light and space—that enabled them to find the source of inspiration within themselves and to respond, with a noble transcendence of the personal, to the challenges presented to them by society.

Just as the artist always draws on something in his past experience and on the tradition in which he works in order to make something new, so the makers of a new civilization are the mediators of the great memory of history. Ideas, thoughts, images, symbols, that seem to have lost their power, are revived and suddenly seem apt and vivid in a new context of thought. Thus the works of Dionysius the Areopagite, brought as we have seen in the ninth century to St-Denis and translated by John Scotus Eriugena, lay virtually dormant until Suger found in them a guide to his own mystical experience and the inspiration that enabled him to recognize the significance of the new style in architecture, art, and stained glass, giving the Dionysian ideas for the first time a visual expression. One feature of the Royal Portal at Chartres is the portrayal of great pagan philosophers, such as Pythagoras (fig. 18), symbolizing the liberal arts. Classical learning and literature were treated at Chartres as having something of the authority of sacred writings; their revival prompted not only commentaries and critical works but also a wealth of religious and secular Latin literature. The same authority probably was attached to surviving examples of Greek and Roman sculpture.[17] A deeper appreciation of classical art is shown by the example of the aesthete Bishop of Winchester, Henry of Blois, who formed a collection of antique sculpture. Classical objects were sought after by Suger who incorporated them into his altar vessels: for instance, the porphyry vase, now in the Louvre, which he transformed into an ampulla with the gold head and wings of an eagle.[18] The ruin-filled soil of the Roman towns of Burgundy had already proved a mine for sculptures and capitals to inspire the sculptors and artists working under the influence of Cluny and later at Autun and Vézelay. Today in Burgundy, passing from the museums to the churches we can see how the figure of the Celtic horse goddess Epona riding side-saddle reappears as the Virgin riding on the flight to Egypt.

Much of the early leaf-carving at St-Denis shows a greater fidelity to classical models[19] than was ever achieved under the Romanesque—an interesting example of how, what seems on the surface an antiquarian desire to return to a truer source or original, turns out to be in part the beginnings of a new style—in this case the leaf and vegetation sculpture characteristic of

the Gothic. There is a profound classical influence to be seen in the drapery
and facial modelling of some of the greatest sculpture at Rheims, such as the
Visitation group (fig. 75). From the thirteenth century onwards Nicola
Pisano led the sculptors of Italy in renewing their work with classical
influences and there are many examples of classical themes and stylistic
borrowings in Gothic sculpture. Whereas much Romanesque work,
especially in the carving of leaf capitals, looks like attempts at imitating
classical exemplars, the Gothic masters, benefiting from the more complete
break in style, were able to assimilate and choose among the ruins and
remains of the past with greater assurance.

Up to the 1170s, apart from a few examples in the Low Countries such as
Valenciennes and Cambrai, the Gothic style remained a phenomenon confined to those parts of Northern France controlled by the Capetian
monarchs. It came to England as a result of two events which overwhelmed
the monks of Canterbury Cathedral. The first was the quarrel between
Henry II and his Archbishop, Thomas à Becket, which culminated in the
latter's murder in the north transept of his cathedral in 1170. Miracles of such
an extraordinary nature followed the death of the hitherto generally de-
tested Archbishop that the cathedral, already sanctified by St Augustine and
St Alphege, became a popular centre of pilgrimage for the pious and the
curious. The second event was the burning down of the eastern parts of the
cathedral in a great fire in 1174. The monks called in French and English
architects to advise them, hoping that the building could be reconstructed
on the basis of what remained. The architects gave conflicting advice, some
saying the surviving piers could be used in the new construction and others
advising that everything should be pulled down for the sake of safety. The
monks were in a state of shock and could not bring themselves to contemplate the total destruction of their beloved choir, believing a new building
could never be built in their lifetime. They decided to appoint the French
architect William of Sens who, in addition to his skills in masonry, carpentry, and engineering, had a shrewd understanding of human nature. The
monk who observed and recorded all the events that followed, Gervase of
Canterbury, reported of him that he was active and ready.[20]

Having chosen him because of his intelligence and good reputation,
they dismissed the others. William spent some time residing with the monks
and surveying the burnt-out choir but kept to himself what he felt was
necessary to be done, until the monks had time to recover from their shock.
Nevertheless he made certain preparations so that when he judged it right to
tell the monks that a major part of the old building should come down and be
replaced, not only did he win their agreement but he was ready to start
work. He pulled down the arcades of the old choir and had stone shipped
across the Channel from Caen. He devised machines for the loading and

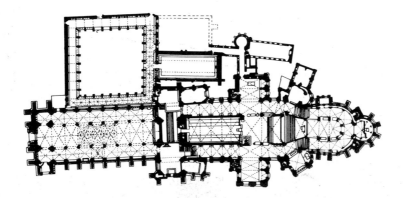

Left Plan of Canterbury
Cathedral.

48   Canterbury. The choir
begun by William of Sens
in 1175, showing the
openings into the choir
transept and a view of the
vault of Henry Yeveley's
nave beyond. Note the
extensive use of Purbeck
marble.

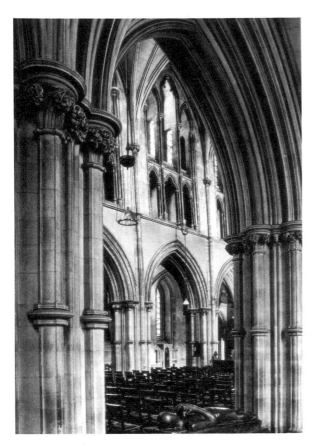

50 *Above*   Dublin. The
north side of the nave of
Christchurch cathedral,
built by Somerset masons
1212–35 following the
Anglo-Norman conquest
of Ireland.

51 *Above right*   Chichester.
The retrochoir of the
cathedral, one of the
earliest offshoots of the
Canterbury style, built by
Walter of Coventry *c.* 1190.

49 *Left*   Wells. The nave
by Adam Lock, *c.* 1220–39.
The first Gothic building
here, from 1175, was in
the choir, now largely
replaced by later work.
The strainer arches are an
addition of the fourteenth
century.

unloading of the ships and supplied the carvers with the templates for their
work. In the course of 1175–6 he was building the new pillars of the choir
with the vaults of the side aisles. In the next twelve months he had reached
the crossing of the eastern transepts with the choir and there he ornamented
the columns with marble shafts. He introduced this fashion to England
where it was to have great influence: his affection for the style is probably
evidence that before his call to England he had been working in Southern
Flanders, where marble shafts had been employed at Tournai and
Valenciennes[21] (fig. 48).

By September 1178 the columns, triforium and clerestory of the choir
were complete to the point when the high vaulting could be constructed.
William of Sens was superintending the erection of the centerings on 13
September when the scaffolding gave way beneath him and he fell fifty feet
to the ground. Timbers and stones fell with him, adding to his injuries. He
was severely crippled and had to give orders for further work from a bed,
making use of a young monk to oversee the masons. Though his trust in this
young monk attracted jealousy, William managed to direct the completion
of the high vaulting of the crossing and the start of the vaulting of the
transepts of the choir. The effort of will must have been astounding, but at
this point he had to give up: because the doctors were unable to heal him, he
resigned his post and went home to France.

He was succeeded as architect by an Englishman, another William, of
whom Gervase says that he was short in stature but honest and well trained
in many skills.[22] William the Englishman completed the choir vaulting and
then extended the crypt eastwards on which he was to raise the ambulatory
and the chapel, known as the corona or Becket's crown because there the
saint's scalp was to be preserved and venerated. The rebuilding of the choir
and its extension took ten years from the time of the fire.

52 *Above*   Venice. The Ca' d'Oro, a Venetian Gothic palace on the Grand Canal, begun 1421.

53 *Right*   Orvieto. The central door and *rosone* of the west front, designed by Lorenzo Maitani 1290–1330.

The prestige of Canterbury was such that very soon, in all rebuilding of greater churches and in the founding of new ones, the Gothic style supplanted in England the later form of Romanesque known as Transitional. This is not to ignore the fact that the choir of Wells Cathedral was already being rebuilt in the new style from 1175, and indeed in one sense it was the most up-to-date construction of its time, because it was the first building to incorporate the pointed arch in every single feature, bays, arcades, windows and vaulting. The influence of Wells spread north to Wales at Llandaff and Pembroke and then across the Irish Sea to Christchurch, Dublin. The influence of Canterbury, sited as it was on the main route to the Continent and drawing pilgrims of all classes, was much wider. Its great length, then extended westwards by the Norman nave (to be replaced in the late fourteenth century by Henry Yeveley's nave) continued the English tradition of building long rather than high and concentrating the vertical impulse on immensely tall crossing towers and towers at the west front.

By the end of the twelfth century the rebuilding of Canterbury in the new style had influenced a number of other great cathedrals, notably Chichester (the retrochoir) and Lincoln. The new choir of Lincoln was built under the direction of its bishop, the Carthusian Hugh of Avalon, known as Great St Hugh. The cathedral had been severely damaged in an earthquake and, so keen on the work was St Hugh, he himself would carry loads for the masons.[23] The way was set for the important architectural achievements of England and Scotland in the thirteenth century and, as crucial to our future pleasure, the adoption of the Gothic style for the building of thousands of parish churches in towns and in the country throughout the next three centuries.

Canterbury illustrates the sensitivity of the early Gothic masters to the particular needs of the nations amongst which they found themselves, once they had left France. It also illustrates how often the adoption of the style reflects the influence of a new religious or political movement, a living or recently dead saint or a miracle of exceptional import. Though the fire at Canterbury was the immediate cause of the introduction of the style, William of Sens' choir chiefly reflects both the constitutional struggles of twelfth-century England and the extraordinary evidence of martyrdom, sainthood and miraculous events that arose from those struggles and which needed expression in a new and significant architectural form. The same course of events may be demonstrated for Italy and Germany. Romanesque traditions south and eastward had been protected by the Alps and the Rhine, barriers against this new French fashion, and it was not until well into the thirteenth century that the Gothic influence was felt in the German-speaking regions and in many parts of Italy. In both regions it was introduced by the Cistercians. The portal of the Cistercian monastery of Maulbronn of about 1200 is often cited as one of the earliest examples of the Gothic style in Germany. Similarly the Cistercians introduced the style in their monasteries at Fossanova from 1187 and San Galgano, near Siena, from 1218 onwards.

Cistercian influence is to be seen in the Northern Italian church of San Andrea at Vercelli (fig. 54), built from 1219 with English funds by a cardinal who was guardian to the young Henry III of England. In Southern Italy, where the Emperor Frederick II Hohenstaufen generally preferred to reside up to his death in 1250, his architects and sculptors united Cistercian Burgundian Gothic influences with the classical styles favoured by the Emperor. Especially in his palace castles such as Castel del Monte, they created a secular Gothic style, mirroring Frederick's reassertion of imperial supremacy and his independence of the Church, both of which are also

54 *Above* Vercelli. The nave of San Andrea, one of the earliest examples of Italian Gothic, built *c.* 1219.

55 *Above right* Venice. The Doge's Palace: a supreme example of secular Gothic architecture built at various stages in the fourteenth and fifteenth centuries.

reflected in the numerous writings of his Chancery in his long battle with the Papacy. Throughout the thirteenth century strife in the cities of Central and Northern Italy, both against outside enemies and in their internal constitutional struggles, also led to another form of secular Gothic architecture: the civic castles of their leaders, their town halls, their palaces of the Captains of the people or of the political parties. Ruskin was to regard one of these monuments, the Doge's Palace at Venice, as the central building of the world for its union of the Roman, the Lombard and the Arab styles (fig. 55).[24]

For the development of church architecture in Central and Northern Italy St Francis is of the greatest significance. The saint was buried at Assisi, not in one of the small Romanesque mountain churches of Monte Subasio, but in the rock beneath what became at the same time a fortress for keeping safe the papal treasure and an enormous basilica, rising from a lower church above the grave to a great single-aisled upper church, built between 1228 and 1253, according to Vasari, by the architect Jacopo da Alemannia. It was later painted with frescoes by Cimabue and by another artist, sometimes, according to the vagaries of art historians, allowed to be Giotto. The richly painted vaults (fig. 56) are among the many wonders of the basilica. Also at Assisi is the church of Santa Chiara, with its warm pink and white polychrome exterior. The Gothic style, often in a particularly pure and inspiring version, was generally adopted for the new churches of the Franciscans in Central and Northern Italy.[25] Of equal importance as an influence on the churches of the Dominicans was the fact that St Dominic died in Bologna and the church erected there to house his sepulchre, carved by Nicola Pisano, was also built in the new style.

Yet another instance of how a newly current belief allied to the wide reporting of a miracle could lead to the building of an important church or

56 Assisi. The brilliantly painted vaults of the single-aisled basilica of San Francesco looking towards the *rosone* of the west front: the work of Jacopo da Alemannia. The church was built 1228–39 and the vaults were rebuilt *c*. 1253.

cathedral is given by the example of Orvieto. The Lateran Council of 1215 had formally pronounced the Church's teaching affirming the Doctrine of Transubstantiation. A German priest who had doubts about the Doctrine was celebrating mass at Bolsena in the course of a journey to Rome. To his horror the host began to bleed and the blood permanently stained his corporal (the cloth for holding the host). Understandably, he regarded the miracle as a rebuke to his unbelief. The Papacy gave its sanction to a cult that confirmed true doctrine and would work confusion among heretics, and from 1290 onwards a new cathedral was built to house the corporal on the hilltop of the papal city of Orvieto. It was faced with bands of black and white marble and with mosaics on its west façade that take flame in the eyes of the traveller coming at evening over the hills from Bolsena (fig. 53). To signify the reason for the cathedral's erection, the interior flooring, rising gently to extend the perspective towards the high altar, is made of sheets of blood-red marble.

The Low Countries, being so close to the north-eastern parts of France where many of the early Gothic churches were first built, had responded much earlier to the new style. The thickly populated, rich and prosperous towns of the Low Countries were, like those of Italy, soon to adopt the style for their civic and secular buildings, again as in Italy using the Gothic to signify their success in establishing their rights in battles and constitutional struggles. The extension of Capetian power into the Low Countries after Philip Augustus's triumph over the Emperor at the battle of Bouvines in 1214 had a similar effect to Philip's earlier conquest of Normandy in 1204. The Gothic style had become identified with the Capetian monarchy, and just as the greater Gothic churches—such as Rouen (fig. 58) and Coutances (fig. 130)—were rebuilt in Normandy after the duchy was ruled from Paris, so we find a new surge of Gothic building in the Low Countries: St-Gudule at Brussels from 1220, St-Martin at Ypres from 1221, Notre-Dame at Bruges (1239–97) and the choir at Tournai.

57 Marburg. A painted panel from the shrine of St Elisabeth.

In the German regions of the Holy Roman Empire the Romanesque style was strongly identified with the imperial tradition. Though there were isolated attempts to adopt elements of the Gothic, as in the choir of Magdeburg from 1200 and in Limburg-an-der-Lahn, it was not until 1235, when the foundation stone of the Elisabethkirche at Marburg was laid, that the Gothic style truly entered the heartland of Germany. The construction took another fifty years, and this lovely sandstone building, alive with vegetation and flowers and presenting a perfect profile of three spires above the valley of the Lahn, again sets the style for a nation because it is the first German Gothic hall church. Though Romanesque hall churches had been built, for example in Westphalia, the Elisabethkirche set a model for the great series of Gothic city churches in Germany. Once again the Gothic followed a living example of holiness. The church was built to house the remains of St Elisabeth of Hungary, the wife of a Landgrave of Thuringia, who, during her short life, had been inspired by the example of St Francis to devote herself to works of kindness and charity (fig. 57).

Contemporary with the first works at Marburg was the adoption of the Gothic style at Strasbourg—then firmly part of Germany—for the south transept, with its wholly original pillar of the angels, of about 1230 (fig. 59), and the nave from 1250 onwards. Battles between the city and the bishop, ending in the victory of the burghers in 1262, did not interrupt progress on the cathedral, because the burghers took over from the clerics complete responsibility for its further building—to such an extent that in 1350 the bishop complained bitterly that neither he nor his canons had any say in further designs and improvements for their cathedral. It was under the patronage of the city burghers that the nave was completed by 1270 and the marvellous façade up to the rose, with its openwork tracery and dynamic vertical impulse, was created by Master Erwin between 1276 and 1318.

58 *Above left* Rouen. The south aisle and nave, built by Jean d'Audeli and Enguerran from 1204 onwards following the Capetian conquest of Normandy. The aisle vaults and floors of the tribunes were never completed.

59 *Above* Strasbourg. Two angels from the *pilier des anges*, *c.* 1220–30, in the south transept.

In many features of the nave and façade Strasbourg reflects the influence of the *rayonnant* style, which under St Louis in France became the court style of Paris. More is said of this style in Chapters 8 and 9, but here it is enough to remark that it was the international prestige of St Louis that secured the universal triumph of the Gothic style. The influence is to be seen at Cologne, begun in 1245, in Henry III's choir of Westminster Abbey, and most especially in Spain, at León, from 1250 onwards.

In Spain the new style had entered slowly, first through Angevin influence in the Cistercian Convent of Las Huelgas (1180–1203) near Burgos and then through more direct Northern French participation. The national style of Northern Christian Spain, devoted as its population was to the driving out of the Moslems from the peninsula, was centred on the shrine of St James the Apostle at Compostela, where the Portico de la Gloria of 1180 is

60   Marburg. The central nave vaulting, looking towards the crossing, of the first German Gothic hall church, built 1235 onwards.

one of the richest achievements of Romanesque sculpture, and in the numerous Romanesque churches and abbeys that hug the Pyrenees. From the earliest days of the reconquest French knights had been prominent in the fight against the Moors. There was intermarriage between the French royal family and the royal families of Spain, the most notable example being the marriage of Blanche of Castile and Louis VIII, the parents of St Louis. It was therefore a natural consequence that the new style should be adopted. The cathedrals of Burgos (1221), Toledo (1227) and León (c. 1250) were all probably designed by French architects, and more is said of them in Chapter 9.

This survey has left out the further spread of the style into Sweden directly from France, into Norway directly from England, and into the Eastern conquests of the Teutonic knights, who were to take it far into present Poland and Northern Soviet Russia. It also leaves out the later development of its highly individual forms in the region of the Hanseatic League, along the Baltic coast and along the North Sea where, because of the lack of suitable building stone, the buildings were nearly all of brick.

Throughout Western Europe and its outposts in the Latin Kingdom and Cyprus the influence of the Gothic masters was to become paramount. They drew upon the energies released by political developments, most notably the ever-growing authority and prestige of the Capetian monarchy which was to culminate in the reign of St Louis; they reflected the intellectual ferment of the schools and the rise of scholastic philosophy; at the same time, while in their sculptural and iconographical programmes they could mirror the rapid development and formulation of new doctrines of the Church, they were able to synthesize and express in an acceptable form influences from the classical and Northern pagan past. They were called upon by the new monastic and preaching orders because they were the masters of a style that could utter in spatial and architectural terms what was new and original in the spirit and teaching of those orders. As the supreme experts in the technology of the age, they were internationally respected for their skills. They were the chief interpreters to a revitalized and prosperous Western Europe of the dreams of change, of transformation, and of expansion that were being woven by the archetypes in the deepest levels of the collective psyche.

Though it is an exploded notion that the great architecture of the Middle Ages was the work of monks and prelates aided solely by faith and muscle-power, the thought still persists that the creation of the style was primarily the work of gifted patrons such as Suger.[26] There is far more evidence of bishops and clerics taking an active part in the design of military fortifications, castles, and engines of war than of great churches.[27] The skills required for the design and building of these churches were far beyond their training and experience.[28] The attribution of the origins of the style to patrons rests largely on the lack of surviving inscriptions to the architects in most early Gothic buildings and on the want of evidence for craft organizations and lodges in the twelfth century. There is much evidence for the existence of these organizations in the thirteenth century and presumably they existed, even if in looser and less formal groups, in the earlier period.

The very fact that the monks of Canterbury were able in 1174 to call on several architect-masons capable of rebuilding the burnt-out choir, from whom they chose William of Sens, should be enough to rule out the patron theory. None of them came accompanied by an omniscient prelate to tell them what to do. The clue perhaps lies in the reasons why the monks chose William of Sens, which were not only his evident range of skills but also their respect for his character—a choice well justified by his courage and perseverance after his crippling accident. The sudden appearance in the

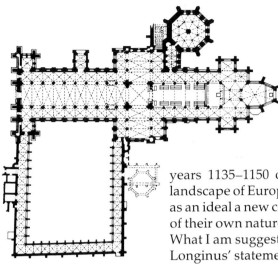

Plan of Wells Cathedral.

years 1135–1150 of a group of men capable of transforming the artistic landscape of Europe was not fortuitous. It happened because these men had as an ideal a new conception of Man to make manifest, a new understanding of their own natures, and a new insight into the springs of art and of science. What I am suggesting comes closer to an ancient theory of the origins of art: Longinus' statement that great literature comes from greatness of the soul.[29] The splendour of Gothic art and architecture derives from the magnanimity of soul of its makers. That was the source of their imaginative grasp of the possibilities of the new technology and of the quality of life revitalized that shines from their work.

This will be explored further in the next chapter, but in preparation for that let us take the rebuilding of Chartres as a further example of the effect of a miraculous event, the powers the clergy and masons of Chartres could draw upon, and the revelation in architecture of the works of the creative imagination.

On 10 June 1194 a fire that destroyed much of the city of Chartres burned out all the cathedral except for the west façade, with its two towers, and the old crypt. The account of the fire in *The Miracles of the Blessed Virgin*[30] says that the inhabitants of the city were more overcome by the destruction of the cathedral, which they regarded as the Palace of the Virgin, than by any private losses of their own. They were particularly appalled at the thought that the fire had consumed the most sacred relic of the Virgin, the silk tunic she had worn in giving birth to Christ, the relic that entitled Chartres to the position of the chief shrine of the Virgin in the West. They believed that there was now no point in rebuilding either the city or the cathedral. Then after a few days the clergy summoned the people together and they watched the reliquary containing the tunic being carried out from the crypt, to which it had been transferred during the fire. Those who had carried it to the crypt had had to remain with it for fear of the falling timbers and other dangers all throughout the period of the fire, protected by an iron door. They were greeted by the clergy and people outside with tears of joy. The preservation of the holy tunic was regarded as a miracle, and a new feeling of hope replaced the first response of despair. The very destruction of the old cathedral was regarded as an intervention by the Virgin so that a more beautiful building could be constructed in her honour.

Thus it came about that what the world agrees is the finest achievement of the Gothic Age came to be built. In 26 years the nave, choir, transepts and the high vaulting were finished, and by about 1260 the glaziers had completed what now survives as the most complete series of stained-glass windows in existence. Inspired by the column statues of the Royal Portal which survived the fire, the sculptors of the portals of the north and south transepts made new discoveries in the portrayal of individual human beings, the influence of which spread throughout Europe.

CHAPTER 5

A New Image of Man

All civilizations possess in their beginnings one feature in common: they present a new image of Man. In each case the image and the way it is manifested will vary according to the resources and the needs of the epoch. For Periclean Athens a new ideal of man was presented in the form of drama, publicly in the tragedies of the great playwrights and for private reading in the dialogues of Plato. At the beginning of the Christian era a completely new conception of man, of man who forgives and loves his enemies and is at one with his Father, was given to the world in the form of the Gospels. For the Dark Ages and the early Middle Ages the ideal became that of the saint or holy man, generally a monk because the monastic way was conceived as the means of creating holy men. Within the different stages of other religions such as Hinduism or Buddhism, we can point to the many stages of renewal of the ideal of the realized man, as given, in the one case, in the *Upanishads* and the *Bhagavad Gita* and, in the other, to the portrayals, in painting and sculpture, of the Bodhisattvas.

In every case it can be shown that the new image arises to transcend the conflicts of the age and to resolve dualisms through a fresh conception of the unity of man with his Maker and the natural world. It is as though the deepest power in the soul of humanity, welling over with compassion and concern for the struggles and divisions of men, surges up with a vision of all that has been lost or disregarded, of infinite possibilities of thoughts and emotions, of achievements that could be encompassed, and of new directions and vocations to which men might aspire.

The new image of man which is the work of the Gothic masters presents man as an individual endowed with free will, who is seen as God and His angels look upon him and is set within a framework of apparently abstract shapes of portals, arches, niches and vaults that nevertheless symbolize aspects of the laws and forms of the universe. The Christian concept of the worth of the individual soul, a concept with which the Gospels and the Pauline Epistles are instinct, only achieved its first full expression eleven hundred years after the death of Christ, in the column statues of St-Denis and Chartres. The statues, seen by thousands of pilgrims at these important shrines, were to set a trend in the exact portrayal of emotion through the varied configurations of the human face, that was to be carried across Europe into innumerable cathedrals and churches, thus exerting a liberating force in the development of the Western conception of the individual. They helped to excise the shame in men's souls at their being men, they spoke, without words, of peace of mind and rationality, and they gave new intensity to the doctrine of the Incarnation through the radiance of the spirit proclaimed by the stone from which they were carved.

What were the dualisms that the Gothic image of man helped to resolve? We have already noted that the development of French Gothic sculpture can be read as a statement of Western Catholic doctrine on the Incarnation, against the many dualist Christian sects, of which the most powerful and threatening was the faith of the Albigensians, influenced as they were by

61 Chartres. Three column statues of the south-west doorway of the Royal Portal with (*left*) the side view of one of the central doorway statues. These statues are by the Master of Chartres, *c*. 1150.

Zoroastrian teachings into believing the world was the creation of the power of darkness. There was, however, a much more deeply based dualism, that between Christianity and the still ineradicable native pagan religions of Europe. The extent to which the old religions still ruled in the collective unconscious of Western man can be seen in nearly every surviving Romanesque church that incorporates contemporary sculpture. It had been in any case the policy of the missionaries of the Dark Ages to take over the holy places of pagan cults and to build churches on their sites.[1] The spirits were not however expelled from their former fanes. The old gods, their symbolic beasts and birds, and the vegetation over which they ruled, sprouted out of the capitals of columns, ranged themselves as courses of corbel heads inside and outside, and writhed, zigzagged and battled in and around the doorways of churches (figs. 62 and 63).

One man woke up to the implications of Romanesque sculpture. St Bernard wrote a scathing attack on them:

> What are these fantastic monsters doing in the cloisters under the very eyes of the brothers as they read? . . . What is the *meaning* of these unclean monkeys, these savage lions, and monstrous creatures? To what purpose are here placed these creatures, half-beast, half-man, or these spotted tigers? I see several bodies with one head and several heads with one body. Here is a quadruped with a serpent's head, there a fish with a quadruped's head, there again an animal (half-horse, half-goat) . . . Surely if we do not blush for such absurdities we should at least regret what we have spent on them.[2]

As we have seen, St Bernard dealt with the problem by forbidding in general all sculptural or figural representations in the abbey churches of his rule. He also, interestingly in the present context, gave his followers a new approach to the mystical way by making them concentrate on the face of God.[3] The Cistercian example, however, did little to hinder the proliferation of grotesque sculpture of pagan origin elsewhere, partly I think because the Gothic masters recognized in the phenomenon forces that were basic to human nature and whose energies they could transform, in the unity of architecture and sculpture the new style permitted.

The old gods and goddesses reappeared in the decoration of Romanesque and Gothic churches because, in at least three ways, nearly everyone still believed in them. The convinced Christian believed in them because they were demons or agents of the devil and therefore they should be portrayed as a warning of the dark forces that had ruled before Christ's coming. They are the dark aspect of the 'elements' or cosmic powers of St Paul.[4] The crypto-pagans, of whom there must have been a considerable number, given the efforts of churchmen to denounce them, believed in them because they held to the rites and beliefs of their ancestors. Then there is the third way, of unthinking belief, which is superstition in its true sense of belief or practice held over from an earlier age. The great majority of people, being largely farmers and peasants, held to both Christian and pagan sets of beliefs without much difficulty: for practical matters of life, such as farming, curing disease and running a household, they performed the rites and dances of their forefathers.[5] These ceremonies often acquired a gloss of Christianity, rather in the way the peasants attributed to their local saints the attributes and powers of ancient gods and goddesses. For the spiritual side of life, especially where their hopes of the hereafter were concerned, they paid equal attention to the public and established faith of Christianity. That this living side by side of two apparently incompatible sets of belief was not confined to the peasant population can be shown from legends of demonic

62 *Above left* Chauvigny. The Romanesque presentation of existence as strife, graphically portrayed by a monster with two bodies and one head devouring a man.

63 *Left* Chauvigny. Sphinxes with their tails devoured by lions on a painted capital: vivid examples of the monsters deplored by St Bernard.

blood in ancient families such as the Plantagenets and the de Lusignans, and from the early development of heraldry, which is more or less contemporaneous with the rise of the Gothic. The devices of heraldry begin with the use of the chevron and lozenge patterns of the Great Goddess or with the totem-like identity of a family or clan with beasts, in a way that was typical of Celtic tribes.

Though this pairing of Christian and pagan beliefs and practices may have been accepted by most of the population over the generations, it cannot always have been an easy matter for the Romanesque sculptors or for their patrons, the priests and monks. One dominant theme of Romanesque sculpture is the battle; life outside the church was a battle to survive against extremes of weather and against hunger, marauders and the spirits of the natural world, and it is in the capitals of the columns in churches that the struggle outside was reflected, through scenes of men committing acts of slaughter or of beasts and birds devouring men and one another (figs. 62 and 63).

The capital marks the change from one stage to another in a building. It is a point of awareness, both in that the eye of the onlooker is naturally drawn towards it and in that it expresses the rising forces hidden in the column. Friedrich Heer says that in medieval Germany the columns of a church were regarded as living creatures. They housed the Tree of Life, and wanton damage to them could be punishable by death,[6] a story reminiscent of what Tacitus says about the veneration earlier paid to trees in Germany, and of the stories of men tortured to death for harming a tree.[7] So we may see the Romanesque sculptors carving into the capitals the likenesses of the monsters rising up through the columns of the collective unconscious. In expressing the physical struggle of life they were also portraying the dualism of their epoch, which has already been described as the struggle between Christianity and paganism, but which may be seen in its essence as an unconscious Manichaeism, a vision of life as a struggle between the spirit and matter.

What is curious and paradoxical about so many of the human beings in Romanesque sculpture is the lack of expression on their faces. They have the anonymity of uniformed men. Whatever the pains and sufferings inflicted on them, however deeply the teeth and beaks bite into them, they bear it all with hieratic unconcern (fig. 62). We can learn to identify characters by the attributes they are given, St Peter by his keys or the Virgin on the throne of Wisdom, we know their importance by their relative sizes, graded down from Christ who is always the largest or tallest, and we can be stirred to the depths by the marvellous dancing rhythms of their bodies, by the cosmic energies flowing through the draperies of Christ and the apostles (fig. 30), and by the touching skill with which scenes of the Gospel story or of the lives of the saints are made to bend down to us from the angled sides of the capitals—but in general their faces stare with the same expression, set in heads like hazelnuts. When they do show a particular emotion, it is generally grief, shown by the furrowed foreheads of women weeping over Christ.[8] On the rare occasions when an attempt is made to show a smile, the effect is coarse—except for the one example at Autun of Gislebertus' Eve, whose expression is so subtle, so charmingly wicked, so alluring, that she is in a class by herself. It was in the German series of bronze and wooden crucifixes from the Romanesque period that the finest advance in one line of development of the expressiveness of the human face had been made, where the artists dwelt on the aspect of resignation in the drooped eyelids of Christ with his head bent forward. There, however, they were portraying a dead man. It was as though quicker eyes and happier minds were needed to

64   Vézelay. The mystic mill, *c.* 1132: a prophet feeds a hopper with the grain of the Old Testament, which becomes flour, ground by the mill of the Gospels, gathered by St Paul.

capture the range of fleeting and vital expressions of which the human face is capable.

Then there appeared the column statues of St-Denis and Chartres. Those of St-Denis were the earlier, but we possess only fragments of them, in addition to a series of eighteenth-century drawings and engravings. So it is to the column statues on the Royal Portal of Chartres that we must turn with relief and joy (figs. 61, 65, 66 and 67). The column statue is so called because it is cut from the same block of stone which forms each of the columnar jambs of the doorway round which it is set. The origins of the form have been much discussed: one school has derived it from manuscript illuminations, such as the letter 'I' turned into a human being in Cistercian manuscripts.[9] Another school sees the influence of Byzantine mosaic figures in it.[10] Neither theory accounts for its three-dimensional emergence from these two-dimensional originals. Probably both sources were an influence in the synthesis that went to its making. I think however that its deepest artistic origins are in the symbolism of the column itself as a living being. Honorius of Autun, in his description of the symbolism of the parts of the church, saw the columns as representing bishops who support the organization of the Church by their righteous lives.[11] Suger saw the columns of his choir as the apostles and the minor prophets and it was under his direction that the first column statues were carved at St-Denis.[12]

One of his sculptors is credited with two column statues at Chartres to the right of the doorway of the Virgin. Another sculptor, who also worked at Etampes, carved two on the far left. Apart from these four male figures and another two female statues, the rest are given to the Master of Chartres.[13] There were originally 24 column statues, of which 19 remain: a few of these are excellent modern copies. They are ranged beside the three doorways of the west front of Chartres. The south door is surmounted by a tympanum showing the Nativity, the presentation in the temple and, above, the Virgin seated on the throne of Wisdom with the Christ Child on her knee, surrounded by the seven liberal arts together with the supreme masters of each art. The tympanum of the north doorway shows the apostles looking upwards to a band of angels pointing to the Ascension of Christ, surrounded by archivolts of the labours of the months and the signs of the zodiac. The

66   Chartres. An Old Testament queen or prophetess from the central doorway of the Royal Portal.

tympanum of the central doorway shows Christ at the Second Coming, enthroned in a mandorla with the apocalyptic beasts of the Evangelists about him, the apostles and Enoch and Elijah at his feet, and angels and the 24 elders surrounding him in the archivolts. In addition, the capitals are carved with a series of minute figures depicting scenes from the lives of Mary or Christ.

The column statues appear to support this ordered conglomeration of doctrine and story, but whereas we know very well the names and place of nearly every character in the upper carvings of the Royal Portal, by an extraordinary paradox—given their importance in the portrayal of human individuality—we cannot give a single certain name to any of the column statues of Chartres. As a group they are probably a sequence of kings, queens, prophets and prophetesses of Judah, who foretold, or in their lives

prefigured, the coming of Christ. They also probably symbolize a theme dear to Suger, the union of *regnum* and *sacerdotium*, secular rule and ecclesiastical rule, both founded on justice: a balance claimed, at times rightly, as the achievement of the French monarchy and the Church.[14]

The iconographic scheme of the Royal Portal as a whole must have been chosen by members of the School of Chartres, possibly under the direction of their great chancellor Thierry of Chartres. It therefore reflects their Neoplatonic belief in the unity of all knowledge under the rule of Christ, mediated through the Virgin Mother in her aspect as Sapientia, the everlasting Wisdom that was with God from the beginning.[15] It also reflects, in the pre-Christian figures such as Pythagoras with his tintinnabulum (fig. 18) and Euclid with his compasses, not only the near-worship of classical learning and literature by the School of Chartres, but their belief that the universe was founded on number, weight and measure. The Royal Portal, therefore, depicts the concordances between the Old Testament and the New, and between the learning of the ancients and Christian education based on the seven liberal arts, as the road of the mind to Christ. The members of the School of Chartres also believed most powerfully in the eternal worlds as the dwelling-places of ideas. Therefore the Royal Portal with its central theme of the Second Coming expresses a view of the age when time will be no more and all knowledge will be revealed complete and whole.

The thoroughness with which the iconographic scheme was devised is also revealed in the subjects of the glass of the three lancet windows above the tympana of the Royal Portal; these frequently reflect the individual subjects of the Royal Portal and show the Tree of Jesse (fig. 87), the Nativity and Christ's life up to the entry into Jerusalem, and the Passion and Resurrection. These windows are contemporary with the Royal Portal, and the glassworkers are thought to have come from St-Denis.

With all the instruction they had to give the sculptors, the canons and clergy must have reached a point at which they had to stop talking and wait for what the sculptors would carve. Faced with these statues in their present state, bare of colours and gilding, with hands and faces in many cases mutilated, we can imagine the shock they must have given the patrons, the townspeople and the pilgrims of the time, because they still have the power to alert and wake us up. They startle us with their calmness. Each elongated figure taken as a whole, with its pointed boots angled sharply downwards, with the neat folds of its clothing running vertically down like cascades in a garden or eddying peacefully at an elbow, a shoulder, a hem, with its neatly crisped hair, often, in the case of the women, plaited, can hardly be said to be naturalistic. Nevertheless, the effect is of free and liberated human beings, men and women endowed with the composure that comes from complete moral certainty, complete development of their talents and faculties, a perfection that is implied in the use of the golden section, which marks its division at the bent elbows of each figure.

Then we study the faces. These can be said to convey a number of individuating features rarely attempted or attained since Roman times. They are clearly of different sex, of different ages and reveal different life histories in their physiognomies, but what is the greater achievement is that in the moulding of their lips, cheekbones and foreheads and in their clear open eyes, they imply not one possible range of expressions but all possible expressions. These are faces that, though they do not move, could move. Their incipient mobility is owed to the fact that their sculptors understood the nature of facial muscles; they could carve the faces in a state of rest so that they express the conserved power of mental stillness.

The statues are presences of matured individuality that leave an im-

67 Chartres. Christ at the Second Coming, seated on a throne within a mandorla and surrounded by the symbols of the Evangelists, in the central tympanum of the Royal Portal. This is one of the most outstanding works of religious art, remarkable for its humanity and inner stillness.

pression in the memory as much of sung music as of visual stimulation. What was the source of their originality and authority? Though there were contemporary debates on the nature of the individuality of the soul,[16] no amount of reading treatises would account for the impression of direct experience revealed by these statues. The source must have been the self-knowledge, the experience of mental stillness and the wisdom of the sculptors themselves. They could only sculpt what they had known in themselves or observed and admired in others. They were

> The lords and owners of their faces:
> Others but stewards of their excellence

and it was from their experience of stillness and from their love of humanity that they created what are, in addition to their place in the sculptural ensemble, in a sense portraits of their own souls. A new age was announced through a new image of Man, which may thus be considered a side-effect of groups of men and women transcending the personal in themselves by means of art, learning, or contemplation.

In the creative imagination of the Master of Chartres, his experience was drawn on to make this sequence of column statues into Old Testament worthies prefiguring the coming of Christ. They are presented here with all their earthly existence imprinted on their souls but, because they are in eternity, they are shown grouped together, each one of them, out of their time, as exemplars of virtues and ideas. Thus, as Solomon is portrayed almost certainly here as one of the crowned male statues, he would appear not only as a man who fulfilled a certain necessary historical role, but as the principle of royal wisdom, prefiguring the supreme Wisdom of Christ shown in the central tympanum.

It is the figure of Christ that gives meaning to all the rest (fig. 67). It is one of the most beautiful portrayals of Christ in existence. He is no longer the huge terrifying Christ of Vézelay or Autun (fig. 29), out of scale with all the other figures. He does not need size to emphasize His grandeur and perfection, because His forehead beams with divine understanding and His eyes radiate love. He is portrayed as the man on the great white throne of the book of Revelation who says 'Behold, I make all things new',[17] a text that has been read with fresh understanding of His own teaching of forgiveness and mercy. Among His works of renewal are the expressions of delight and surprise in the faces of the angels and elders of the archivolts around Him and of the apostles beneath His feet.

The Royal Portal is unique. It had few immediate stylistic successors that survive—there are some examples of column statues at Le Mans and Rochester and some remarkable statues survive from the ruined abbey of St Mary's, York. Its later influence, however, was immense, through its iconography, its mood, and the potential it suggested for extending the range of human expression. This influence was to stretch across Europe, reaching Germany and Italy by way of the sculpture of Rheims and Amiens, crossing the Channel and the Pyrenees. Its chief immediate influence was, however, on the later sculpture of Chartres. In the rebuilding after the fire of 1194 described in the previous chapter, elaborate iconographical schemes were planned and executed in the portals of the north and south transepts. As was said earlier, the long axis of the cathedral forms the line of eternity, so that the short axis of the transepts forms the line of time intersecting with eternity at the crossing before the high altar. The north side of the church symbolizes the Old Law, and therefore the sculptures there portray the precursors of Christ and His Mother (fig. 113). The south side of the church symbolizes the New Law, and the sculptures show Christ with the symbols

68   Strasbourg.
Synagogue (*c.* 1225–30),
blindfold and dejected,
signifying the Old Law.
She and her pair, Ecclesia,
stood formerly outside the
south transept door. They
are now in the Musée de
l'oeuvre de Notre-Dame.

of the Passion, accompanied by the apostles, and the saints, martyrs and doctors of the Church (fig. 11).

This theme of the continuity of history and of the debt owed to the past, both Judaic and classical, also appears in the glass of the south transept. Here the apostles are shown perched upon the shoulders of the prophets as though illustrating the remark of one of the great teachers of the school, Bernard of Chartres; according to John of Salisbury, he said that in relation to the wisdom of the past, 'we are pygmies upon the shoulders of giants'.[18] The same vivid idea appears in some of the thirteenth-century windows of Canterbury and with particular poignancy in the yearning faces of both prophets and apostles in the doorway known as the Portal of the Princes at Bamberg.

Another sculptural theme illustrating the same relationship of the Old Law to the New appears in the figures of Synagogue and Ecclesia. In the most perfect representation of this theme at Strasbourg (now in the Cathedral Museum), Synagogue is a beautiful woman with her wand of authority broken, her eyes blindfold and her body bent with doubt and obscurity (fig. 68). Ecclesia is an open-eyed crowned queen, also beautiful, but upright, gentle and certain. It is Synagogue, though, who touches our emotions; so finely carved is the veil moulding her hidden eyes that it seems to make palpable to us the barriers to understanding of the inner and outer worlds that befog our lives.

The sympathy with Synagogue revealed by the Strasbourg master must be linked with the deep knowledge of the Old Testament shown by the patrons and the fascination of the artists with the dramatic and visual possibilities of the stories of Jewish history. An immense labour on the part of the Church had been carried on for centuries finding typological concordances between the events of the Old Testament and those of the life and resurrection of Christ.[19] There had evolved a method of reading the Bible for four levels of meaning: (1) the literal, which concerned the narrative or physical details of a particular story; (2) the allegorical, which related the story to the whole history of Christ and mankind; (3) the moral, which drew out the psychological lesson to be gathered from it; and (4) the anagogic, which revealed the innermost mystical meaning of the story as a parable of the relationship of the soul to God. Suger commissioned a window for St-Denis illustrating the levels of meaning,[20] and Hugh of St Victor described how the method should be used[21]—a technique very interesting for showing how the visual education of the clergy fitted them so well for their role as patrons. He made his pupils, when reading a passage of scripture, imagine the physical details described there as clearly as possible in their minds and let the higher allegorical meanings rise up naturally from this method of controlled dreaming.

Yet another method of finding the connexions between the Old and the New Testament was that of *figura*.[22] A personage such as Samson had a historical existence in his own right, but he was also a *figura* of Christ. He carried off the gates of Gaza as Christ made the gates of Hell fall down before Him. There are many examples in the relationship of statues to one another in Gothic sculpture that show the influence of the *figura* method—as again at Bamberg, where, paired in the outer arcades of the south side of the west choir, prophets and apostles are shown like soul brothers in conversation with one another.

How does all this relate to the new image of man and the new ability to express human individuality and human emotion? According to the Christian view of history, every event had meaning and purpose. This meant too that every human individual had not only meaning and purpose but also the choice of furthering or attempting to limit the manifestation of God's glory in creation. The great individuals of the past were therefore persons to be studied, the meaning of their lives had to be interpreted, and above all their characters had to be entered into by the creative imagination. The Gothic discovery of the individual therefore is not a Romantic elevation of the single human personality into a self-dependent being, but a drawing-out from the unconscious depths of the past of the primal worth of the soul in relation to God.

The marvellous living beings of Chartres, Rheims, Notre-Dame de Paris, Amiens, Strasbourg, Bamberg and Naumburg owe their creation to the fact that they were seen within a greater whole. We can approach this greater whole through examining the development of the way in which they are placed in the doorways or on the buildings. First they step out from the columns to which they are still joined, then they are carved freestanding, but with canopies above them and socles or stands beneath their feet that often portray the villains or the vices they overcame, and then they are given niches, little houses often called aedicules or tabernacles which place them in the whole iconographical and architectural scheme. The niches are like illustrations of the many mansions of the Father—and their column shafts and their canopies, though emphasizing the individual nature of the saint or holy person depicted, also convey the hidden extension of his or her being, the unseen connectedness that each of us has with history and with a greater consciousness.

From the canopied stall or niche we extend our gaze to the depiction of the whole of creation as it will be at the Resurrection, and we find the towering cliffs of statues and rose windows, a phenomenon that derived from the west front of Chartres and grew to its grandest at Notre-Dame, its highest at Amiens, and its most sublime at Rheims.

It is a corollary of the appearance of a new image of man at the start or renewal of a civilization that it accompanies a new vision or interpretation of the universe. Putting it another way, we can say that the view of the universe current at any one time within a culture, nation or other large homogeneous group is a measure of its psychological state, of the relative dominance of fear or confidence within that group. Thus our astrophysicists have given us the Big Bang theory of creation which is the macroscale of the big bangs achieved or anticipated on earth. Going further back, Newton's description of the solar system with its checks and balances reflected the then current ideal of the Man of Reason with his balanced nature.

The appearance of the Gothic image of man, though it came at a period of renewed interest in cosmology, accompanies a conception of the universe as immensity of mind rather than as the endlessness of space, a subject of which more is said in Chapter 9. One of the west fronts that illustrates this

69 Peterborough. The screen of the early-thirteenth-century west front, with its immense archways.

70 *Left*   Wells. Part of the west front showing buttresses layered with niches containing statues of kings, queens, and holy men and women, *c.* 1220–40.

71 *Below*   Freiburg-im-Breisgau. Eve beside the tree of knowledge of good and evil round which the serpent is entwined: from the inner porch of the Minster tower, *c.* 1270–1300.

72 *Right*   Chartres. Adam in the mind of God: one of the series of archivolts in the north portal telling the story of creation, *c.* 1210.

view of the universe as the natural order founded on a harmony of musical and mathematical laws is that of Peterborough (fig. 69), which, it has been shown, is constructed according to the intervals of classical music.[23] The proportions of the screen are based on the double square, with ratios of width and height of arches and corner towers that correspond in music to diapason (the octave), diapente (the fifth) and diatesseron (the fourth). Though Peterborough has few figure sculptures, and those chiefly in the gables, its abstract design of three immensely high doorways, each framed by clusters of six shafts, helps to illustrate how the new ideal of man extended into the macroscale of the great church as a whole. Each doorway can be seen as a niche for a gigantic figure, so much are they enlargements of the aedicule form, but they are kept to a human scale by the clusters of slender columns which sweeten the oppressiveness of great size and convey the shafting downwards of beneficent energies from heaven.

Another great English screen west front, that of Wells, is entirely made up of niches (fig. 70). Here the doorways disappear to insignificance as out of every buttress and wall front over a hundred life-size statues of prophets, apostles, saints, kings, queens and clergy soar up to the region of angels and to Christ in glory. Once painted in a variety of gilding, reds, ochres, maroons, blues and greens, they must have made an even more astonishing impact than the honey-coloured Doulting stone, from which they are carved, does at sunset today. Still, here most gloriously we see the placing of souls in the order of Eternity; we also see one of the possible origins of the Gothic presentation of man: the labour of the imagination by both clergy and artists on the question of what we will be like at the moment of resurrection, when the perfected soul is joined again to the regenerate and stainless body and the individual spirit is made one with the Universal Spirit. There has been much debate on the overall theme of the Wells west front. Attempts to

73 *Above left* Amiens. The creation of Eve: a scene set below the statue of the Virgin and Child from the trumeau of the south-west doorway of the west front, *c.* 1220.

74 *Above* Freiburg-im-Breisgau. The creation of Eve, one of a series of sculptures of the Creation (see also fig. 107) from the north doorway of the choir, *c.* 1354.

fit it into the pattern of the Last Judgment scenes of other cathedrals have always run up against difficulties. A recent and satisfying suggestion is that it is a huge representation of Noah's Ark in its allegorical interpretation by Hugh of St Victor as the Church.[24]

There is another popular sequence of sculptures that tells us of man in his original perfection and of the Fall. The figural association between Adam and Christ and between Eve and the Virgin Mary, so often stressed in the liturgy, prayers, poems and commentaries, also inspired the artists and sculptors. From the toy nudes of Romanesque art we start to see a new nobility portrayed in the naked forms of Adam and Eve and a visual realization of the essential goodness in their first creation. One of the most beautiful of all these sequences is in the north portal of Chartres, where we see Adam's face peering over the shoulder of the Father as a thought in the mind of God before He creates (fig. 72). It is a startling concept—and one that we are struggling to regain—that what we regard as our most precious treasure, the sense each one of us has of himself or herself, has its origins in the selfhood of the Creator.[25]

One of the most beautiful delineations of the human body in repose is that of Adam on a socle of the west front of Amiens, bent in slumber as God the Father raises Eve from his breast (fig. 73)—a conception equalled only by the carving of the same scene at Freiburg-im-Breisgau, where Adam is so fast asleep, so relaxed in every limb, it seems that the stone is about to reabsorb him into its unconsciousness (fig. 74).

With the effort of showing Adam and Eve in their primal beauty there arose a new impulse to show the naked human form as part of the goodness

75 Below Rheims. The Visitation of the west front: Mary and Elizabeth with their robes suggesting a strong classical, possibly Greek influence, *c.* 1220.

76 Below right Bamberg. The Virgin, from a Visitation Group, *c.* 1230. This statue, now separated from that of Elizabeth, shows in her drapery classical influence, as does the angel (*right*) with his face reminiscent of archaic Greek sculpture. The cathedral carved on top of the canopy above the angel is said to be Laon, before the chevet was replaced by its present square east end.

77   Bamberg. The Rider, placed high on a pier at the entrance to the west choir, c. 1235. Though various identifications have been offered for him, including the young St Louis, he is best regarded as the supreme expression in sculpture of the medieval knightly ideal.

of creation. The finest surviving example comes from Notre-Dame in Paris, where once Adam and Eve in their nakedness smiled over the inner side of the doors of the south transept. The figure of Eve was, alas, destroyed, but that of Adam survives, even though much restored, to remind us of what was lost by the Fall (fig. 78). He is lithe, intelligent and happy; the expression on his face reminds one of that passage in Dante where it is said that, on awakening at the moment of his creation from the dust, Adam looked on his Maker and gave a cry of joy that was the first human word ever spoken.[26]

The expression of happiness on the human face was another gift the Gothic artists gave back to the world. Smiles flicker or are incipient in many of the faces of Chartres, but it is at Rheims that the faces of angels and of men were first made to smile, in that their eyes were given characteristic lines whose curves tend towards the expression of happiness, and their cheeks and lips were moulded for laughter (figs. 108 and 109). The happiness of Rheims infected Europe, radiating to Strasbourg, Cologne and Bamberg in one direction and to the angels of Westminster Abbey and of Lincoln in the other. This spirit of happiness in human form derives directly from the same inspiration—the writings of Dionysius the Areopagite—that led to the rebuilding of St-Denis. There and at Sens and Chartres it was first expressed in the combination of the new architectural forms, the many-coloured win-

78   Adam, the head of a full-size nude figure, *c.* 1250, formerly in the south transept of Notre-Dame de Paris and now, much restored in part, in the Musée de Cluny.

dows of stained glass, and the incipient happiness of the column statues. As many depictions of the wise and foolish virgins remind us, it is a happiness not sought in forgetfulness but realized in states of higher consciousness, those states to which the Dionysian writings have acted as a guide over the centuries.

It was not only the good who were allowed to smile. A new geniality spread over the faces of many of the unregenerate gods and spirits of the pagan past who still thrust their way into the churches. This was one of the ways in which the Gothic artists reconciled the dualism mentioned earlier in Romanesque decoration and carving, extending to the grotesque and even to the demons an infinitely wider range of expressions, weakening the effect of the blind terrors they signified, not by denying them, but by portraying them with exactitude in the light of clear-eyed imagination.

The sculptures in the south aisle beside the west choir of Bamberg illustrate many of the themes we have been discussing here. Against the screen of prophets paired with apostles in conversation, already mentioned, stand figures of Mary and Elizabeth at the Visitation, their robes clearly classical and even Greek in their texture and the way they cling to the body. The influence of the Rheims sculptures on them (fig. 75) is clear, even to the difference in age between the two women and their lively characterization. Next to Mary stands an angel (fig. 76) with the archaic smile of a *kouros* or early Apollo, who from his now broken-off hands once presented the wreath of martyrdom to the statue of St Denis, then thought to have been identical with Dionysius the Areopagite. We turn the corner and see raised on a stone shelf carved with acanthus leaves one of the most famous of German medieval sculptures, the Rider of Bamberg (fig. 77).

As with many of the statues we have discussed, we have no certain identification for him. His lack of name does nothing to lessen his individuality or the ideal he seems to suggest of a young knight riding through the forest of the world to bring justice and reconciliation where he can. We do know something of the symbolism of the rider in command of his horse from other representations: it depicts a man disciplined and in control of his senses. At Notre-Dame and Worms the disciplined rider is paired with a foolish or careless man who is thrown by his horse. The west front of Strasbourg is given an extra majesty by the huge horsemen who ride in arcades in the upper stages of the façade, symbolizing the control and assurance of those who wield imperial power.[27] The citizens of Magdeburg erected opposite their town hall a noble rider escorted at his stirrups by female figures of justice and charity.[28] It was a theme particularly cherished in Germany and it drew on ancient hero legends for its power. The Bamberg figure draws deeply on one aspect of these legends, the hero who is in contact with nature and who can understand the language of birds and of leaves. The shelf on which his horse treads is supported by two consoles, one of which is carved into a most powerful depiction of the vegetation god known as the Green Man (fig. 79). He has the face of a great monarch, with fleshy sensual lips and eyes hooded under leaves, suspicious of any derogation of his power. The knight is no threat to him and can pass even with his blessing. The knight does not want conquest: he has the mark of the search on his face and perhaps, like Parsifal, he seeks the Grail hidden in Muntsalvaesche. Here we see reconciled, in one of the masterpieces of Gothic art, the Christian and the pagan through the new conception of man, not as a monk or a recluse, but a bold and sensitive explorer of the world.

Chapter 6

The World of the Green Man

Once you look for the Green Man he appears everywhere, returning your stare. The Green Man is one of the recurrent images of western art. In the eleventh century he underwent a resurrection from his earlier portrayals in the art of the La Tène Celts and in Gallo-Roman sculpture, and he revelled in the churches up to the fifteenth and sixteenth centuries, when he found a new career among the swags and scrolls of Renaissance decoration.[1] In England he is known as the foliate head, the Green Man, or Jack o' the Green. In France he is called less evocatively either a *tête de feuilles* or a *masque feuillu* according to whether his face is formed of many leaves or is centred in one leaf. In many cases the leaves of which his hair is formed spring from his mouth. In rare instances, as at Toscanella, he is three-headed or tricephalic, with vegetation growing out of each mouth.[2] He probably descends in part from the Celtic horned god Cernunnos, a god of forest, fields and hunting who had serpents as his attributes. Under the general rule that the gods of an older religion become the devils of a new faith, the horned visage of Cernunnos provided the model for medieval depictions of the devil and his cohorts. As the devil had to be portrayed in sculpture and painting for the purposes of instruction and warning, so, by being depicted as Cernunnos, even to the extent as at Schwäbisch-Gmünd[3] of having serpents coming out of his mouth, the devil provided a means for one of the most powerful of the ancient gods to maintain his presence in a Christian context.

The Green Man would seem to have infiltrated the churches in much the same way. In the ninth century the influential Hrabanus Maurus had identified the leaf as a symbol of sexual sin[4]—an association that to us may seem astonishing. Such an association would have provided the licence for the carving of foliate heads and vegetation in churches, again as a symbolic warning to the faithful of the perils of the flesh, but whereas Cernunnos in his horned aspect always remained the irredeemable devil throughout the Middle Ages, in his contribution to the figure of the Green Man he underwent a remarkable transformation at the hands of the Gothic artists into a symbol of renewal and resurrection, as befits a god of vegetation.

The popularity of the Green Man was widespread throughout western

79 *Left* Bamberg. The Green Man, his face formed of acanthus leaves, who acts as a console to the ledge carrying the Rider of Bamberg: one of the most powerful depictions of the Green Man to have survived.

80 *Right* Strasbourg. A benign Green Man of vine leaves and grapes, now in the Musée de l'oeuvre de Notre-Dame.

81 *Left*   Dijon. A Green Man with vine leaves and grapes, a vault boss from the Chapelle de Bauffremont, formerly attached to St-Bénigne, now in the Musée archéologique.

Europe, increasing with the passing of time and the full establishment of the Gothic style. He is portrayed in corbels, vaulting bosses, arcades, or tombstones, screens, pulpits, misericords, and choir stalls. As a decorative device he was useful for bringing the eye to the point of a gable; at Notre-Dame and Cologne he appears in the gables of the exteriors of the chapels ringing the chevets of both cathedrals. That Villard de Honnecourt felt it necessary to draw many of his forms in his sketch-book shows that he thought the Green Man a vital element in the decorative vocabulary of the master mason.[5]

Given the popularity of the figure, it is strange that there is no written mention or description of the Green Man surviving from the Middle Ages. The nearest we have is the description of the Green Knight from the fourteenth-century northern English poem of *Sir Gawaine*. The Green Knight, green in skin, hair, clothing, riding a green horse, with a holly bush in his hand, enters Arthur's court during a feast and demands that one of the knights of the Round Table should strike his head from his shoulders. Sir

82 *Right*   Norwich. A Green Man in the east walk of the cloisters of the cathedral, first half of the fourteenth century.

83 *Far left*   Ulm. A Green
Woman. It is unusual to
find female foliate heads,
though this is one of
several, *c.* 1400, in the
north aisle of the Minster.

84 *Left*   Dijon. One of the
earliest Green Men in
Romanesque sculpture:
part of a capital in the
crypt of St Bénigne, built
by Lombard masons from
1000 onwards. Compare
this savage face with that
in fig. 81.

Gawaine accepts the challenge and decapitates the knight who, with his
head under his arm, rides out challenging Gawaine to meet him in a year's
time so that he may perform the same service for Gawaine.[6] The story draws
on ancient vegetation myths and rites of prophecy and sacrifice which, as we
shall see, connect very well in some instances with the origins of the corbel
head and the Gothic transformation of the image.

Another clue may lie in the fountain of about 1200 that now stands in the
Musée lapidaire of St-Denis.[7] The bowl of the fountain is carved with the
heads of classical deities, amongst which is a Green Man with vegetation
coming out of his mouth, inscribed with the name of the Roman god of
forests, Silvanus. Silvanus was never shown in this way in classical times
and the ascription may have been a way of rationalizing or justifying the
portrayal of a native pagan god whose presence was too powerful to be
repressed.

The transformation of the Green Man affords one of the most striking
examples of how the Gothic masters drew on the psychic energies contained
in an archetype of the ancient European mind that might have stayed a blind
unconscious force working against all civilizing influences. By giving the
Green Man a place of honour in their buildings, they channelled those forces
into creating an image capable of reflecting the vast range of emotions
evoked in man by the vegetation of the Earth in its seasonal changes and the
variety of its forms. One comparison demonstrates the difference between
the early Romanesque treatment of the image and what the Gothic masters
did with it. A short stroll in Dijon will take one from the Green Man (fig. 84)
and other monsters in the capitals of the crypt of St Bénigne, built at the
direction of the severe and energetic monk Guillaume Volpiano in the early
eleventh century,[8] to the Musée archéologique to see what, to my mind, is
one of the most enchanting Green Men ever carved, a roof boss with its
painting intact, from the destroyed Chapelle de Bauffremont. This Green
Man reflects warmth, direct contact, a subtlety of humorous and delicate
response, and he seems to declare to us that the love we feel for nature is
reflected back to us in measure for our appreciation and that the source of
this love is the same for us as is the driving force of sap in leaves and
branches (fig. 81).

Another contrast that takes us on much wider journeys is between the

Green Men sprouting foliage from their mouths at the tiny church of Kilpeck in Herefordshire, and later Gothic portrayals. At Kilpeck they are neither kind nor malevolent, with their staring lentoid eyes, but fulfil their function of providing vegetation for the Earth with unwinking duty. They have no messages for men and the leaves and tendrils that flow from their mouths have no identity with any plant species (fig. 85). These were carved in about 1135. Travel in any direction from Kilpeck, crossing mountains and seas to all the limits of the European littoral and land borders, to churches built a hundred years or more later, and you are bound to find Green Men whose faces, transformed and humanized by the magic of the Gothic, partake of its new gift of expressing precisely felt and individual emotion. Some will tell you of spring with their fresh young faces, some of summer with their full cheeks and luxuriant leaves that sprout from them, some will sigh with the burden of autumn and some will be like corpse heads in the shrouds of their vegetation. Some will stare you into the state of their own horror, conveying, as though from a forest at twilight, the original meaning of the word 'panic'; and some will leave within you a smile that lasts for days. Some dream like Merlin slumbering in the courteous briars of Broceliande and some show aspects of the multifarious nature of Wotan, whether as the god of forests and of battles, as at Bamberg, or as the source of inspiration, the *minne* of the poets as he hung on the World Tree to gain wisdom.[9] And some seem the human face of a landscape as with the Burgundian Green Man.

85   Kilpeck. The Green Man as a capital on one of the richly carved columns of the door of this remarkable small Herefordshire church, *c.* 1135.

The words Virgil applied to another god: *cruda deo viridisque senectus*[10] ('a god's old age is hardy and green'), could well apply to the Green Man. As early as the sixth century Bishop Nicetius had taken foliate head capitals from the Hadrianic temple of Am Herrenbrünnchen and incorporated them in his new cathedral at Trier.[11] Though these are now walled up behind later buildings, their presence over several centuries in so important a cathedral must have had a wide influence in establishing their right to a place in other churches. Though the later versions of the Green Man draw on these and other influences, in their vitality they bear witness to the process that has been called 'the transformation of images', the fusion of symbols during the merging of races and traditions in the Dark Ages. Just as the early workers in stained glass dug among the ruins of old towns for caches of Roman glass which they melted down to create the new Christian images of their windows, so the Green Man is a freshly realized archetype formed from the fusion of many gods and spirits. Even if one were to regard him, at the lowest level, as a mascot of the masons, his presence in so many regions and over so long a period indicates that he had a particular meaning for them. Did he sum up for them the energy they had to transform, the energy both of living nature and of the past stored in the collective unconscious? And did he at the same time express the spirit of inspiration, the *genius* hidden in created things?

In this last case, we can connect the new character given to the Green Man by the Gothic masters with the visual realizations they could draw from the doctrine of the Incarnation. The flowers and leaves of the field were given a new worth as signs of the Virgin Mary. There is in Exeter Cathedral a corbel of the Virgin and Child above a Green Man which is no scene of triumph over evil or of duality. The infant Jesus chucks His Mother under the chin, angels cense them from above and the Green Man, with the face of a happy clown, pours out with delight the vegetation that rises up on either side of Mother and Child, no longer emblematic of sin but rather of the signature of God in creation.

So too the Green Man in the miraculous leaf sculptures of the Marburg pulpitum (fig. 88), carved at the place of honour where the Gospel was read

86 *Above*   Freiburg-im-Breisgau. The Easter sepulchre, *c.* 1330, showing part of the figure of Christ lying on the tomb slab with Green Men weeping in the canopy above.

88   Marburg. A Green Man, one of many in the leaf carvings of the pulpitum, *c.* 1270.

and in front of the high altar of the church, shows how far the image had travelled, readily accepted into the Christian fold. The example that, however, shows best the absorption of pagan elements into Christianity is in the Easter sepulchre at Freiburg-im-Breisgau. Here, lying on a slab, Christ is carved life-size, laid out dead with the soldiers of his guard wrapped in sleep in the panels below. The Christ is profoundly moving and profoundly reminiscent of old Germanic legends of the deaths of heroes, of Siegfried treacherously slain or of Balder who could not return from death because, of all nature, only one creature refused to mourn for him. In the canopy above the Christ is a range of Green Men with their faces harrowed by grief, endowed with all the intensity of emotion that was one of Germany's transfusions of new energy into the Gothic style. It is as though the death of the god in the vegetation myth and the death of Christ are seen as one; indigenous experience and folk memory are redeemed and used to exemplify, through great art, the greater theme of the sorrow of creation at the death of Christ (fig. 86).

The Green Man is nearly always shown just as a head—unless he is also related to the Wodwo or wild man—and we will come to him again in discussing the origin and significance of the corbel head. What concern us first are the creatures and plants of the Green Man's world. A revolution in man's understanding of nature took place, related to the new presentation of man as an individual, and of equal significance. Just as it became desirable and possible to carve the face and form of a saint so that the whole statue presented a recognizable portrait of an individual with the history of his life and experience printed in his features and implicit in his gestures and garments, so, in the carving of vegetation, the generalized leaf and flower forms of Romanesque sculpture changed into plants and petals of recogniz-

87 *Previous page, right* Chartres. The lower part of the Jesse window, *c.* 1150, one of the three lancets of the west front, made by craftsmen from St-Denis, which survived the fire of 1194.

able and keenly observed individual species. The same process that had given individuality to the saint had at once humanized the faces of the Green Man and ensured that the oak, hawthorn, ivy, or vine leaves that issued from his mouth or made up his features were immediately identifiable. This was an achievement of the highest significance in the development of western science because it brought a new area of the natural world under close observation. Earlier medieval botanical illustrations, as part of a series of copies from late classical models, had lost much connexion with the plants they were meant to portray. The clear eye transforms the world, and it was the clear eye of the Gothic sculptor that freed vegetation from its Roman-esque association with sin and that looked at the habits of leaves and boughs in three-dimensional space.

The journey to the great naturalistic leaf carvings of the thirteenth and fourteenth centuries as at Rheims, Gelnhausen, Marburg, Naumburg, Southwell and Lincoln was a roundabout one. The tendency of the early Gothic masters was to ignore the association of sin with vegetation, exempli-fied on the Romanesque jamb columns at Lincoln of men entrapped in tendrils or in artefacts such as the Gloucester candlestick. At Sens, under the influence of St Bernard, the sculptors of the capitals would seem to have gone to an ideal Platonic world in search of an *Urpflanze*, to use Goethe's phrase for the archetypal plant, from the contemplation of which they derived leaves of the calmest and most simple forms. At St-Denis, under Suger's direction, there would appear to have been a movement to return to purer classical models, especially in the use of the acanthus; that abbey also produced the first form of an iconographic theme of long-lasting import-ance, the Tree of Jesse, which showed the genealogy of Christ and the Virgin Mary perched on the branches of a trunk rooted in the loins of Jesse. It was stained-glass workers from St-Denis who made the Tree of Jesse window at Chartres in about 1150, thus giving wider influence to a theme which helped transform the tree and its parts from an image connected with the Fall into the means of redemption. At the summit of the Tree of Jesse sits or stands the Virgin who, in the hymns, poems and sermons of the twelfth and thirteenth centuries, became increasingly associated with the beauty of the natural world, especially with flowers. It is in her cathedral of Notre-Dame at Paris that the delineation of a wide range of recognizable flowers and plants is practised, first on the later capitals of the nave and aisles and then amongst and around the statues of the exterior.[12]

The new tendency to height in Gothic building which begins with Notre-Dame meant that the capital was often placed too high to be histori-ated or used for telling stories. Sculpture of this kind had been brought nearer to eye-level in the portals of the exterior and in the arcades of the interior faces of the walls. The capitals were left free for the luxuriance of vegetation. In this they followed two ways: one was a development of the ideal and generalized vegetation of Sens and this was what the architect of Chartres chose for his nave, introducing what are called crocketed capitals after the knobs that stick out from corners, rising like curled bracken fronds or the tight round leaf-buds of sycamore in April. This is the kind of capital known in the Early English style as stiff-leaf—formal, severe, reserved. The other line of development was that of the later capitals of Notre-Dame which was taken up with enthusiasm at Rheims; there, as though to give a perpe-tual reminder of the wreaths and garlands that would accompany the coronations of the Kings of France, the capitals burst into leaf and flowers and fruit, with oak, waterlilies, roses, fig and vine. These too are very high up to be fully appreciated, and it is to the west wall of the three aisles of the nave—the inner side of the three portals surmounted by the coronation of

89   Rheims. Panels and spandrels of accurate leaf carvings frame the niches of Old Testament figures which are part of the interior west façade of the nave, *c.* 1250–60. Oak, maple, hop, and ilex are among the leaves shown here.

90 *Below*   Naumburg. Hazelnuts on a capital of the west choir pulpitum, *c.* 1240. This is one of a series of leaf capitals in which the symbolism of the plant can be related to the story of the Passion.

the Virgin—that we must go to see some of the finest of Gothic leaf carvings. The wall of the central aisle is inset with niches containing 52 figures, each rank of niches being divided by bands of vegetation set in panels and with vegetation carved also in the spandrels of the arches. Well over 20 identifiable species of plant, some repeated, are carved here as the setting for the forebears of Christ and Old Testament figures, including Melchisedek, robed as a priest, giving bread and wine to Abraham in full chain-mail armour. The niches rise up to scenes of the massacre of the Innocents and the baptism of Christ. It is almost certain that each plant was chosen for its symbolic significance, connecting with the individual figures or with the whole, as with the sequence of wormwood leaves hinting at the bitterness of passion.[13]

The whole composition framed in its leafage is an extension of the theme of the Tree of Jesse, though without Jesse himself and with that interplay between the figures with which the Rheims school introduced a new note of the drama into their sculptural ensembles. Here we see, in almost a literal sense, the Judaeo-Christian stories and tradition brought from the eastern Mediterranean and grafted on to the native tradition, made more accessible by the vitality of the figures and their contemporary dress and bowered within vegetation of North-West Europe (fig. 89). As though to make sure his leaves and flowers sprout and bloom in full health and splendour a Green Man looks out from one of the spandrels, while in the topmost band God appears in the burning bush to Moses, telling the lesson that His glory can be revealed in all the vegetation of the earth.

Plants provided almost the entire pharmacopoeia of the ancient and medieval world, possessing connotations of healing often foreign to us, and therefore linked, in the Gothic transformation of vegetation, to the healing of the wounds inflicted on the will and intellect by original sin.[14] This can be seen most clearly in the screen or pulpitum to the west choir at Naumburg. It is one of the incidental unhappinesses created by the Iron Curtain that the Naumburg sculptures, amongst the finest ever achieved in Europe, are comparatively difficult of access. Naumburg, in common with several other German cathedrals, has the unusual characteristic of two apsidal choirs, one at the conventional east end and the other at the west end. The west choir of Naumburg was built in the 1240s under the direction of Bishop Hugo von Wettin to commemorate the Margraves of Meissen and their wives who founded the cathedral.[15] The statues of the founders will be considered in the next chapter. Naumburg in the middle of the thirteenth century was very close to the borders of the East Prussians and the Poles who, under their heathen rulers, remained the last outposts of pagan religions in Europe. The bishop probably needed all the resources of art both to dignify Christian patrons and to impress the Gospel story upon his flock. The sculptor he chose was one who had already worked on the west portal at Noyon, north of Paris. There, though the tympana were brutally destroyed at the French Revolution, enough of the vegetation carving survives to show his characteristic style. He also worked at Mainz in about 1239, on a pulpitum there, and of it a group of Christ with the Virgin and the Baptist raised on a bracket carved with lovage leaves is preserved in the Diocesan Museum. Lovage was sovereign against poison and venomous bites and therefore was an exact emblem for the healing power of Christ.[16]

At Naumburg he placed in the upper register of the screen or pulpitum a series of tableaux portraying the scenes of the Passion. The two final tableaux were replaced in the eighteenth century. Looking at those by his hand

91 *Below right* Naumburg. The Last Supper, one of the panels in the upper register of the west choir pulpitum, *c.* 1240.

that remain, one feels that never, to this date, had the range of human emotions implicit in the story of the Passion been brought to so full a sculptural realization. Each face and each gesture convey directly to the heart what every character in the drama is feeling, whether it is the sublime resignation on the face of Christ, fully aware of every horror and degradation that awaits Him, the appalled expression of Judas returning the silver to the High Priest, or the guilt of Peter taunted by the handmaid. If we turn to the leaf capitals he carved in the arcade below, we find the same directness and simplicity. The sequence of plants in the capitals runs: wild cucumber, buttercup, wood anemone, mugwort or wormwood, vine, hazel, larkspur, wormwood again, and vine repeated twice. Oakleaves also are carved on a corbel; they rise from a rare depiction of the Green Man with his features made of bark. The symbolism of some of these plants is obvious in relation to the Passion. Adam of St Victor said of the hazel-nut that it symbolized Christ: the green sheath was His flesh; the wood of the shell the cross; and the kernel of the nut His hidden divinity.[17] The meaning of other plants is obscure and must be sought in the herbal lore of writers such as Hildegarde of Bingen and Albertus Magnus.[18] Every plant, though, has been looked at as if with the words of another medieval writer who said that we do not see the reality of any created thing until we see God in it.[19] The effect is liberating: we are brought into a new world of observation: we forget symbolism, we ignore iconographic relationships, we are made to look at the sheer beauty of leaf forms as they have not been revealed in art before. They touch the heart immediately as they issue from the stone with the naturalness of their originals warmed by the sun after a shower, halting the visitor on his journey to the equally marvellous and different wonders beyond the screen (fig. 90).

The chief experience comparable to that of Naumburg is afforded by the chapter house of Southwell with its vestibule.[20] This was built and decorated some forty years later than the Naumburg pulpitum, in about 1290. Even less is known about the sculptor mason than about the Naumburg sculptor. The composition is void of figure sculpture except as humans, animals, birds

92 *Top left* Southwell. Nature humanized and understood: the man peering from the outer band of vine leaves at the apex of the archway of the portal to the chapter house.

93 *Above left* Southwell. Hawthorn, maple, and buttercup leaves in the capitals of the entrance portal to the chapter house.

94 *Above* Southwell. The portal to the chapter house, *c.* 1290.

and Green Men incorporated among the foliage. The concentration is therefore almost wholly upon the vegetation, which begins in the twin doorway in the chancel aisle and continues in the straight arcaded corridor to the vestibule where another portal, arched with buttercup and vine leaves and shafted with Purbeck marble, leads into the octagonal chapter house. The central boss of the chapter house is a large bulbous generalized plant form—perhaps another version of the Platonic *Urpflanze*—from which the particularized species emerge first in sixteen bosses, through which the ridges of the vaults swing down to mark the eight sides of the chapter house. Thirty-six stalls, each with its leafy tympanum and capitals, are set round the chapter house, where the canons of the Minster once discussed their own affairs, dealt with their tenants and exercised their ecclesiastical jurisdiction. In the complex of chapter house, vestibule and corridor there are 93 leaf capitals. Amongst these, many species, such as buttercup, vine, maple, hawthorn, ivy, hop and tormentil, recur several times but always as though seen anew. Here at Southwell, because of the absence of a sequence of figure carvings like the Naumburg Passion, one is led even more deeply into the

95   Amiens. Part of the immense band or garland of vegetation that marks the division between the main arcade and the triforium in the nave, built 1220–36.

World of the Green Man who, in many aspects, broods like a guardian spirit over his garden. The pagan spirit here is purified through the higher awareness of the sculptor. He must have studied the plants in their natural state with such intensity that their habits of growth, the way the nodules on their twigs have sealed over leaf scars, and the angles at which the leaves spring from their stalks and overlie one another in their hunger for light, were absorbed into an inner vision of the divine signature in created things. The leaf capitals were an exercise in self-knowledge for him; at the same time as he carved the limestone, he investigated and brought to the light of consciousness pure emotions that were inner reflections of the varied beauty in which his eye delighted.

So intense is the experience of looking at these carvings that we too find ourselves taking a journey of discovery into the world of nature within ourselves. Thus the wild forest becomes the Garden of Eden and the faces of men and women, birds and beasts, unseen or unregarded, start to emerge as though they are part of the increasing humanization of nature. The ensemble of sculpture speaks of the reward for freeing ourselves from the false duality between the world and our inner selves: the achievement of a higher state of awareness, like the figure of a man holding the tendrils of the vine that symbolizes Christ, looking out relaxed and free of sin at the apex of the pointed arch of the main portal (fig. 92).

Once the models for the realistic carving of vegetation in three dimensions had been set, not only by the sculptors of Naumburg, Rheims, and Southwell but in a widely spread number of churches, many of which are lost to us, a new impulse was given to the Gothic love of fantasy: the artists could now give greater credibility to their invented foliation, their strange animals, and their monsters by drawing them out of a synthesis of their close observations of natural forms. To this movement we owe the luxuriant decoration of some of the English rood screens or pulpita, as with the fourteenth-century screens at Southwell and Lincoln, the fantastic vegetation on the west façade of Regensburg of the same century, and the leaf and bark decoration associated with the Parler dynasty of master masons wherever their influence spread, from Prague to Cologne. Much of the ingenuity was exercised on sepulchral monuments, which proliferated in churches as the nobility and the richer burghers sought and won the privilege of burial within the church—in general up to the thirteenth century this had been reserved for bishops and the higher clergy, monarchs, their families, other ruling princes, and founders of abbeys and churches. Thus we find in Beverley Minster in the fourteenth century the monument of a lady of the Percy family next to the high altar, bursting with foliage in every direction: it is as though the green life of the world had been brought in both as witness to the illusory extinction of physical death and as an emblem of the eternal life revealed in the figure of Christ in the canopy, receiving the soul of the woman buried below in the tomb chest.

What of the animals and birds that inhabit the forests of the Green Man? Romanesque art is replete with wild and savage animals, often ingeniously incorporated into the architectural forms of the style, as with the beaked heads, probably derived from the Celtic motif of the winged beaked horse,[21] that surround the arches of so many Romanesque doorways. In the greedy monsters and savage birds of Romanesque capitals, still more than in the entangling vegetation, we see that duality of the old and new religions, that struggle which seemed to summate man's whole experience of life in the early Middle Ages. The early Gothic masters obviously agreed with St Bernard and dealt with these creatures of nightmare by abolishing them or transforming them by their powers of accurate observation. Only some seventy-five years separate the scrolled dragon heads which protrude from the west wall of Kilpeck and the salamander of Wells which is caught about to dart over some foliage, though both ultimately derive from the pre-Celtic dragon attribute of the Great Goddess. These animals and monsters had been permitted into Romanesque churches, not only because they were seen as aspects of the devil or of the old gods who were the devil's allies, but because they could be interpreted as symbolizing the sins and virtues of mankind.

This method of interpretation was founded on the *Physiologus*, an Alexandrian work from which the medieval bestiaries derived.[22] Through its African provenance details of numerous real and mythical desert and subtropical beasts, birds, and insects were made familiar to a north European audience, to whom, in the case of the exotic animals, an amphisboena was as real as an elephant. Yet further opportunities for portraying animals and birds were afforded by the stories of both Testaments, from the Creation to the ram caught in the thicket, from the sheep under the star of the Nativity to the beasts of the Apocalypse. To this zoo of stone we can add the various animal symbols of the signs of the Zodiac, the creatures like the hog slaughtered in November in the labours of the year, the lions, eagles, leopards, swans and elephants of heraldic devices, and the extraordinary range of animals and semi-human figures from the classical past, like the centaur, or from Nordic myth like the Fenris wolf who devours the world, or, from the Celtic pantheon, like the figure of Nobody, and the grinning toothy Giant. Some creatures come from travellers' tales, like the Sciapod who has one enormous foot and lies beside the Ganges shielding himself from the sun, using his foot as a parasol. Others have no name, which is curious because they are indigenous and cousins to the Green Man. These can only be described generically as glaring figures or devouring figures,[23] for example, by their chief characteristic action, but their bodies and faces, humanoid rather than human, are like the results of mistakes in an embryologist's test-tubes. These creatures frequently appear among the gallimaufry of

96   Chartres. Sheep grazing as the angel tells the shepherds of the Nativity: a scene from the south doorway tympanum of the Royal Portal, *c.* 1150.

features that often surround the eaves of Romanesque churches and are known as corbel heads. The corbel head, another feature of the Romanesque transformed by the Gothic artists, has a strange origin.

Sequences of corbel heads were not, in general, a feature of classical architecture and they were denied to the Byzantine sculptor because of the Orthodox ban on three-dimensional depictions of the human face. The most obvious source for them, according to Dr Anne Ross, is in the Celtic cult of the severed head:

> Together with the cult of sacred springs and wells, the severed human head, or animal head, was one of the most worshipful of all the ancient pre-Christian symbols. Both were almost ineradicable. The cult of the head was taken into the Christian Church, and as a result the severed head is one of the most widespread and common motifs in the Gothic period. Grotesque heads are exceptionally numerous, as is the motif of the head with foliage coming from the mouth, or the human head mask embedded in greenery, the eyes staring balefully out, harking back to memories of human sacrifice and tree worship, widely practised in Europe, as elsewhere. The Celts, from whom so many of the later European people were descended, were like other northern peoples, head-hunters. But apart from cutting off the heads of their enemies in battle they worshipped the severed head, and believed it to be imbued with every divine power—prophecy, fertility, speech, song and hospitality and, perhaps more than anything else, the power of averting evil. Thus, the presence of so many heads in our churches— janiform, tricephalic, foliate and purely grotesque—over and above the straightforward portrait heads, would have a very obvious explanation. In the same way heads set up on the gateposts of dwellings, or placed on walls or above doors, would have the same ultimate significance—the protection of the dwelling from evil forces, and the imbuing of it with everything lucky and desirable.[24]

The extent to which the veneration of the severed head survived the introduction of Christianity and the means by which its cult was transmitted are both obscure. It is certain, however, that the Saxons, the Teutonic tribes and the Slavs all erected horse and human skulls in their temples and that the skulls of saints from early days were separated from their skeletons and encased in gold and silver jewelled masks, as happened to the head of St Foy at Conques. The exposing of heads inside and outside buildings may have been widespread in domestic buildings: the practice of nailing animal skulls over barn doors survived in many farming communities in Europe up to the present century. Similarly, the decoration of castle halls with antlers and deer skulls may not have been intended to show off the hunting prowess of the castle's lord and family but to ensure luck, fertility, and increase. With the revival of stone building from the early eleventh century it was probably considered quite natural that churches should be provided with the protective cincture of severed heads that was customary for ordinary buildings: only, because of their greater dignity, the heads were carved in stone. Thus it came about that between the early eleventh and the later twelfth century churches were built all over Europe, from the west of Ireland as at Clonfert, to Kilpeck in Herefordshire, to the borders of the pagan Pruss and down beyond the Pyrenees and the Alps, with their sequences of corbel heads round and above their doors, about their eaves and string courses and along the arcades of their interiors, mingling pagan and Christian motifs in a seemingly indiscriminate manner.

In the Gothic period the severed head flourished to a new order of

97   Auxerre. Three corbel heads from the choir ambulatory, begun 1215, showing (*left to right*) a Green Man, a Sibyl, and an Old Testament prophet. The Sibyls signified the Church of the Gentiles as the Old Testament prophets signified the Church of the Jews; their role in prophesying Christ is expressed in this Celtic form.

extent, not only because of the greater repertoire of architectural features the new style commanded or introduced but because the severed head could be transformed by the same individuating hands and minds which had called the Gothic image of man into existence. With the rediscovery by western man of the powers of reason latent within his nature, the severed head retained its aura as the vehicle of prophecy and clairvoyancy but could now convey a spirit of rationality. The severed head could also now, through the Gothic ability to characterize, be brought into the exposition of the Judaeo-Christian tradition. Just as the vegetative world of the Green Man was made the framework for the genealogy of Christ on the inner west wall of Rheims, so sequences of severed heads were used for Christian instruction. Nowhere is the synthesis more clearly seen than in the cathedral of the ancient Gallo-Roman city of Auxerre, where along the walls of the ambulatory jut out massive superbly carved heads of all the Jewish prophets and all the Sibyls of antiquity who foretold the coming of Christ. They are, it must be said, interspersed with faces of the Green Man, who is there to remind us that the very device by which they are grouped together, and which enabled their sculptors to convey their qualities of inspiration and interpretation of divine messages, was an invention of his Celtic peoples who once on this very spot looked to the severed heads for prophecy and guidance (fig. 97).

It is tempting to ask how far the Gothic masters were aware of the pagan antecedents of the decorative and figurative themes at their command. There are certainly strange anomalies such as the Gallo-Roman altar of the Celtic god Erec that was built into the choir stalls of Notre-Dame at Paris like an act of propitiation to the old religion, but these instances are rare. I think that they were aware of them to the extent that survivals of the pagan past surrounded them from childhood as part of the natural and accepted order of things, that they were much closer than us to the physical remains of Roman towns and Celtic settlements and that with the expansion of towns and the bringing of land into cultivation, there was a constant discovery of ancient statues and artefacts to stimulate their imaginations and to reinforce the visualization of archetypes present in their creative dream-life. The artists of the Romanesque had performed the enormous task of recovering the wealth of imagery left by the old religions and of assimilating it into buildings based on Roman and Byzantine models. It was for the Gothic

98   Lincoln. The Judgment Portal, the south entrance to the choir. The head of Christ in glory and the statue of the Virgin and Child are replacements.

masters to choose amongst this wealth what they would discard and what they would treasure and develop in the interest of their greater aim, which, to repeat Frankl's words, was 'the purest and most intensive realization of the spirit contained in the New Testament'[25] and which seemed to direct them towards making their buildings gigantic symbols of the whole psychology of man.

Urged on by their clerical patrons to demonstrate through their art that the whole of creation existed for the redemption of man, they transformed their own attitudes and those of succeeding generations to the natural world, showing it to be truly beautiful, truly instinct with the creative power of its maker. As a corollary of that achievement, again helped by the labours of the clerics to find an individual signature or meaning in every mineral, precious stone, plant and beast that related to the passions, virtues, and vices of man, they created buildings symbolizing man in his totality from which the thought could grow that the whole of creation exists in every man.

To make their achievement complete, the Gothic masters had to conquer the world of the Green Man, if they were to draw on energies more powerful than those at their command in their teams of workmen, their oxen and draughthorses, their ingenious machines, and the resources of power, spiritual authority and finance placed at their disposal by their patrons. Those energies are those of the collective unconscious and its archetypes which, as artists, they had to draw out from their dream worlds, transforming them from the nightmares of a tribal past into fully seen and realized images. Their only safeguards in this dangerous task must have been their powers of attention and their capacity for love, for the art of sculpting in stone allows of few mistakes and the creation of a new image of man and a new presentation of the natural world could only derive from the deepest love of humanity and a delight in natural form that is inseparable from love.

Let us use Lincoln Cathedral as an example of the development of the themes of vegetation and of the severed head from the Romanesque into the high Gothic period. The remaining door jambs of the Romanesque period in the west front are carved with figures of naked men entangled in vegetation as in the bonds of lust and sin. If we move round the exterior to the Judgment portal in the south choir wall (fig. 98), executed about a century later, we find a wholly different world. Ithyphallic demons exclaim with annoyance at the very feet of Christ at the Second Coming, surrounded by hosts of angels, elders, and wise and foolish virgins, while in the outer arch of the portal is a miraculous frieze of vegetation with birds enjoying the berries as though they and their world had been redeemed from their false association with sin. Walking in and out of the many exterior angles of the buttresses and transepts we are dazzled by the countless heads of men and women, spirits, gargoyles and animals that spring from every side, an impression that seems to overwhelm us with the feeling that each one of these is part of the thousands of personalities within our own natures. Going into the cathedral, especially on seeing the pulpitum with its luxuriant foliage and entering the choir, we are again assaulted by the same diversity of faces, figures and attitudes, and we gain an inkling of what the Gothic sculptors were aiming at in their transformation of the tradition of the severed head. They meant to change the perceptions of everyone who saw their work through the impression of being watched by hundreds of pairs of eyes, and they used the most powerful images of the past to make their contemporaries live more fully in the present by enhancing their awareness of themselves. Thus through this assault course of our own natures we are brought into that glory of the Middle Ages, the Angel Choir, built by Simon of Thirsk from 1256 (fig. 99), where our eyes are raised above courses of heads of men and of women, above that loveable demon, the Lincoln imp, to the angels and the portrayals of Mary and her Son in the spandrels of the triforium. As we have seen the transformation of the world of the Green Man, whose very nature is transience and rebirth, in the works of the Gothic masters, so we must turn to another of their great works, the interpretation of the everlasting worlds of the angels and of the redemption of the Eternal Feminine through their portrayal of the Virgin Mary.

Chapter 7

The Angelic Orders and the Eternal Feminine

The Cathedral of Regensburg on the Danube contains one of the most beautiful, and certainly the most dramatic, of all Gothic representations of the Annunciation. On piers of the crossing, Angel and Virgin face one another across the nave; the Archangel Gabriel, radiant with the divine command he announces, smiles at the Virgin who responds with right hand upturned. These figures are the work of a sculptor known as the Erminoldmeister, and date from about 1280.[1] The contrasts between the two figures are so sharp that they set up a force field in the high space of the nave, affecting our emotional response. They are so dominant that it is as though the whole cathedral grew out of their encounter.[2] The interplay between them is a palpable image of the great tension that it was the duty of the Gothic masters to resolve as a major part of their mission—the tension between the world and man, between a universe created as an act of goodness and thronged with invisible intelligences praising its creator and fulfilling his decrees, and the species which shares the natures of angels and of beasts and which has gone astray through original sin. The sculptor used the two figures to express and resolve this tension in every detail of their features, the rhythms of their drapery, their attitude and gestures. Gabriel's stance gives out the impulsive joy of a vision that has just appeared. He has chosen the form of an adolescent boy in which to deliver his message; his features, however, are not those of a boy breaking into smile but those played with by the essence of a smile that needed the face of a boy to manifest its nature. His flesh is the medium of the unearthly and the surging uprising folds of his robes, signifying his freedom from gravity and terrestrial constraints, emphasize the active role of his mission, which contrasts with the passivity and the down-flowing movement of the Virgin's veil, hair, mantle, and skirts (figs. 114 and 115).

Her face could be the portrait of a good and beautiful girl in thirteenth-century Regensburg. She is the ideal of womankind, but it is an ideal expanded from one individual woman, with graces of feature and movement that are as particular to her alone as were the virtues of Mary that singled her out to bear the Son of Man in her womb and as the seven joys and the seven sorrows associated with her name. In the city that, as the seat of the Imperial Diet, once greeted the ambassadors of the earth, the Archangel Gabriel remains the envoy of God. In the cathedral built above the river whose basin eastwards was the cradle of one of the first European civilizations, devoted to the worship of the Great Goddess,[3] Mary preserves the saving grace of the Eternal Feminine. In the space between them, so striking, so modern are these figures, we feel the power of the event they commemorate as a living presence.

How did these images gain their power, their beauty, their goodness? It is a question that includes and goes beyond the genius of their sculptor: they are public works of art, commissioned by clergy for an established cult and

99 Lincoln. The Angel Choir, built by Simon of Thirsk from 1256: a view up into the triforium, showing leaf decoration in the capitals of the Purbeck columns, corbel heads supporting the hood mouldings, and some of the exquisitely carved angels in the spandrels.

revealing attitudes to the cosmos, to the nature of intelligence, and to the role of women that amount to nothing less than a social and religious revolution in Western Europe. We have already seen how the achievements of the Gothic masters, in the new representation of man as an individual and in their objective portrayal of the forms and creatures of nature, can be ascribed to the resolution of dualisms, notably that between Christianity and pagan survivals and an unconscious Manichaeist dualism between spirit and matter. Let us turn to the dualisms that particularly affected the estimation in which women were held and the descriptions and beliefs in the angelic orders.

The Church denied women a place in its hierarchy, and its only solution for women who wished to pursue the spiritual life was to lock them up in nunneries. By the late eleventh century the Church, under the influence of reforming monks, tried to impose celibacy on all secular priests. If it can be said also for the Church that at the same time it was trying to raise the status of women by insisting on monogamy and on marriage under the auspices of a priest, the fundamental view of women of the monks who set intellectual and social attitudes was one of fear, dictated by hatred of sex and a denial of their own mothers. Here are some of the milder sentences in castigation of the female sex in the poem *De contemptu mundi* by a notable poet, Bernard of Cluny, writing *c.* 1130:

> Woman sordid, perfidious, fallen, besmirches purity, meditates impiety, corrupts life . . . Woman is a wild beast; her crimes are like the sand . . . There is no good one, or, if you do find any good one, the good one is a bad thing, for there is almost no good woman. Woman is a guilty thing, a hopelessly fleshly thing, nothing but flesh, vigorous to destroy, born to deceive, and taught to deceive—the last pitfall, worst of vipers, beautiful rottenness, a slippery pathway, public doorway, sweet poison. All guile is she, fickle and impious, a vessel of filth, an unprofitable vessel. . . .[4]

Thus the ranting continues to the breathtaking point where he says 'the sins of a man are more pious, more acceptable to the Lord, than the good deeds of a woman'.

100   Auxerre. Delight in the beauty of the female body sometimes, in the sculpture of the Gothic Master, transcends the moral lesson the subject was intended to convey. This figure, *c.* 1300, from the south transept, is Sensuality, shown riding on a goat, the symbol of lust.

101   León. The White
Madonna, formerly on the
trumeau of the central
doorway of the west front,
and now inside the
cathedral, *c.* 1250.

The author of these lines was not removed from society as a demented lunatic; he was applauded as one who gave forceful expression to a generally accepted truth. What is equally extraordinary is that the poem of which they form part begins with one of the most moving descriptions of the Heavenly Jerusalem ever penned, the source of the hymn in English churches known as 'Jerusalem the Golden'. The longing for another world, one of beauty, radiant light and peace, burns in his words like the nostalgia of a perpetual exile. Here is yet another dualism, that of this world (bad) and that world (good), and the denunciation is not just of woman as the female of Bernard's own species but of woman as the symbol of Nature, transient, corrupted by change and time, and dragging men down to damnation in her coils. She is contrasted with the world of the angels, the arena of bliss from which, by the sin of the first woman, men are excluded in this life and which will be denied to the majority of mankind on death because of the sins they have committed through the enticements of the daughters of Eve. We will come in Chapter 8 to the cathedral as the reconstruction on earth of the Heavenly Jerusalem, as yet another manifestation of the spirit in matter achieved by the Gothic masters. Here we are concerned with the transformation of woman into an ideal, largely through the representations of the Virgin Mary but also through the poetry of the troubadours and the minnesingers, the compilers of the Arthurian legends, and through allegorical figures such as Fortune, Philosophy, and Sapientia.

We have already seen how the need to fight against heresies denying the Doctrine of the Incarnation had led prelates and the clergy to give ever greater prominence to the Virgin Mary, culminating in sculptures such as the coronation of the Virgin on the façade of Rheims and the Dormition at Strasbourg. There was an inner need also of the monks to find the feminine in themselves, to sublimate their sexual urges by devotion to the Virgin. It was another Bernard, of Clairvaux, who gave his authority to this movement. So, too, in the influential Abbey of St-Victoire, the poet Adam of St Victor was writing hymns in praise of Mary, and bishops would take the opportunity when their cathedrals were rebuilt in the new Gothic style to reconsecrate the new buildings, not to the local saints or the apostles to which they were formerly dedicated but to the Blessed Virgin.[5]

The new feeling of devotion to the Virgin was not confined to the monks and the intellectual classes: it was backed by a huge popular surge of devotion throughout Europe, linked to the penitentiary movement, as people in their desire for salvation saw in the Virgin their chief mediatrix with the Deity. Ancient shrines containing her relics or marking the scene of her appearances and miracles, such as Chartres, were to be joined by newer holy places associated with her such as Walsingham, Prato, Loreto, and Czestochowa. All required churches, sculptures, and paintings to set out her majesty and glory and a widespread literature, gradually penetrating into vernacular tongues, told apocryphal stories of her life and death[6] together with legends of miracles she continued to perform, many of which were drawn upon by the artists and sculptors.

If the new devotion to the Virgin resulted from the correcting of an imbalance in the doctrine, practices, and needs of the monks and clergy, the popular movement was drawing on much more ancient sources. The cathedral of Chartres stands on a site originally devoted to the Great Goddess and later occupied by a temple of Venus. I have earlier pointed to the use of the neolithic symbols of the Great Goddess, the lozenge, the chevron, the spiral, in the carved decoration of Durham, probably handed down in the harvest figures and corndollies still seen today. One of the strangest phenomena of the survival or revival of this ancient cult is the appearance from the early twelfth century of the figure known as the Sheela-na-gig.[7] Found frequently in Ireland, from which her name comes, and surviving in scattered concentrations from England to Czechoslovakia, she is the figure of a woman displaying her vulva as in an example from Kilpeck (fig. 102). Although never so popular in numbers of surviving instances as the Green Man and, for obvious reasons, the target of puritans and restorers, she is to be found in the most unlikely places, on the tomb of a bishop at Kildare, amongst the scatological and pagan emblems carved down the side of the ramp at Bourges leading to the shrine of the protomartyr Stephen, in the cloister of the canons of Bridlington, and as one of the most startling gargoyles of Freiburg-im-Breisgau. There is a less gross female figure, very popular in later Romanesque art, which may well be a more sophisticated version of her, and that is the mermaid or siren whose tails are divided at the crutch and who seems to symbolize the bestial quality of the lower nature. Why were the artists permitted to carve her either as Sheela-na-gig or as a siren? There are several explanations: the tradition that the devil could be driven away by the display of the sexual parts, a tradition linked also to the many gargoyles and heads with tongues protruding as penis substitutes;[8] the suggestion that because so many of these figures are haglike, they emphasized the inner ugliness of sex which the celibate had sworn to avoid; and the theory that they were fertility figures from the older religion, incorporated, like the many other survivals we have noted, into a semi-Christian context.

My own preferred identification is that she is the Morrigan, the Celtic hag who appears to kings and heroes.[9] When they consent to have intercourse with her, she transforms into a beautiful woman. The Morrigan, who is a form of the Great Goddess, appears in the Arthurian legends as the King's half-sister Morgan le Fay. Her legend is a parable of the image of woman presented to the medieval artists by their clerical patrons and transformed into beauty as they, in their generations, absorbed her into their creative imaginations and discovered wisdom, compassion, and gentleness in her. Nightmares are the revenge of the soul for our rejection of the gifts of life and their images are often the reverse of the spiritual and emotional objects we deny ourselves. The denial of Europe's ancient religious past, insisted upon by the leaders of Christianity, forced the return of the old gods and goddesses as nightmares. The Kilpeck Sheela-na-gig (fig. 102) is the nightmare and the Auxerre girl (fig. 100) is the transformation of the theme by a Gothic sculptor into an image of fresh beauty, even though she is meant to portray sensuality.

102   Kilpeck. The Sheela-na-gig, one of the corbel heads of the eaves of the north side, c. 1120.

Great art is prophetic because it looks into the world of causes in the human psyche. It sees the possible futures in the present forms of the archetypes. It can help mankind to choose a better future by interpreting and giving form to the messages and symbols of the archetypes. It is a law of its correct functioning that it draws on the stored energy of the past. In terms of the energy on which art draws, the past recurs only at certain times, like a comet with a fixed trajectory. Such a period, offering such an opportunity, was that covered by the eleventh and the early twelfth centuries, and it was seized by those already prepared to grasp the possibilities of the new order and capable of interpreting them and giving them comprehensible expression. It was a time when, in response to the intensified exposure to the artistic and technical superiority of Byzantium and Islam, North-Western Europe found the mother and father gods of the old religions, who survived only in its peasant culture, forcing themselves in myth and attributes upon the consciousness of the artist and the poet.[10]

Another way of describing what happened, again as an analogy, would be to posit again the idea of a great memory. Just as, in our individual experience, our memories can suddenly give us back ideas from which we thought we had sucked all the meaning, emotions that we thought had died, experiences we had buried as having no current import, and return them charged with new life and vigour, so on the greater scale of history there is a regular process of recollection, of the return of old beliefs and cults, of nostalgia for some vanished state of primal innocence and goodness.

In this way, at the beginning of our period, we see a reassertion of the feminine both within and outside the Church. The Great Goddess worshipped by the Neolithic peoples who introduced farming to Europe reappears as the Sheela-na-gig at a time when vast stretches of waste land and forest were being claimed for agriculture. The attributes of the Magna Mater of Gallo-Roman times are adapted for the numerous representations of the Black Virgin that, most notably, were revered at Chartres, Vézelay, and Le Puy.[11] The power that could be wielded by women in stories of passion and conflicting loyalties was exemplified in the *Nibelungenlied* on the one hand and in the Arthurian cycle on the other. Thus the male-centred epics and poems of early vernacular poetry gave way to the ideal of the lady in the poems of the troubadours, trouvères and minnesingers.

Though it is rare to come across a Gothic female figure, apart from the Virgin Mary, that can be said to owe a direct debt to the troubadour or minnesinger tradition, in that treasure house of originality, the cathedral of Naumburg, the sculptures of the Margravines Regelindis and Uta have the glamour of the ladies of countless lyrics. On either side of the high altar of the west choir, whose leaf decoration was described earlier, stand the four founders of the cathedral. On the south side is the Margrave Hermann with his Polish wife Regelindis, who is portrayed with a gay entrancing smile. Facing them on the north side is the Margrave Ekkehard, a bull of a man with bushy eyebrows and thick locks, whose left hand grasps the butt of a great scabbarded sword. On his own, he would be one of the finest medieval sculptures of a ruler to have come down to us—but his wife, standing beside him, outshines him to extinction. She holds the collar of her cloak up against her chin. The carving is so life-like that one sees the moulding of the side of her hand underneath the cloth. Her other hand gathers up the train of the cloak as she looks in the same direction as her husband towards the high altar. But what thoughts is she thinking? The sculptor, one feels, once saw a beautiful woman, finely but simply dressed, pausing in reverie at the top of a staircase, either unaware or uncaring that anyone should be looking at her, when into her face and most especially into her eyes there came a look of

104 *Above*   Naumburg.
The Margravine Uta.

103   Naumburg. The
Margrave Ekkehard and
his wife, Uta, *c.* 1250, from
the series of founders of
the cathedral placed
around the high altar of
the west choir.

abstracted longing. He could never forget that moment and seized his
chance, when given the commission, to make the figure of the long-dead
princess the expression of the ideal of his life. She bears that mark of
supreme beauty, surpassing those women with merely perfect features, in
that the particular configuration of her eyes, brow, lips and nostrils conveys
a wide and delicate range of emotions, as mysterious as the feelings aroused
in us by certain jewels, as indefinable as the scale of tones there may be in a
clear sky on a fine day. Uta, like her husband, is a ruler: she wears a coronet;
but the feeling she portrays is of a woman who rules through love and
adoration (fig. 104).

Previously, the monks learned, under the influence of Boethius, to see
Philosophy as a personification of female beauty, and in their interpretation
of the Song of Solomon they transformed the ancient Hebrew love songs
into an allegory of the love of Christ and his Church—equating the Church
(Ecclesia) with Wisdom or Sapientia, the lovely woman who is 'fair as the
morning, bright as the moon, radiant as the sun, and terrible as an army
with banners'.[12] The image of Wisdom as the female companion of God,

present at and rejoicing in the acts of creation, was one of the most powerful sources of renewal for the feminine ideal. It extended far beyond the bounds of the Church into the works of many poets who idealized their ladies as living exemplars of the eternal Wisdom. The female figures of Philosophy and Sapientia probably led to the female characterization both of the liberal arts and of the virtues (see page 135). There is another extraordinary story underlying the introduction of the sibyls, the prophetesses of classical antiquity, into Gothic schemes of sculpture.[13] They were thought to have prophesied the coming of Christ and were therefore incorporated into Christian iconography as symbols of the Church of the Gentiles, the body of virtuous men and women who could be said to have foreshadowed Christ, as opposed to the predominantly masculine Old Testament prophets and worthies who made up the Church of the Jews. Thus they appear, as we have already noted, at Auxerre among the prophets and the Green Man, in the pulpits of Giovanni Pisano (see page 195), and in the choir-stalls of Ulm, another example of the way in which the balance of the sexes was brought into equilibrium.

From all these sources there was an ineluctable drive to reassert the feminine, and the figure of the Virgin became the focus into which they all merged. It was Abbot Suger who helped to develop the iconographical scheme of the Tree of Jesse culminating in the Virgin and her Son that was to lead to the triumphal portrayal of Mary as the Queen of Heaven in so many cathedrals and churches. Through the association with her of so many ancient images of the moon, the stars, the Milky Way, she came to possess a cosmic significance, seen most clearly in the great rose windows of France, as though she were the womb of the universe containing Christ the sunchild.

If the Virgin of Regensburg represents the redemption of matter and the return to the source, then what of the Angel, the *puer aeternus* who greets her? It was again Suger as patron who, through his love and understanding of the works of Dionysius the Areopagite, released new meanings from the doctrine of the angelic orders for the artist to play with and proclaim. His account of the consecration of St-Denis ends with his prayer to Christ that

> by these and similar visible blessings, Thou invisibly restorest and miraculously transformest the present (state) into the Heavenly Kingdom. Thus, when thou shalt have delivered up the Kingdom to God, even the Father, mayest Thou powerfully and mercifully make us and the nature of the angels, Heaven and earth, into one State; thou who livest and reignest as God for ever and ever. Amen.[14]

What did Suger mean by the union of men and angels into one state? To him the aim of the new art and architecture at whose beginnings he presided was the creation of a holy environment, where the liturgy, music, vestments, sacred vessels and jewelled ornaments, the symbolic processions of the clergy, and the atmosphere of exalted devotion, amid candles and incense fumes, under gilded vaults and enclosed by windows brilliant with colour, should approximate to the service of praise perpetually offered in heaven. He wished to make the churches of earth resound with the happiness of the celestial paradise.

Angels are the higher emotions and intellectual powers of the universe. Belief in them as the messengers of God and as intelligent beings is common to Judaism and its two offspring Christianity and Islam, and they have their counterparts in Hinduism and Buddhism. Their depiction as beautiful creatures with human faces and wings derives from a medley of sources, from the Old and New Testaments, from Iris, the messenger of the gods, from the winged Victories and geniuses of Hellenistic and Roman art as well as from the winged bulls and lions of ancient Mesopotamia.[15] Encounters with angels are constantly described in legends of the saints and missionaries of the Dark Ages, such as the story of St Patrick on the mountain of Croagh Patrick or the appearance of the Archangel Michael on the mausoleum of Hadrian in Rome. St Michael's exploits as the general of the heavenly hosts inspired in a warlike age the consecration of many shrines, notably on hilltops and mountainous islands, from the Adriatic coast to the west of Ireland. It was one of the great achievements of the Romanesque to convey with immediacy and authority in sculpture and painting the images of these beings. Their wings and robes inspired in Romanesque artists a particular delight in manuscript illuminations and in carvings such as those by Gislebertus at Autun (fig. 105).

The rise of the Gothic coincided with the birth of scholastic philosophy and the beginnings of an independent western science. As men discovered the latent powers of their own minds and speculated on the nature and form of the universe, so their interest grew in the nature of the intellect of the angels and the role they played in a Christian cosmos.[16] If, behind the surge of devotion to the Virgin Mary in the twelfth century, there was a profound drive to redress the balance of the Church and society against its masculine domination, so behind the Gothic portrayal of the angel there was the equally strong drive for men to learn how to think. The angels were created as perfect beings with immediate insight, according to their degree, into the mind and purposes of God. They possess *intellectus*, what St Thomas Aquinas calls the immediate apprehension of the truth, as opposed to *ratio*, the searching for the truth which is the general characteristic of human thought.[17] The angels are images of being while men are the creatures of becoming, capable of reaching the condition of *intellectus* through grace and right intention.

As western cosmology developed, first through study of the *Timaeus* and of Aristotle and then of Ptolemy, a marvellous congruence or synthesis was perceived. The nine heavens corresponded to the nine orders of angels described by Dionysius and it came to be thought, as Dante expresses it so

105   Autun. The angel wakes the three kings to warn them of Herod: a capital by Gislebertus, *c*. 1130.

106 *Above* Freiburg-im-Breisgau. The Prince of the World offering a rose to a naked figure of Lussuria on his right, *c.* 1280. Though he is dressed like a nobleman and is crowned with roses, his true nature appears in the toads and serpents on his back.

107 *Above right* Freiburg-im-Breisgau. God as Architect and Creator: the making of the spheres of the fixed stars and the planets, from the creation series in the north door of the choir of the Minster, *c.* 1354.

finely in the *Convivio*, that the spheres of the heavens and the planets were moved as an effect of the contemplations of the angels.[18]

The nine orders of angels according to Dionysius are divided into three triads, and all of them express a principle or virtue that is latent or active in man.[19] The first triad is of those closest to God, the Seraphim, the Cherubim, and the Thrones. The second triad of the Dominations, Powers, and Virtues mediates the divine commands to the third triad of Principalities, Archangels, and Angels, which is that closest to man. Principalities are the guardian angels of nations, regions, and races; and the Archangels and Angels are the only members of the hierarchy who appear to men. Though there are few representations that I know of showing all the angelic orders together, apart from the west front of Wells and the dome mosaics of the Baptistery of San Marco at Venice,[20] the educated visitor would have known well the name and function of the angels carved and painted in churches, from the seraphim bearing the crucified Christ in the vision of St Francis at La Verna to the guardian angel who supports the head of a knight or his lady on an alabaster tomb-slab. They are all creatures of light and therefore can be seen as emblems of the degrees of higher consciousness.

C. S. Lewis compares our current view of man with them thus: 'In modern, that is, in evolutionary, thought Man stands at the top of a stair whose foot is lost in obscurity; in this, he stands at the bottom of a stair whose top is invisible with light'.[21] One could add that the steps of that stair entice with happiness.

This attitude is most perfectly expressed by Dante in his paraphrase of the Lord's Prayer in *Purgatorio*. There the proud, among them famous artists of his time, repeat this form of the third petition, 'Thy will be done on earth as it is in heaven',

Come del suo voler il angeli tuoi
fan sacrificio a te, cantando osanna
così facciano li uomini de' suoi.[22]

As of their will Thy angels unto Thee
Make sacrifice, singing hosanna
Men should make sacrifice of their own wills.

The service of praise by the angels provided a constant image for the Gothic artists. At the same time the idea of sacrifice gave them a standard of impersonal art to which they should aspire. Among countless examples we may note: the angels shouting in amazement at the Ascension of Christ in the north tympanum of the Royal Portal at Chartres; the ring of smiling angels engirdling the exterior of Rheims with wings that spread outside their housing in the pillared tabernacles perched on the buttresses; the *pilier des anges* in Strasbourg cathedral; the angels in the fifteenth-century high choir of Norwich cathedral; and the many angel roofs in the churches of Norfolk. Here again the writings of Dionysius the Areopagite on the nature and hierarchies of the angels were a constant inspiration, because in their analysis of the different works of praise performed by the angels they depicted an art whose origins and whose effects were joy.

It is at Rheims (figs. 108, 109) that we see the way in which the Gothic sculptors responded to the challenge of portraying the joy of the heavenly hosts. As the coronation church of the Capetian monarchy, Rheims cathedral required in its decoration a permanent sense of renewal and celebration. The angels carved there, not only those in the buttress

108   Rheims. A section of the series of angels with outspread wings in tabernacles that form part of the buttresses receiving the thrust of the double flying buttresses along the south side of the nave.

109 *Above*   Rheims. The angel of the Annunciation, *c.* 1245–55. From placement marks found after the First World War it was discovered that he should occupy another place on the west front.

110 *Above right*   Dijon. One of the six angels of the Well of Moses, set above the statues of Moses and David. The well, designed and largely carved by Claus Sluter, 1395–1405, is the base remaining from a calvary now destroyed. It stands close to the Chartreuse of Champmol, formerly the burial-place of the Dukes of Burgundy. The angels were carved by Claus Sluter's nephew, Claus van Werve.

tabernacles but also the Gabriel of the Annunciation and the angel *au sourire*, are characterized by an extraordinary smile, a smile that has an unearthly authority. It was achieved by enhancing the feminine qualities of the face. Perhaps behind it too lay the influence of a smiling bronze or marble faun dancing with tilted head, as there is undoubtedly an antique influence present in the Demeter-like face of the Virgin in the Visitation group and in the Praxitelean folds both of her garments and those of the figure of Elizabeth. That smile spread across Europe, to the noble angels of the transepts of Westminster Abbey, to the sculptures of Lorenzo Maitani on the façade of Orvieto and to its greatest influence in Germany, at Strasbourg, Cologne, Bamberg and Freiburg.

It was at Strasbourg and Freiburg that the smile was adopted for the portrayal of its opposite: the depiction of falsity instead of truth. This is in the figure of the Prince of the World who, in the Freiburg version, offers a rose to the naked figure of Lussuria: he is a handsome smiling finely dressed villain—we know that by looking to his side where we see toads and serpents crawling on his back and lower limbs (fig. 106). He is crowned with roses because the sculptor knew the words of the ungodly: 'Let us crown ourselves with rosebuds, before they be withered: let none of us go without his part of our voluptuousness.'[23]

The Prince of the World at Freiburg forms part of a wonderful sequence of sculptures in the porch of the west tower of the Minster.[24] The Virgin and Child stand on the *trumeau* of the double door, while ranged round the walls are the liberal arts, wise and foolish virgins and saints. In the arts we can see how the process of allegorization, by which figures such as Philosophy and the seven virtues had long been portrayed as beautiful women, had led to the depiction of noble qualities also as women, these eternal qualities being those possessed by each order of angels. We distinguish between the wise

111   Bourges. St Michael protects a naked soul from a waiting demon while weighing his good deeds against his bad. Another small demon clings to the bad deeds, hoping in vain to make them heavier. This scene is part of the central portal, *c.* 1255–60, of the cathedral.

112 *Below*   Bourges. Demons bear the damned towards Hell's mouth while in the lower register souls reunited with their bodies issue from their graves: sculptures to St Michael's left (see fig. 111).

virgins who are awake and prepared for the coming of the bridegroom by their upright lamps and their ready smiles, and the foolish ones by their down-turned lamps and their wretched expressions. Thus the always male angels gave to the virtues, as women, their inmost essences as principles or ideas, and to the wise virgins their quality of perpetual watchfulness, which is an attribute of the state of higher consciousness in which they exist. Through such lofty means did the Eternal Feminine reassert an ancient dominion.

The angelic orders were also portrayed in scenes of the Last Judgment and as the attendants of Christ and the Virgin. St Michael had acquired the task of weighing the souls of the dead. The most memorable depiction of him at this work is at Bourges where he stands with huge wings outspread, holding an iron balance with his right hand and with his left shielding the soul whose sins and virtues are being tested against a demon waiting with a grappling hook. Other demons, with monstrous faces appearing on their bellies or, in one case, out of the nipples, are bearing off the naked damned to the Mouth of Hell (figs. 111 and 112).

On the other side the saved, who are clothed, are conducted by angels to the bosom of Abraham. Here, and also most notably at Amiens, one feels the sense of immediate though invisible impact the presence of angels had for medieval man, both in his living and his manner of death. The place where one feels it most strongly is at Mont St-Michel, not through any particular medieval portrayal of the archangel (the magnificent golden figure on the spire is a work of the last century) but because of the series of buildings that were erected on the granite tidal island of Mont Tombe from the ninth to the sixteenth century.[25] The first building here was at the command of the Archangel to a bishop of Avranches in AD 708. The Benedictine monks, who from 965 settled on Mont St-Michel, built a Romanesque abbey church on the summit, and then, in the twelfth and thirteenth centuries, the range of buildings rightly called the Merveille revetting the escarpment on the Atlantic side. Here floor after floor rose from the cellars to the granite hall of the knights and the many-windowed refectory, giving onto a cloister whose vegetation is richer in its stone carvings than in its flower beds. Huge fortifications arose about the base of the rock and barbicans protected each stage of the winding road up to the abbey church. Then, in the fifteenth century when the choir of the Norman church collapsed, the monks replaced it with the two-tiered construction of a well-lit crypt or lower church supporting on massive piers the chevet of the upper church with its clusters of pinnacles and flying buttresses.

There are few experiences for ordinary mortals more awe-inspiring than the climb up one of the spiral staircases leading up to and over the flying buttress known as the *escalier de dentelles*. There as you step onto the high roof of the abbey church you are hit by the Atlantic wind that beats like archangelic wings, churning the grey waves, hundreds of feet below you and miles out to the west, and driving the race of waters to meet across the mudflats in arcs of ripples that intersect like cusps of giant tracery. You stand so high, like one of Bernard of Chartres' pygmies, because a bishop had a vision, because generations of monks fulfilled that vision with their life of prayer and praise and because artists, architects and engineers of genius, inspired by their patrons and by the desire to express the superhuman power and majesty of the island's patron, followed the fascination of the difficult.

If the angels inspire awe by their presence and authority in their dealings with mankind, when in attendance on Christ, God made Man, they themselves show surprise and subservience. The angels who announce the

113 *Overleaf left* Chartres. John the Baptist in the central doorway of the north portal, *c.* 1210: seen here on one of the comparatively few occasions when evening sunlight penetrates into the portal.

114 *Overleaf right* Regensburg. The Archangel Gabriel, *c.* 1280, by the Erminoldmeister in the cathedral nave.

115 *Overleaf far right* Regensburg. The Virgin Mary, also by the Erminoldmeister, who faces Gabriel, forming a group of the Annunciation.

Ascension at Chartres are as astounded by what they witness as the apostles on earth beneath them. As was said earlier, angels are images of being and man is the image of becoming: in the perfect man, Christ, we find the reason for the wonder of the angels. In Him the angelic capacity for pure thoughts and pure emotion is embraced and surpassed. The great Gothic statues of Christ, such as that on the west front of Chartres—Christ in majesty as the summation of all knowledge—or that at Amiens known as the *beau dieu*, act as focal introductions to the cathedrals at whose portals they preside. Each cathedral is an attempt to show the totality of man with the whole universe created for the reflection of his consciousness. The buildings may be seen as strange portrayals of the physical universe governed by number, weight and measure, with every known creature depicted within the light of history and of eternity. They may be seen as projections of the individual soul, designed to make the mind and heart of every pilgrim and visitor expand through the grandeur of art to catch a glimpse of his or her latent possibilities of spiritual growth. Or they may be seen as emblems of the four bodies of Christ, the physical body that suffered and rose again, the mystical body which includes potentially the whole of mankind, the sacramental body made present daily in the liturgy of the church, and the divine body which is the everlasting nature of Christ at one with the Trinity.[26]

The huge conceptions with which the Gothic masters had to wrestle found their most satisfying expression in the rose windows where the universe is expressed either as a wheel or as a flower. Here time and again the angelic worlds radiating out from Christ or His Mother as Queen of Heaven, or from both together, express their messages of praise and contemplation through sun-shot spectra of colour. The rose window derives from the oculus or round window of Provençal and Tuscan Romanesque churches.[27] The decorative and rhythmic emphasis of the first oculi was on the circumference, with its decoration of leafage and heads; sometimes outside its 'four imagined corners' are carved the beasts of the Apocalypse. The centre of the oculus could be filled with alabaster or glass, but for the making of large round openings it was necessary to add internal supports, which could take the form of a cross or, more generally, the spokes of a wheel. There is a remarkable example at St Etienne, Beauvais, of the oculus transformed into the wheel of Fortune, with men round the circumference dragged up to worldly happiness until at the summit they meet a giant with a club who casts them down again.[28] Two serpent heads stress the meaning of the wheel as that of time. The feeling expressed by the window is that of the crushing domination of Fate as though its wheel belonged to the chariot of Juggernaut. With their greater mastery of the techniques of metalwork, glazing, and stonework, together with their skill in applied geometry, the Gothic masters were yet again to take a Romanesque theme and turn it inside out in its emphasis, mood, and symbolism. The emphasis was placed on the centre of the circle or wheel so that it became a focus of force radiating as from the calyx of a flower. Through the use of stained glass, the round window grew into a dominating feature of the interior of the church as well as being an adornment, greatly increased in size, to the outside. Its symbolism changed from the external power of Fate to the celebration of grace that transcends time and bestows liberty and renewal from the Self of the Universe to the self in every individual.

We have seen the creation of the Gothic ideal of individuality in man as the effect of a new love of humanity. We have looked at the transformation in attitudes to the world of nature as the result of a new love of created things. The rose window leads us yet nearer to the love that inspired the makers of Gothic civilization, because it is a means of depicting the whole of

116 Amiens. The statue of Christ known as the *beau dieu* from the central portal of the west front.

creation as an act of love. Dante approaches the final vision of *Paradiso* through seeing heaven as a rose, and close to that point he is told of the angelic orders winging about him and of the divine impulse in creation that led to the making of 'new loves in whom the Eternal Love is shown'.[29]

The first true rose window to be filled with stained glass is at St-Denis, made in about 1144 and now much restored. This keeps to the wheel form of its Romanesque antecedents. The wheel form is also dominant in the west front rose of Chartres, whose theme of the Last Judgment is an inner and later reflection of the same theme on the Royal Portal. Here one's eye goes immediately to Christ in the centre, within a quatrefoil and a cusped circle containing eight orders of angels and the beasts of the Apocalypse. From this radiate in turn twelve lobes between the wheel spokes, containing amongst their subjects the twelve apostles. In the outer roundels are the emblems of the Passion, borne by angels, and scenes of resurrection and judgment. The designer of this rose is also thought to be the author of the rose of the north transept of Laon, where Sapientia or Philosophy is shown surrounded by the liberal arts. There are four great roses at Laon and in the eastern one the Virgin at the centre holds up a flaming scarlet flower as though to give a message of how the world should be perceived.

In this rose, as in the earlier rose at Mantes of about 1180, we see the designers making use of their skill in constructing tracery within the round form to break away from the wheel form into flower-like patterns of petals or else elaborate geometric shapes. One of the most exciting experiences afforded by these rose windows is from the crossing of Chartres, where the rose of the north transept gives us the Virgin and Child with the graces of heaven as a fourfold dove and angelic forms, surrounded by angled squares like lozenges containing Mary's genealogy. The movement here in rhythm and symbolism is thus to the centre, to the womb of Mary (fig. 118), showing all the divinely inspired forces that led to the Incarnation. This window was

118   Chartres. The rose of the north transept presented by Blanche of Castile *c.* 1221.

117 *Below*   Mont-St Michel.

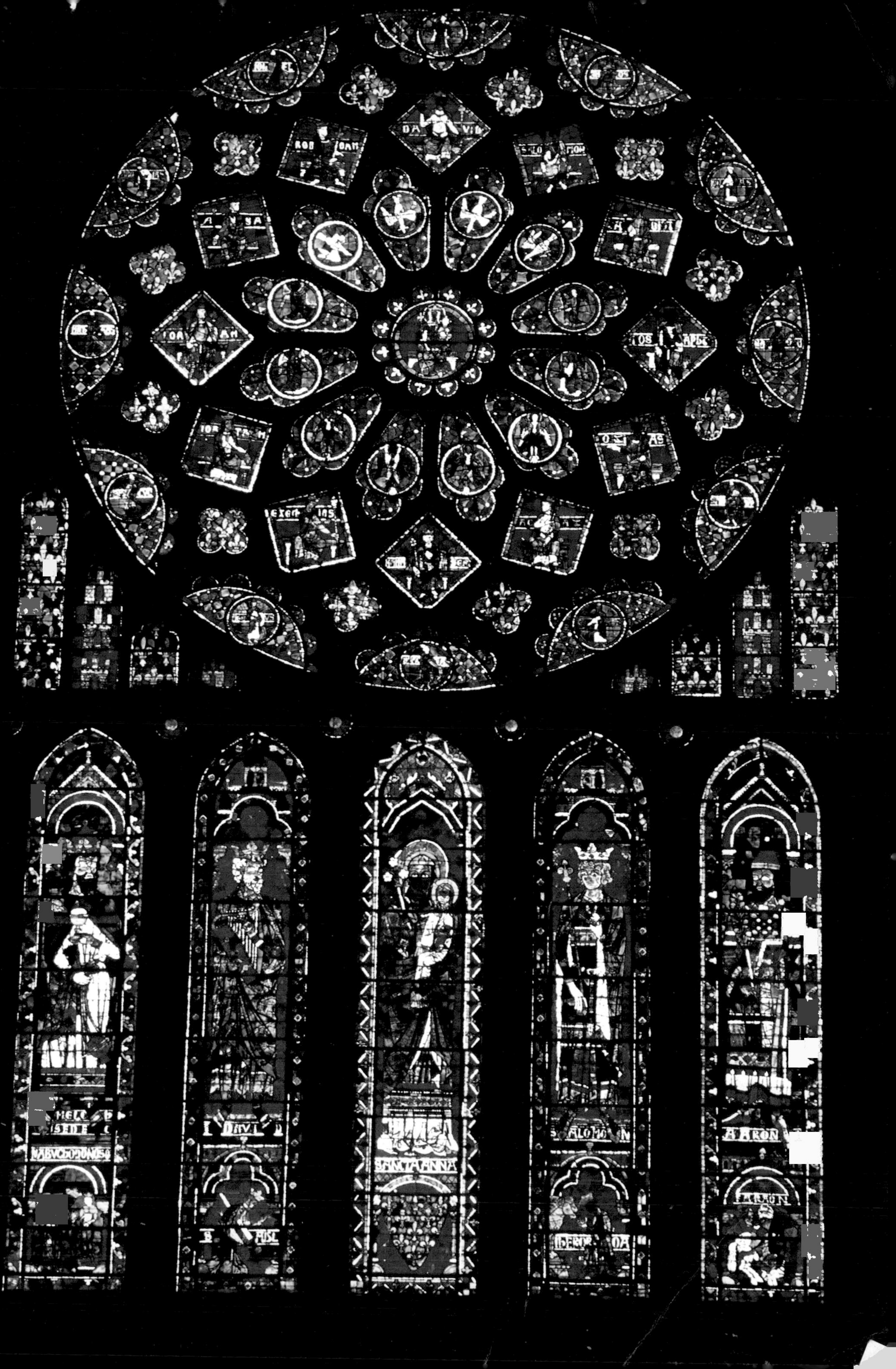
SANTA ANNA

given by Blanche of Castile, widow of Louis VIII and mother of St Louis, so that it is supported by the *fleur de lys* of France and the gold castles of her native land burning on scarlet. The window of the south transept was given by her deadly enemy, Pierre de Dreux. It shows the Christ of the Resurrection, blessing us with one hand and holding the chalice in the other; the movement rushes outwards to angels and music-making kings. It is a triumphant expression of the energy released amongst mankind by the hope of the Resurrection and one of its rarest features is that Christ is depicted as smiling. There was much debate in the Middle Ages as to whether Christ smiled or laughed. Dame Julian of Norwich had a vision in which she and those with her saw the devil overcome and laughed at him—'but I saw not Christ laugh'.[30] The master of this rose window had no doubts on the matter.

In addition to its three great roses Chartres contains 34 rosettes above the dual lancets of the clerestory windows. These rosettes impart a marvellous repetitive pattern to the high parts of the cathedral's interior. These, together with the three great roses, give a point of rest to the mind and the eyes and therefore meaning to the powerful vertical forces in the columns and arches that constantly bid us with authority and mystery to rise above ourselves.

The same effect is granted by the even higher and larger roses of Notre-Dame at Paris. Though these have been severely damaged, altered and restored, they retain their power to uplift and amaze. The west rose, largely hidden by the organ, is centred on the Virgin, surrounded by the works of time in the Zodiac and the months of the year. The north rose, like that of Chartres, shows her surrounded by her genealogy, facing the south rose which once mirrored her with God in Majesty. The roses of Rheims depict a similar exaltation of the Virgin, though they received great damage from fire and bombardment. There the great rose of the west front is contained within a pointed arch, at the peak of which Christ receives the soul of His mother who is shown at death in the centre of the rose.

France, the cradle of the Gothic, contains the majority of rose windows. England has few, among them the much restored examples of Westminster Abbey and the highly original transept roses of Lincoln known as the Dean's Eye and the Bishop's Eye. The latter has as its tracery design two reticulated leaves placed side by side as though taking up the theme of superabundant vegetation that ramps over so much of the cathedral. Apart from its use as rosettes in lancet windows there are few great examples in German Gothic, though Strasbourg has a fine one. Italy, though, developed its own version of the wheel window, particularly delightful with barley-sugar spokes and richly patterned shapes in the basilica of San Francesco and at Santa Chiara, both in Assisi. The most breathtaking of these *rosoni* is that of Orvieto with the head of Christ carved at its centre, the whole circle set in a square with 52 heads round its borders symbolizing the weeks of the year (fig. 53).

In France, the rise of the Flamboyant style gave an impetus to wilder tracery patterns of swirling lobes, constructed right into the sixteenth century as at Sens and Beauvais (by Martin Chambiges) and at Tours where the circle was transformed into a remarkable lozenge. The circle that had been the symbol of the transitory nature of human fortunes was transformed into the most powerful symbol of the Middle Ages: the certainty and eternal strength of Christ and of His Mother as the Queen of Heaven, radiating divine love on to mankind. The circle is essentially an emblem of the feminine, and the delight we feel, as the traceries and glazing of these rose windows make their mark of shadow or shaft their colours on the mothering air, is the redemptive power of the Eternal Feminine awoken in ourselves.

CHAPTER 8

The Drama of the Gothic

In many manuscript illuminations God is shown as the Divine Architect, measuring and dividing the world with a pair of compasses. Bishop Grosseteste, in developing this image, said that, as the design in the mind of the architect is the design of the house, so do art, or wisdom, or the word of Almighty God form the pattern of all creatures.[1] So dominant a position had the medieval architects established in society by the thirteenth century that their skills in design and the tools of their profession could be used as analogies for understanding the primal act of creation. From the design of God followed the drama of creation, the elaboration of nature into multiplicity of forms: this could be regarded as a game enticing man to seek the world of causes behind appearances, or as part of a great play in which man had the right to choose a role enabling him to reflect the divine glory.

The symbolism and the iconography of the great churches were intended to reveal the hidden redemptive purposes of God in nature and in history. With their rich variety of human and animal faces and bodies they provided also a macrocosmic image of the drama of the selves within the individual soul, so that every side of human nature, physical and spiritual, is acknowledged, whether in the extreme physicality of gargoyles, the portrayal of trades and professions, or the exalted contemplations of the saint. In the last three chapters we have considered the static drama of the carvings and the stained glass: to understand the new employment of architectural space by the Gothic masters which is dealt with in Chapter 9, we need to see the construction of the cathedrals and great churches in the light of many aspects of the drama.

While they were being built, they were a form of theatre to the clergy

119   Amiens. The flamboyant rose window, *c.* 1400, of the south transept set within the Wheel of Fortune rising on the left and falling to the right.

and citizens living about them. The stories of their construction cannot be separated from the vicissitudes of medieval history. A favourite image of mortal affairs, sometimes depicted as we have seen around the perimeter of rose windows, was the wheel of Fortune, an image which taught men to expect nothing lasting in earthly life. The primal impulse for the erection of these buildings was to provide a noble and splendid setting for the drama of the mass and also for all the many liturgical plays and dances, performed and elaborated since the early days of the Church and which now required a grander space for their *mise-en-scène*. The great churches were also the desired end of one of the most influential examples of the drama entering life: pilgrimage, for which men and women of all classes would put off the masks of their usual lives and occupations and try to assume the role of a human being, naked in soul and devoted to God. There also is the part so many cathedrals still play as the settings for national and regional thanksgivings and acts of dedication, as when under the threat of destruction by Florence the whole city of Siena was offered up to the Virgin

121   Burgos. The fretwork spires built by Juan de Colonia, 1442–56 onwards, using designs made for the west towers of Cologne Cathedral. The spires of Cologne were not in fact built until the last century.

120 *Below* Auxerre. The cathedral seen across the river Yonne; a superb example of the great Gothic church dominating its city. Built on a Gallo-Roman site and rising on Romanesque foundations, the Gothic cathedral was begun in 1215.

before the battle of Montaperti in 1260. Finally there is the element of drama their spires and towers afford to so many European landscapes.

From our own fascination today with watching men working on deep foundations or engaged on some dangerous and skilful task a hundred feet or more above us in the air, we can gain an inkling of the absorbing interest a whole community, sometimes over generations, would experience as they watched their new cathedral rise. Every stage could be filled with excitement: at Auxerre in 1215 the bishop, aware that other cities had new and beautiful cathedrals, ordered the destruction of the old cathedral. The old choir was pulled down leaving two towers which just before an important service was to be held in 1217 were seen to be in a dangerous state. The canons sent to the architect for advice. He assured them it would be safe though his assistant denied it. Constantly pressed, he at last said, 'I mean nothing at all is certain: I cannot tell the future.' This remark, curiously enough, inspired them to hold the service. The moment it was over, one of the towers crashed against the other, bringing both down.[2]

Everyone would be interested, partly because they could watch the progression of the work and partly because nearly everyone had helped to pay for it: the bishop and dean out of their often enormous incomes (some ten years ago it was estimated that the annual income of the Dean of Chartres was the equivalent of £250,000 a year); the canons, again out of their revenues, or by keeping one of their benefices vacant so that the income could go to the building fund; the guilds and trade corporations of the city who would donate windows and statues and sometimes whole chapels; the serfs of the cathedral lands, sometimes less willingly, by a poll tax, and the pilgrims and the devout of all ranks from kings, queens, and nobles to the humblest labourer giving their offerings. At a time when banking was a comparatively recent innovation, developing through the Templar Order and in the cities of North and Central Italy, there was little chance of long-term borrowing to finance the construction of churches and, if the cash was not to hand, the masons would be laid off and sometimes many years would elapse before work was resumed. This would be sad news, not only to the masons and the canons, but also to the rest of the town, which benefited from the influx of workers to house, feed, and clothe and would look forward with eagerness to completion. Better news would have been that of a completion of a bay, the successful raising of the bells, announced by their first peal from the tower, the unveiling of a series of freshly painted sculptures, or such a moment as when the citizens of Chartres saw for the first time the golden angel on the roof over the chevet follow the direction of the sun at which it pointed, moved by a hidden clockwork mechanism.

Every stage of construction was at risk from the vicissitudes of war. The rebuilding of both Chartres and Bourges was begun in the 1190s when the strife between Richard the Lion-Heart and Philip Augustus was at its height. The success of Philip Augustus with the conquest of Normandy in 1204 was only possible because of the sudden and unexpected death of Richard, by far the abler general, in 1199. Had Richard lived and defeated Philip Augustus, the development of the Gothic style might have been quite different. As it happened, with the conquest of Normandy, wherever a great church was rebuilt or newly begun in the duchy, as in the case of Rouen or Le Mans, it followed the style of the new rulers. Philip Augustus established his hegemony over much of Flanders, with the same effect on architecture, and his heirs made use of the Albigensian Crusade to conquer southern France, building cathedrals within fortified towns as at Carcassonne or Albi, a cathedral that is itself fortified.

122 *Above* Auxerre. Looking towards the choir begun in 1215 from the nave, begun 1309: a view taken from the site of the maze where the dean and canons of the cathedral performed their Easter dance and ball game.

123 *Above right* St Ouen, Rouen. An outstanding example of late French Gothic: the north aisle and nave from 1459.

We have seen how three royal patrons, one a saint, one an aesthete, and one an eclectic genius, Louis IX of France, Henry III of England, and the Emperor Frederick II, ensured the triumph of the style. They also changed the basis of patronage, helping to secularize the Gothic by making it the architecture of the palace, and giving it the prestige of a court style. St Louis rebuilt the nave and transepts of St-Denis, designing the abbey church as a fitting necropolis for his dynasty, and constructed, as a shrine for the Crown of Thorns bought from the Latin Emperor of Byzantium, the Sainte Chapelle, the apogee of the Gothic transformation of stone walls into windows of glass. He was able to draw on financial resources, augmented from conquered territories, on a scale unknown to his predecessors.

This great wealth now came to Paris, which became the centre from which the style developed internationally. Paris, with its population of about 200,000 by the mid-thirteenth century, was the largest city in Western Europe, and its goldsmiths and metal-workers, its carvers in wood and ivory, its scriptoria where manuscripts were copied and illuminated, had taken over many of the functions once confined to monastic cloisters and workshops. The artefacts of the Paris workshops, which all expressed the mood and line of the new style, were exported to all parts of Europe. The University of Paris also attracted intelligent young clerics from far outside the confines of France, men who would be great prelates and influential theologians in Germany, Italy, Scandinavia, and the Iberian peninsula and who, as they rose to eminence, decreed that the style of new buildings should be that of the *opus francigenum*,[3] the work of France, as, for example, the Gothic was known in Germany.

It was this seeding of foreign tastes that saved the Gothic for another two hundred years, and more, of masterpieces, a period during which the combined effects of economic decline, the narrowing of intellectual horizons

124 *Left*   Albi. The jubé or
pulpitum, one of the few
to have survived in the
greater French cathedrals.

following the condemnation of errors and the crushing of debate in the University of Paris in 1277, and the inability of St Louis' descendants to live up to the standards he set, brought a halt to much of the building or completion of great churches in France. For example, the choir and crossing of the wonderful church of St Ouen at Rouen were built between 1319 and 1339; work on the nave was suspended until 1459 (fig. 123). Recession, inflation, and plague weakened France which, by the middle of the fourteenth century, was set for a hundred years of war with England and a consequent decline in the planning and execution of great projects.

While France suffered, other countries continued to build, amongst them England which in the course of the fourteenth century completed the cycle of one style, the Decorated, and then produced its characteristic national version of the Gothic in the Perpendicular style. The vitality of the kingdoms associated with the royal house of Aragon in this period is preserved in the many remaining examples of Catalan Gothic such as the cathedrals of Barcelona and Palma, a style of intimate grandeur and sophisticated purity. Germany too, guided by the Parler dynasty of masons, developed its own late Gothic style, known as *Sondergotik*, as the Emperor

Charles IV at the western end of his domains built the choir to Charlemagne's Palatine chapel at Aachen and at the eastern end virtually refounded the city of Prague with its castle, cathedral, and university. One quality characterized the cities of Germany, Italy, and the Low Countries and that was their civic pride, which drove them to erect magnificent city halls, fountains, and gates and to outdo their rivals in the height of their belfries and the numbers of churches within their city walls. Civic pride was also responsible for such late Gothic wonders as the completion of the north-west spire of Strasbourg cathedral in 1439, at 466 ft (142 m) the highest building in the world for some four hundred years.

The independent court of the dukes of Burgundy at Dijon brought back a new splendour to sculpture and architecture in France. At the Chartreuse of Champmol the work of Claus Sluter on the funerary chapel of the dukes and on the Well of Moses (fig. 126) gave a new impetus to the realism and expressiveness of Gothic art. By the time France, in the mid-fifteenth century, recovered her integrity of rule and possessions, she experienced a period of renewed building activity which is to be seen, not only in completely new churches such as Caudebec and St Maclou at Rouen, but in great works of improving and completing cathedrals which had never been finished—works such as the transepts of Sens and Beauvais, the west façades of Troyes and Tours, and Jean de Beauce's spire to the north-west tower at Chartres. This final burst of the rocket for the style was an extraordinary achievement, given that the twin phenomena of the Renaissance and the Reformation were preparing, the one to oust it artistically, the other to supplant a religion of the image by a religion of the word. The achievement was not confined to France, as the examples of Bath and Sherborne Abbeys remain in England to show or, greater than these, Milan Cathedral and the gigantic Minster of Ulm.

It has been pointed out that not a single one of the great cathedrals was ever completed during the Middle Ages. Chartres was meant to have nine spired towers. Cologne remained with most of its nave and west front unfinished until the last century, when it was completed as a patriotic act by the new Germany. Ulm likewise only acquired the higher stages of its spire in the same period.

In 1291 Bishop Wishart sent a request for timber to complete a bell tower or spire on his cathedral at Glasgow to Edward I of England, at that time attempting to annex Scotland. Edward, hoping to get the bishop on his side, sent a gift of 60 oaks from Ettrick Forest to Glasgow. They were never used on the cathedral; the bishop had them made into siege engines and mangonels for attacking Kirkintilloch castle, which was held by Scottish allies of the English.[4] Glasgow had to wait a hundred and fifty years for its spire to be built.

Apart from the effects of war in delaying building, one of the chief causes for unfinished work was that funds ran out and the masons and workmen left for other sites. The thirteenth-century west front of Wells was

126   Dijon. The prophet Isaiah by Claus Sluter, 1395–1405, one of the six prophets on the Well of Moses. Sluter is said to have employed Jews from the Dijon ghetto as his models.

127 Wells. A view looking into the Lady chapel (1310–22) by Thomas Witney, from the slightly later retrochoir by William Joy.

intended to be completed by two spired towers, at least twice the height of those later added at the turn of the fourteenth and fifteenth centuries. The expense was too great to bear and, with the passing of time and the change of styles, what had been at first an imperative necessity appeared a needless extravagance. We owe one of Wells's finest features to another way in which Edward I was foiled. In 1297 he ordered inventories to be taken of church treasures with a view to seizing them for funds for his wars in France. It is most probable that the bishop and chapter used the treasure rapidly, before it could be grabbed, to construct the retrochoir and Lady Chapel which give us such exquisite pleasure today (fig. 127) with the prospect of columned space leading the eye back beyond the high altar. Gloucester too gives us examples of the vicissitudes of fortune. In 1327 the Abbot of Gloucester was brave enough to accept for burial the body of Edward II, murdered at Berkeley Castle. The corpse had been refused by the Abbot of Bristol. The honour of possessing a royal and a murdered body attracted pilgrims and visitors in large numbers, and their offerings paid for the reconstruction of the choir and the erection of the great east window, the largest in the country, which was also a thank-offering for the defeat of the Valois at Crécy.

Some of the Italian cathedrals give examples of the varied troubles that dogged the building of the great churches. The new Duomo of Florence was begun under Arnolfo da Cambio in the 1290s as the city was approaching the height of her wealth and international influence. Constitutional struggles were soon to cause delays, followed by the collapse of the great banking houses; the vaulting was skimped (Ruskin snarls that it is 'vaulted indeed—but so is many a tailor's garret window for that matter'[5]); the west front remained largely bare brick until the 1870s and the problem of the crossing was left until Brunelleschi in the fifteenth century produced his solution of the dome. The cathedral of Siena too suffered; its west façade, designed and sculpted by the greatest artist of the time, Giovanni Pisano, became the subject of a row within the city. It was decreed that he and other masters should be held in chains until they could explain the lack of progress and waste of money. We do not know if the threat was carried out but Giovanni left Siena and the façade was never executed to his intentions.[6] Also at Siena, the huge windowed walls that protrude from the south transept are all that was achieved of a grandiose project in the mid-fourteenth century to build the largest cathedral in the world, making the already existing cathedral a mere addendum of the total concept. To these sad stories we can add quarrels between groups of masons, as shown by the debates on Milan Cathedral, and the insurgence of townspeople against the clergy of the cathedrals, as at Norwich in 1272 when the citizens slung burning missiles onto the cathedral and monastic buildings, leaving nearly everything roofless in the ensuing conflagration.

What kept the will to build going in so many parts of Europe over so long a period of time? The answer is to be found in the needs of the souls of medieval men and women, their need for a religion and rites that synthe-sized the rhythms of the farming year both with rites from the pagan past and with the festivals of the Church, their hunger for instruction that could often be best provided through the Bible of the Poor in the sculptures and stained-glass windows, their need for visible tokens of other worlds and of the presence of Christ, the Virgin, the saints, and the angels in their relics and realistic depictions, and their need for pilgrimage, for breaking the cycle of a dull fixed working life, for the making of their souls. In the doctrines associated with the sacrifice of the mass and in its daily and manifold celebrations, the Church provided a constant reminder of the entry of the divine into ordinary life. The drama of the mass, the offering of man that made God present, was central to established worship and therefore essen-tial in maintaining the will to build. Both religion and art were close to daily life. Thus the naves of great churches were frequently used for the business of the city or trade. London merchants carried out negotiations in the nave of Old St Pauls and the canons of Chartres, at one time, had to tell the wine merchants of their city to conduct their business in the crypt, instead of the nave. It became essential therefore to make a sharp division between the nave and the eastern parts of the church, through constructing screens of stone or wood. The finest must have been in France, to judge by the fragments such as those of the screen or *jubé* of Chartres, but nearly all of them were destroyed in the eighteenth century to suit the taste of the *grand goût*. One that has survived is that of Albi. Among the German examples are those of Naumburg (see p. 115) and Marburg, while England retains a great number, from the stone *pulpita* of Lincoln and Southwell and the screens of English kings at both Canterbury and York, to the series of wooden rood screens to be found in so many of the West Country churches. These screens or pulpita served several purposes, liturgical because they were used for readings from the Gospel and sometimes for sermons, dramatic because of their use in religious plays, symbolic because they marked the entry into the holiest part of the church, and practical because at once they divided the many secular uses of the nave from the regular services of the cathedral. They were part of the house within a house that the canons and choristers needed for protection against the cold. There are many Spanish examples, such as at Barcelona and Burgos, that give exactly this impression.

Within the inner house of the choir marvellous opportunities for invention and design were afforded by the choir stalls. Those at Amiens are worthily credited with being the world's finest. One walks among them as though through the population of a late medieval city made Lilliputian in size but losing nothing in intensity of expression or feeling. These again are a rare survival in France because of the same eighteenth-century taste for clearing out the areas around the high altars. Here we must turn once more to Spain for the examples just quoted; to England for the pinnacled stalls of Lincoln, Beverley, and Chester with their fantastically carved misericords and bench ends; and to Germany for the poppyheads of the stalls of Erfurt Cathedral and the somnolent sibyls and worthies of the ancient world, who at once dream of the Christianity they predicted or foreshadowed and find it fulfilled around them in Jörg Syrlin's choir stalls at Ulm.

Changes in the requirements of religion could also bring about alterations or additions in churches. We have already noted (p. 63) the changes in the design of churches brought about by the mendicant orders much of whose authority was owed to their skill in preaching. An increasingly literate population in the towns demanded not just instruction but long explications, especially in Italian cities where they were, in any case, accustomed to long political speeches as part of their constitutional practices. The great churches and cathedrals had to respond to the challenge from the churches of the mendicant orders. Amongst the most powerful creations that arose from this need are the pulpits by Nicola Pisano and his son Giovanni, between 1260 and 1311. These, the pulpit in the Pisa Baptistery by Nicola, the pulpit in Siena Cathedral by father and son working together, and the pulpits in the church of Sant'Andrea at Pistoia and Pisa Cathedral by Giovanni, represent a revolution in Gothic sculpture: the works of the father by their revival of the deepest moods and plastic qualities of classical sculpture; the works of the son by their voicing of extremes of feeling that had until this time only been achieved by some of the German masters as at Naumburg. These pulpits are octagonal in form, eight being the number of baptism—which is why so many fonts are octagonal—and of regeneration. Their shape proclaims regeneration through the Word of God, a theme emphasized by the open mouths of all the animals, men and women and angels that are crowded into their panels or stand at their angles, from the growling lions lifting their heads from their kill that support the pillars to the prophets and sibyls that frame the scenes of the Incarnation and the Passion they predicted (fig. 156).

Each of the pulpits was built at times of great crisis in the histories of their cities: the Pisa Baptistery pulpit when Pisa was on the point of losing the dominant position she had held for two centuries; the Siena pulpit shortly after the battle of Montaperti when the city had narrowly avoided total destruction by Florence; the Pistoia pulpit at the time of the struggles between the Black and White factions of the Cancellieri family, a quarrel which spread to Florence and caused Dante's perpetual exile; and the Pisa Cathedral pulpit at a time when Pisa was the centre of the Emperor Henry

VII's attempt to conquer Tuscany. It is as though the intensity of civic strife and passions surrounding the sculptors provided the raw energy of their art which they transformed into their speaking sculptures, and produced the variety of expressions of men and women living under stress which they copied for their dramatizations of the Gospel stories. *Doctum super omnia visa*, 'learned in all things seen', was how Giovanni described himself in the inscription to the Pistoia pulpit.[7] Those pulpits have the immediacy of the contemporary chronicles on the constitutional struggles of central Italy.

There are also features surviving from religious and celebratory rites that have almost completely vanished from the Church today. The round shape of the rose windows of Chartres is reflected in one of the most mysterious features of that cathedral: the immense labyrinth 40 ft (12 m) across set into the floor of the nave.[8] It is said to have had at its centre a bronze plaque depicting Theseus and the Minotaur. For a Christian justification of the use of this ancient Cretan legend we have to go to Lucca, where a similar labyrinth is incised on a pier of the west front with an inscription speaking of the labyrinth of sin which is so easy to enter, so difficult to escape from.[9] Labyrinths of different shapes were placed in many other naves. Those at Amiens and Rheims were inscribed with the names of the chief architects of the cathedrals, fortunately recorded before the destruction of the labyrinths. This indicates the esteem in which the architects of such masterpieces were held; the loss of similar inscriptions from the Chartres labyrinths has left us with one of the chief puzzles of the Middle Ages, the names of the geniuses who built the cathedral. The Chartres labyrinth was also called the Jerusalem because pilgrims would carry out a figural journey to the Holy Land by following the pattern of its maze on their knees. This was part of their preparation for their homage to the great relics of Chartres and the statue of the Black Virgin. The Chartres labyrinth may have had another part to play in the sacred ritual, if we can go by the extraordinary and well authenticated story of the similar labyrinth at Auxerre which formerly was set in the floor at the west end of the nave (fig. 122).

On the afternoon of Easter Day the Dean of Auxerre surrounded by his chapter would stand on the labyrinth. The Dean carried a large gold or yellow ball under his arm and with his other hand took the hand of the priest near him. As he struck up the Easter hymn *Victimae Paschali laudes* he would start to dance. The circle joined hands, revolving round the labyrinth while the Dean threw the ball to each member of the chapter who returned it while they all danced in triple rhythm to the hymn. At the conclusion of the dance the watching dignitaries of the city would accompany the clerics to a congenial feast and then to evensong.[10]

This ceremony at Auxerre has been linked to the old belief that by going to a high place on Easter morning you will see the sun dance.[11] It probably, in its association both with the Bronze Age emblem of the maze and with the Sun, drew on pre-Christian traditions as well. This may be said of many of the other rites and ceremonies of the medieval Church such as the Feasts of the Fools and of the Asses, traced back to the Roman festival of Saturnalia, which survived under the guise of Christmas celebrations.[12] One such rite was widely practised on Holy Innocents Day up to the sixteenth century in the churches of Northern France and Flanders, when the young men of each parish would appear naked or semi-naked in the churches and pursue the marriageable girls, who would fling ashes at them.[13] The same day was often chosen for the ceremony of the boy bishop: at Strasbourg, the choristers, at the point in the Magnificat where it says 'he has cast down the mighty from their seats', would turn the canons out of their stalls and under the guidance of a boy would carry out the rest of the service themselves.[14]

This was one of four ceremonies at Christmastide when there was dancing and revelry in the great churches, the others being the Deacon's dance on St Stephen's Day, the Priest's dance on St John's Day, and the subdeacons' dance at Epiphany or the Circumcision. This last was called the Festival of the Fools, when the clergy would appear in masks and women's clothes at mass, cense the congregation from old shoes, dance round the altar and then travel round the town singing obscene ballads.[15] At Laon on Christmas Eve a donkey was led into the cathedral to be greeted by a chorus of *Hé! Sire Âne! Hé!* A procession of canons dressed as prophets, introduced by a master of ceremonies standing on the choir screen, then took place and Balaam appeared on the donkey with a choirboy hidden under its caparisons. The angel appeared to Balaam and the choirboy spoke the words of the Ass while the congregation brayed in encouragement, after which they were all served wine.[16] At Beauvais a beautiful girl signifying the Virgin on the flight to Egypt was led in to mass riding a donkey and the celebrant led the congregation in braying the responses.[17] At Rouen someone twisted the donkey's tail to make sure it responded to the priest's benedictions.

Such jollities were interspersed with more solemn dramas when the stories of the Gospel would be enacted. The most important of these were connected with Easter. On Palm Sunday choirs would sing sometimes from towers and sometimes from galleries as at Rheims or from over the porch as at Winchester. On Maundy Thursday the great cross of the church would be taken down and laid with the Host in its pyx on the Easter sepulchre, which might be guarded by watchers dressed in armour, simulating Pilate's soldiers. The Resurrection could be signalled by smoke and thunder and the drama of the angel and the three Maries would be played with song, music and dancing. On Easter Eve the Archbishop of Sens would lead his clerics and the town corporation in a dance round the cloister into the cathedral, round the choir and into the nave to the accompaniment of the partsong *Salvator mundi*.[18] One hopes the Archbishop wore his mitre; one hopes it went a little askew.

Christ's journey to Galilee after the Resurrection was also a time for great symbolic processions round the churches, a memory of which survives in the name of Galilee given to the Lady Chapel at Durham and the great south porch at Lincoln. The Ascension was portrayed literally at Lille by the priest being lifted by a stage device out of the pulpit and disappearing. Whitsun, when all the parish priests would come to the cathedral to receive the holy oil with which they would anoint the dying in the coming year, was an occasion for marvels. In some churches burning tow was dropped to symbolize the gift of tongues and in others the tow was trailed from the tail-feathers of a dove. From the hole in one of the nave bosses at Norwich a censing angel was lowered, while at Old St Pauls, from a similar hole, first a dove was released, and then a censer was lowered nearly to floor level and swung above the heads of the congregation in great sweeps, almost the length of the nave, pouring out billows of perfumed smoke.[19] A huge silver censer is still swung in this way at Santiago de Compostela.

These examples of ceremony and the drama illustrate that pagan themes in the sculpture and decoration of the Gothic had their counterpart in rites that, though frequently denounced as in the case of the Festival of Fools, were indelible in their attractions to the majority of the clergy as well as their flocks. They also help us to imagine the brief that would have been given to the architects for a new great church and how immense its requirements would be: it extended from the minutest details of the iconography and liturgical needs for the clergy who governed the cathedral, to the necessity of providing an enclosed space that could contain the entire population of a medieval city with room to spare for hordes of pilgrims.

The great cathedral can be seen as the centre of play in another drama of medieval life: the pilgrimage. Set on a high hill or dominating a plain, it was a figure of Jerusalem on earth: it stood for the goal of what was called the Great Pilgrimage, the journey through Egypt and Mount Sinai to Jerusalem, returning to Rome. It was also the image of the Heavenly Jerusalem—as glistening a simulacrum of the Apocalyptic city as human hands could make. The relics it contained, whether portions of Christ's or His Mother's clothing or instruments of the Passion, or the bones of apostles and of saints of the Dark Ages or of more recent martyrs such as Thomas à Becket, made it a place where miracles were to be expected, where the mortally ill and chronically sick could be cured, where long-cherished desires could be granted, and where special graces in consolation and recollection of the soul might be bestowed.

The pilgrimage routes were a vital element in the creation of medieval civilization, bringing about the spread of the precursors of Gothic in the

128   Canterbury. The central crossing tower known as Bell Harry, begun by John Wastell in 1493, a generation before the pilgrimages to Becket's shrine were stopped by Henry VIII.

series of Romanesque pilgrim churches that extend across the Pyrenees to Santiago de Compostela. It was the interruption of the rights of pilgrims to visit Jerusalem that partly provoked the First Crusade, with its consequent effects on learning, science, technical development, and the arts. It was the need to stop the pilgrims from trampling one another underfoot that provided Suger with a further reason for enlarging the abbey church of St-Denis. Much of the funding of the building campaigns came from the accumulated offerings of pilgrims in cash and jewellery. These funds helped to pay for later constructions such as Henry Yeveley's nave at Canterbury in the late fourteenth century, and the central tower of the crossing known as Bell Harry which was begun in the late fifteenth century—just in time to act as a signal to the last generation of pilgrims who made their way to Becket's shrine. Similarly, a new chapel was built in the fifteenth century behind the high altar for the shrine of the patron saint of Wales at St Davids, and at Glasgow in the same century was built the remarkable series of staircases on either side of the crossing leading down to the shrine of St Mungo in the lower church or crypt and up through the pulpitum into the richly carved thirteenth-century choir.

To the medieval pilgrim of pure intent the great churches that sheltered famous shrines were places of renewal of the spirit and places of awe. To enhance these feelings was another consideration for the Gothic masters to take into account in their plans and designs.

Many of the statues they made acquired in the popular mind the ability to work miracles, just as images of earlier times had done. Some became like charms, to be touched for luck as you passed. Some, like the St Christopher on the exterior of Amiens, had to be looked at every day to ensure that you went to heaven. Some, in the frightening days of the epidemics of dancing fever, probably caused by ergotism, were believed to provide a miraculous cure and bands of peasants would dance their way over long miles to these shrines and leap and gesticulate in front of the images themselves.[20] Some were pious tricks like the figure of Christ on the Holy Rood of Boxley which had hidden mechanisms to roll the eyes and twist the head in grief.

It was devices such as this that helped to destroy the popular faith of the medieval period. When Dublin declared for the Reformed religion in 1547, a famous miracle-working image of Christ as the Man of Sorrows in Christchurch Cathedral was reported to have streams of blood pouring down from the crown of thorns set in its head. The mayor and corporation came hurrying to see and fell on their knees, weeping with repentance—until one bolder soul went up to the statue and pulled out from the crown of thorns a sponge soaked in calf's blood.

The number of well-attested miracles, unexplained by conventional medicine, that take place at the shrines of today are enough for us to believe that, beyond the trickery and the self-delusion associated with medieval pilgrimages and shrines, there were indeed miraculous events and true visions. Here, however, we are concerned with a greater miracle, the fact of art, its inspiration, and its power to regenerate, and the command of art the Gothic masters revealed in their creations.

This may be seen in their capacity to create the planned surprise on every scale, from the placing of an individual statue such as the statue of St Christopher by Tilman Riemenschneider in Cologne, to the immensity of a spire suddenly rearing before a traveller's eyes, as in the way Salisbury dominates so much of the Wiltshire landscape. Great ingenuity often went into these surprises. The sculpture of the north portal of Chartres which sums up the history of man before the birth of Christ is so arranged that it only receives the direct rays of the sun on summer evenings, so that figures

129 *Left* Freiburg-im-Breisgau. The view up into the fretted spire, *c.* 1300–30, from the lantern.

such as the sublime statue of St John the Baptist (fig. 113) are suddenly transfigured by a light that symbolizes the meaning given to the past by the appearance of Christ, the Sun of Righteousness. Some of these surprises are only to be seen by those of strong wind and sturdy legs: the first reward of climbing the tower of Freiburg is to stand in the marvellous open lantern and look out on to the Black Forest and up into the fretwork of the spire; the second reward, by a further ascent up to the parapet crowning the lantern, is to see the eight masks of the Green Men from whose heads sprout the leaf forms of the crockets that issue as the very ribs of the spire (fig. 146).

The architects were often spurred on by enthusiastic patrons. It was the canons of Seville who wanted to be thought mad by future generations for the immensity of their cathedral, begun in 1402. The great engineer Vauban exclaimed at the sight of the octagonal crossing tower of Coutances that it was the work of a madman. There was, however, a saner and truer instinct at work: to change perception and awareness through stupendous and

130   Coutances. The octagonal lantern over the crossing of the cathedral, built between 1218 and 1250, one of the most important of the Norman Gothic cathedrals.

dramatic constructions. Such an aim must have lain behind the building of
the lantern of Ely.

When the Norman tower over the crossing at Ely collapsed in 1322, the
sacrist Alan of Walsingham sent for an architect and for one of the most
notable craftsmen of England, William Hurle, the King's carpenter.
Together they collaborated in devising an original contribution to the
various manners in which hitherto the Gothic masters had played with light.
Instead of the high lateral lighting of the clerestory, they invented the
seemingly vertical descent of light from an octagonal lantern of wood cased
in lead cantilevered out on hammer beams hidden behind the vaulting. It is
like a chapter house raised into the sky and with its floor taken away. The
octagon shape appears below in the four great arches of the crossing and in
the four diagonal walls set with high clerestory windows, and the drama of
the whole effect of an aureole of light suspended above our heads is given
seeming motion by the way in which the angles of the lantern face a straight
side of the octagon beneath. Here we find a natural union of the symbolic
language of number and technical mastery, set to the solution of a new
problem. 'Let us respond to disaster', they might have said to themselves,
'by founding our design upon the number eight which signifies regeneration, the new life, and the just balance between the powers of the spirit and
the powers of nature. We have heard of, but never seen, octagons raised to
transmit light in the mausolea of Persia. We know the hexagonal dome of
Siena Cathedral and the octagonal tower of Coutances. Let us create something new that will be stronger than the tower it replaces and yet will seem
more daring, more dangerous, more thrilling than anything ever built before. Let us astound the future.'

131   Freiburg-im-
Breisgau. One of the eight
Green Men from whose
heads rise the leaf crockets
and ribs of the spire. The
spikes are iron ties to
pinnacles on the parapet.

132   Ely, The octagon.
Suspended over the
crossing is this lantern
cantilevered out on
hammer beams hidden
behind the ribbed faults,
built 1322–46.

CHAPTER 9

Gothic Space

The appearance of the Gothic style in the twelfth century represents the most important aesthetic revolution in Europe between late antiquity and the start of the modern age.[1] It is synchronous with the rise of scholastic philosophy, which was itself a revolution in man's discovery of the powers of his own mind. Where the saints and monks of the Dark Ages had shown how the acts of the body and the stirrings of the heart could be devoted to Christ, the philosophers aimed to make the processes of logic and speculation a means of entry into the mind of Christ. The effect of the interiors of the great Gothic churches is not dissimilar to that aim: our minds, through the unifying perception of Gothic spaciousness, Gothic linearity, and Gothic height, are changed and expanded into the barely definable state of being part of an infinitely greater mind. The means by which that state is brought about is quite different from the processes of philosophy: by comparison its effects are immediate. We see and know with the winged eye of the artist instead of following the laborious steps of the philosopher through darkness.[2] It is to the St Thomas Aquinas whose very presence gave the grace of consolation and who, after the mystical illumination near the end of his life, thought all his writings were as straw, that we must turn in this connexion, not to the author of the *Summa theologiae*, if we are to

133 Venice. The centralized architecture of the dome seen in this remarkable fusion of Byzantine and Romanesque features in St Mark's.

134 *Overleaf left* León. A view of the clerestory and glazed triforium: part of one of the most complete ensembles of medieval stained glass to have survived.

135 *Above* Strasbourg. The Emperor Frederick Barbarossa, one of the series of 19 Holy Roman Emperors in the windows of the north aisle of the nave.

understand the expansive force of Gothic space on our hearts and minds.[3]

As the effects of Gothic space differ from those of speculative thought, their causes must also be different. As they also differ from the spatial effects of classical architecture, the aims and mental habits of their makers must also vary strongly from those of their predecessors of antiquity. The origin of the difference from speculative thought may be explained by the modern neuro-physiological theory of the two hemispheres of the brain: the lefthand hemisphere, whose dominance in our cultures can be said to date from the twelfth century, is concerned with the linear progression of thought expressed in words, equations, and time-bound conceptions; the righthand hemisphere is concerned with the immediate present, with emotional response, with dreams and the emblems and archetypes of legend and, especially to our present purpose, with the appreciation of spatial forms and proportions. The righthand hemisphere is also probably the gateway to the higher, contemplative sides of our natures.

All great western architecture has aimed at creating in its interior spaces a sense of that higher contemplative side. One of the dominant forms used to create that sense has been the cosmic symbol of the dome. It was used by the Romans in, for example, Hadrian's Pantheon, by the Greeks in St Sophia, by their Islamic followers in the Dome of the Rock, by architects of the Romanesque in St Mark's at Venice and in the dome of St Bénigne in Dijon, destroyed at the Revolution. It has the powerful merit of creating beneath and around it a sense of centralized and unified space. It is a three-dimensional symbol of divine and imperial authority. You stand under Justinian's dome in Istanbul and you know Holy Wisdom sustains all things through Christ's regent, the Emperor. You walk a few hundred yards to Sinan's dome in the Sulimaniye Mosque and you know that God is one and that Suleiman the Magnificent is the rightful heir, as Caliph, of the Prophet. You ascend Michelangelo's dome of St Peter's and, daring to look over the balcony, you are dwarfed not only by the immensity of the space but also by the great gold letters of Christ's charge to Peter that march round the interior of the drum; there indeed you know the *auctoritas* of the Roman Church as the heiress of Emperors and the sole bride of Heaven.

The Gothic masters did not utterly reject the dome. It was developed, as we have seen, in the Angevin lands as a solution to the vault construction of bays, and it is to be found in Italian baptisteries and in some of the few surviving Templar round churches such as those at Laon and Pisa. It spoke, however, a spatial language they did not for their great conceptions want to utter or hear. They did, indeed, want to express the higher contemplative reaches of the mind but not through the centralized immediate certainty of the volumes of classical space. They wished to make the circuit of their buildings a journey that revealed surprise after surprise. They aspired to the effect of the northern forest, not to that of the rounded clear space of the Mediterranean sky.[4] They loved long vistas, interrupted by the sight of columns beyond columns that give promise of further exciting prospects. As the forest is an emblem of the mind, with its dangers and its enticements, they were saying, not 'accept, accept' which is the message of the dome, but 'explore, explore', through which they helped to determine the destiny of Western man.

They employed, therefore, devices that fragmented and multiplied the volumes of their interior spaces to transmit the effect of a unity that is always beyond, not only the habitual concepts of our minds, but their own constructions. Their sequences of arches spreading horizontally, their column shafts rising vertically, all utter the dual message 'aspire', and 'not this'. This message conveys what Ruskin called the noble disquietude of

136 *Far left* Bourges. The nave from the south aisle.

137 *Left* Chartres. The north transept from the nave.

Gothic,[5] its Faustian injunction to strive and never to rest.

As an effect of the journey we undertake in visiting a great Gothic church, we are granted a special experience of peace to counter that restlessness. Sometimes almost immediately, sometimes after a longer period, the building creates a new state in us, the state of intensified aesthetic delight which is like a singing in the mind, an effortless concentration on the beauty of fine and subtle lines, of tracery that takes the eye on easy travels. Then we start to appreciate in a new and deeper way the point of raising the vaulting so high as the spiritual centre of the building becomes apparent, placed in the space above us enclosed by the clerestory and felt in the long vista most powerfully in its concentrations over the high altar. This is a generally perceived experience and one that turns inside out our usual ways of describing spatial volumes. Great interiors have to be built from the ground upwards but they are conceived from a high point downwards. An analogy would be with a crystal, growing in space instead of a supersaturated solution and radiating out along the main axes of growth in three dimensions. To take the analogy further, we have to imagine ourselves as the seed of the initial inspiration in the architect's mind, placed high in the space of the destined crossing and extending transparently outwards in all directions but most strongly along the east–west axis of choir and nave, the north–south axis of the transepts, and deep below the solid floor into the hollowed hidden stairs and crypts.

How deliberate were the Gothic masters in calculating their spatial effects? Given the utter difference of mood and effects of light between contemporary Romanesque buildings and the very earliest Gothic buildings of St-Martin des Champs and St-Denis we must say that they were utterly aware of the new language of space they had hit upon—taking into account the limits of technical experimentation available at that time.[6] Is there, moreover, a link that can be made between the new expressiveness of Gothic figure sculpture, stained glass and painting, whose themes and forms we have considered up to now, and the new spatial effects of Gothic architecture? They have often been treated quite separately, the first as a series of styles and influences and the second as the solution of inevitable problems related to the chief aim of raising stone buildings to even greater heights. It is inconceivable, however, that one could have developed without the other. We have seen how under the guidance of the style, ancient pagan themes and images long repressed were redeemed and found a welcoming home in the context of Christian liturgy and architecture, so that fierce dualisms, wounding the spirit of man, found their resolutions. Was there a comparable synthesis of the past and the new that brought about the creation of Gothic space? There certainly was in the technical sense, in that it was the combination of the new practice of rib vaulting combined with the archaic Parisian practice of building with thin walls that created the choir of St-Denis.[7] But a technical synthesis of that kind is only selected because it responds to deeper emotional and spiritual pressures.

To explore this question further, we have to look into the nature of Gothic spatial effects and to deduce from them not only something of the aims of the Gothic masters in creating atmospheres of light and awe, and the geometrical and numerological methods they employed as aids, but also the natures and temperaments of these men themselves. The first great change necessary for the creation of the Gothic interior was in the disposition of horizontal space. The liturgical needs for that wider space around the high altar were dictated by Suger's desire for splendour and drama in the celebration of the mass at St-Denis. Its new conception therefore may be seen as an attempt to create a worthier space for the presence of Christ in the

138   Toledo. The spacious interior of the cathedral built from 1227 onwards, which owes much to the influence of Bourges.

consecrated elements. There is a charm and intimacy conveyed by the round piers of the double ambulatory at St-Denis, and the rounded ribs of the vaulting which is characteristic of other remaining early Gothic buildings as at Senlis. The round piers, which were to set the style for Gothic piers for many years to come, were a significant change from the massive sharp-angled composite piers of much Romanesque work. They provided clear access for the multi-coloured light of the ambulatory chapel windows, which were continuous in their progression and were linked with the central space by uninterrupted vistas through the double row of columns. This choir was a triumph of originality in comparison with earlier and contemporary Romanesque work, in which the double aisle, though it had been used in the naves of grander churches such as Cluny, had never been applied to the ambulatory round the choir.[8]

Sens, as we saw earlier, provides the best example of an almost complete early Gothic interior where the Romanesque achievement of creating long volumes of space by the device of repetition of bays, distinctly defined by strong pier shafts and transverse arches, is given a new feeling of intimacy and invitation. The wall surfaces are made more interesting by the manner of their piercing and by the integration of each bay façade in the skeletal frame formed by the vaulting ribs linked to the shafts.[9]

The next step in the reorganization of spatial concepts was to gain height and side illumination as at Notre-Dame and Laon. This was done by expanding horizontal space at the level of the first storey above the side-aisle vaults. The basic idea came from Anglo-Norman interiors[10] such as those of Ely, Norwich, and Peterborough and those of Lessay, Caen, and Evreux, where, given the thick walls of the structure, the architects had wished to open up the interiors and, presumably, to provide more room for large congregations. The Gothic designers working north and north-west of Paris

139 *Above left*   Strasbourg. The flying buttresses of the south side of the nave, *c.* 1270, seen from the south-west tower.

140 *Above*   Chartres. A view of the nave flying buttresses and the west side of the north transept, after 1194.

took up this conception with eagerness. Its aesthetic virtues are that it further dissolves the wall space, it adds to the mystery of receding vistas, and, in a contrary motion, increases the upper space of the nave. It also allows a corresponding gain in height because the higher lateral volumes of aisles surmounted by tribunes give greater support to the high vaulting. A consequence of this structural form was that the triforium stage, the roof of which masks the buttressing of the clerestory, had to be built above the tribune vaulting and appears on the interior nave façade, giving a four-storey elevation such as we see at Noyon, the south transept of Soissons, and Laon.[11] At Laon the tribune extends nearly all round the interior, across the transepts on wide platforms that open into upper chapels, giving a marvellous sense of circulating life on its higher horizontal plane. Here the architects had followed the Anglo-Norman style in giving forceful projections to the shafts and mouldings but the designers of Notre-Dame, true to the original Gothic love of thin walls giving the effect of a pierced screen with their perforations, though they adopted the tribune with the four-storey elevation, strove to flatten the surfaces as much as possible. At Notre-Dame the double aisles of round piers, richly decorated with foliage in their capitals, extending down the nave and round the choir, and the light pillars of the tribune arcade giving onto the galleries are totally dominated by the spatial grandeur and height of the central nave, transepts, and choir.[12] It is as though they were sliced off by the flatness of the main elevation, the architects saying to themselves, 'these multiplied spaces are charming, delightful, deceiving trivia compared to the massive sense of unity, the sense of being part of a three-dimensional cross of air we want to convey.'

That greater sense of unity was soon to be developed into two very different paths, in the contemporary rebuilding of Chartres and Bourges. It

141   Bourges. The immense vessel of the cathedral, begun 1192, with its exterior dominated by the steeply raked flying buttresses uninterrupted by transepts.

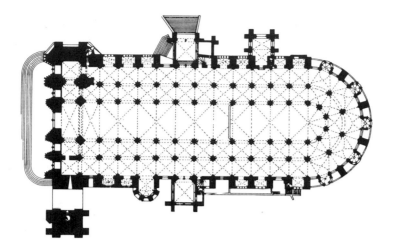

was achieved partly through the discovery of the device of the flying buttress, used, perhaps, for the first time at Notre-Dame[13] and later extended there when the clerestory windows were enlarged downwards (c. 1225) and the oculi of the triforium stage were removed.[14] The flying buttress had existed as an embryo in the dark womb-space of the roofs of the side aisles and tribunes, generally as a quadrant arch supporting the springing of the vault from behind the interior façade.[15] It was now made free of the roofs to become the dominant feature of the articulated exoskeleton of the great church, uniting the height of the roofs to the weight of the exterior buttresses in leaps of energized stone.

The flying buttress permitted the building of higher and wider churches. The tribune was no longer needed for large congregations because the ground floor of the nave was big enough to accommodate them; it was no longer needed for lateral support because that function was now supplied by the flying buttress; and it could be said to detract from the new aim of the grand, simple and high space that we see developed at Chartres and Bourges and at Rheims and Amiens.

The solutions of this search after unity are quite remarkably different at Bourges and Chartres. Like Notre-Dame, Bourges was given double aisles all round the nave and choir but, unlike Notre-Dame, it has unbroken continuity because it followed the original style of Sens in having no transepts. It rises to what was then an unprecedented height of 123 ft (40 m) through the successive raising of the heights of the aisle roofs so that, through the main arcades, you see the plane of the outer aisle and then the plane of the inner aisle given the normal elevation of a three-storey church with bay, triforium, and clerestory, framed within a bay of the main arcade above which rises another triforium and clerestory. Jean Bony says that the effect is as though a church of normal height had been cut in two and another enormous church had been inserted in between.[16] The lack of a transept not only emphasizes the unity of the interior of Bourges: it permitted the unbroken sequence of the steeply raked flying buttresses of the exterior which give the cathedral its awe-inspiring sense of contained power, as though it were a many-winged butterfly just emerged from the chrysalis and dreaming of flight.

For all its height and grandeur Bourges preserves much of the human scale because its interior elevation progresses through five gradations that alleviate its massive impact. It is interesting to note, for when we come to consider numerology, that five is the number of man. Chartres, in contrast, asserts the number three—the number of creation and the Trinity. In its interior, it rejects the multiplicity of the four-storey elevation and insists on

Plan of Bourges Cathedral.

colossal size as though to affirm the words of Hugh of St Victor: 'If you consider well the nature of man, you will not wonder at the great things he can do but rather at the little things to which he devotes himself.'[17] The interior of Chartres forces grand conceptions on us. The requirement to follow the ground plan of the burnt-out ruin of the Romanesque cathedral faced the architects with the problem of covering the central space with a vault wider than had ever been achieved before. Their answer was not to support the central nave with a tribune or staged double aisles as at Bourges but to raise the main arcade on high massive piers of the type known as *piliers cantonnés*, whereby the central round pier has four shafts attached to it. The shafts face the main axes of the building, two rising to the vaulting of aisle and central nave and two rising to the curves of the arches of the main arcade. Above this, the builders set the small narrow passageway of the triforium surmounted by the deep lancets of the clerestory, each window surmounted by a roundel or rose, all set under simple quadripartite vaults. The central nave with its giant clerestory rises to more than twice the height of the aisles; the walls are opened up over an area never possible before in windows into whose stained glass is poured the major decoration of the interior, at once limiting and allowing to continue the chain of spatial effects. The height of the clerestory also permitted the great size of the rose windows of the transepts, off which there opens the further surprise of the double ambulatory round the choir.

The interior space and height of a Gothic church decree to a great extent the arrangement of its exterior. If Bourges is a gigantic chrysalis, then Chartres is a two-headed beast facing westwards with the transepts making

142   León. The exterior of the chevet, begun *c.* 1250.

its haunches and the flying buttresses of the nave its rib-cage. Where, in the interior, the construction of stone is made subordinate to the colours of the windows and the unification of space, outside, the play of stone at its lightest and its heaviest is free to multiply and fragment space. Every major division of the exteriors of the nave and choir, however, corresponds to the internal disposition of the church both in monumentality and in the points from which the flying buttresses issue from the wall surfaces. There is a sharp difference between the exterior of the nave and that of the choir, most noticeable in the openwork of the lower double set of flying buttresses. Outside the nave it is a hoop of round arched columns like a section of the centre of the western rose. Around the choir it is a fan of pointed arches corresponding to the inner line of the double ambulatory, leading out to another spur above the outer line and falling to tabernacled buttresses between the ring of chapels. The nave buttresses express conserved power: those of the choir a joyous release of energy as though they were the media of the creative outflow from the great mind immanent in the space of the interior.

The influence of Bourges and Chartres was widespread. In the choir of Le Mans, one of the most perfect creations of the period, the influences of both were combined, with the staged double ambulatory of Bourges for the interior, and outside, the rotating screen of flying buttresses taken from Chartres, but with the original difference that the spurs break into two in a Y formation, inviting the eye upwards from the side of the cliff on which the choir is built.

Both Bourges and Chartres invited prelates, masons, and townspeople to conceive new buildings on a greater scale. The chief influence of Bourges went abroad to Spain but Chartres had a multifarious influence within France, inspiring the great unified interiors of Rheims and Amiens and the uncompleted Beauvais and, especially through those examples, the rebuilding of Cologne and new work at Strasbourg. Rheims saw the invention of bar tracery, the device of supporting and separating the main divisions of a window by stone mullions instead of the iron armatures that had hitherto been necessary.[18] This invention alone was of widespread importance because it invited the further dissolution of wall space into transparencies of glass, soon leading to what became the Capetian royal style of the thirteenth century, the *Rayonnant*, first seen in the new nave and transepts of St-Denis, with its glazed triforium, and the single-aisled jewel-box of the Sainte Chapelle. This style was far more influential abroad than was the simpler grandeur of the French high Gothic cathedrals which in their aspiration towards ever higher nave vaults remained, in general, a phenomenon of France.

Traditions that, by the mid-thirteenth century, were considered ancient helped to dictate the formation of national Gothic styles. It is characteristic of Gothic space in its searching after vistas that it could be employed in making additions to existing buildings. The English tradition of building long churches went back to the great Anglo-Norman constructions, such as Durham, Ely and Peterborough, of the late eleventh and early twelfth centuries. Many of these stand today with extensive Gothic additions. Others were worked on piecemeal over the centuries: Winchester, for example, is an anthology of every style from the eleventh to the sixteenth centuries, one of its finest features, its late Gothic nave by William Wynford, being an encasement of the old Norman nave. Great length together with a general desire to conserve from the past meant compartmentalization of the English interiors. Where Romanesque buildings were taken down or destroyed by fire, their round apses were often replaced by square east ends. There were

143   Exeter. One of the most unified of all English interiors: a view from the nave (1328–42) looking towards the pulpitum (1324) and the choir (1288–1308).

few attempts to introduce double aisles and then often only in the nave as at Chichester and Elgin. There was an urge instead to drive the eastern ends of churches outwards far beyond the choir and high altar to provide new resting-places for the shrines of saints and Lady chapels in honour of the Virgin. To light the high altar from the sides and to permit the regulation of the flow of pilgrims circulating in these holy areas, many of the greater churches were given a second pair of transepts. This feature can give a magical effect, as at Worcester where, beyond the screens formed by the enclosure of the choir, the spaces of the Lady chapel, the choir transepts and the retrochoir flow together into unity intensified by the tight clusterings of shafts and the pure forms of lancet windows.[19]

That the vaults were generally lower in English cathedrals than in many of their French and German counterparts meant that it was worth while embellishing them with richly decorated ribs, with patterns of ribs that became more and more varied and with sequences of intricately carved bosses visible from ground level. The impulse to build high, where English masons were concerned, was concentrated on the exterior, on creating gigantic spired and pinnacled towers. These too could affect the interior space when their lanterns were allowed to interrupt the vaulting at the crossing and to give the surprise effect of light pouring down from above, a practice already known from Anglo-Norman times as at Norwich but followed through centuries later in the crossing-towers of Canterbury and York.

There are many other features peculiar to English and Scottish Gothic. One that was particular to the part of Flanders where he had been working before he was called to Canterbury was the introduction by William of Sens of the use of dark-coloured shafts to vary the colour of the stonework.[20] England possessed quarries of Purbeck marble, a dark metamorphosed limestone which could be shipped from Dorset, up the Channel and then by river to any site then with a great church in the building. It was employed with great effect to delineate the vertical lines of internal façades, emphasizing the triforium stage as at Worcester or giving a jolly bouncing rhythm as in the transepts of Beverley. Nearly everywhere it was employed in conjunction with the Gothic development of the chevron pattern known as dogstooth ornament, imparting a feeling of richness and variety. The Purbeck shafts at Lincoln were compared in a contemporary account to Sapientia, the Bride of the Song of Solomon, their smoothness expressing her candour, the polish her virtues, and their darkness her distress.[21]

Another feature of English cathedrals—that they are frequently isolated within wide closes like a town within a town—is owed to the fact that, unlike continental practice, many cathedrals were monastic foundations requiring not only living quarters for the monks but ample cloisters and chapter houses as well. The canons of cathedrals that were not monastic also felt that their dignity and needs required similar additions—so that from the polygonal chapter house devised for the monks of Worcester was adapted the form of the Gothic chapter house supported by a great central pillar zooming out vaulting ribs for the canons of Lincoln, Salisbury, and Wells, one of the most delightful and inspiring chamber spaces of the Middle Ages, one copied in Scotland and said to have been adapted by the Teutonic Knights in Prussia. The chapter house at Salisbury is part of the grandest of all English cloisters with its unglazed cusped tracery.

Salisbury possesses one of the few greater English cathedral interiors to have been built largely in one period. Its nave, with huge bay widths to enable the congregations to see the exceptionally splendid rites and processions practised there, is bare and cool, lacking most of the grisaille glass that must have made it as subtle as well-lit shallows of water, but it retains greatness in the disposition of its choir transepts and the beautiful opening into the Lady chapel. Its style was to be superseded by the renewed influence from France of the *Rayonnant* in Westminster Abbey, to be taken up in the grandeur of the nave of York and made thoroughly English in the style known as Decorated in the marvellously light but intense shafting and ribbing of the interior of Exeter. It was also the new opportunities offered by the stone tracery of the *Rayonnant* that invited the English to experiment with a range of geometric and organic forms that gave such stupendous windows as that known as the Heart of Yorkshire, in the west façade of York, and the east window of Carlisle, both probably the work of Ivo de Ragheton. Then followed the more sober mood of the later days in the Perpendicular style, in which the conquest and control of the window tracery was extended to the wall spaces so that they, in their blind tracery, echoed and carried through the church the message of the windows. The finest examples of this are in King's College Chapel, St George's Chapel, Windsor, and Henry VII's chapel at Westminster, all royal foundations and all carrying the English love of intricate ceiling decoration into the original invention of fan vaulting.

Just as England kept stubbornly to what had become native traditions in its development of the Gothic style, so Germany with its proud imperial past had to achieve a synthesis of the old and the new. There was for example a style of simple massive grandeur set by the imperial cathedral of Speyer. There was also the feature of providing a west choir as well as an eastern choir, a practice said to be based on the balance that should obtain between *regnum*, in the Emperor's end at the west, and *sacerdotium* in the Church's end in the east.[22] Because in churches of this type, as with the Romanesque Worms and the early Gothic Bamberg and Naumburg, the west end was apsidal to mirror the east, this meant that there could be no dominant west façade. The main entrance is, therefore, from the south, giving the visitor, accustomed to the immediate long vista down the nave of French and English churches, a curious new experience, in which he feels the lateral expansion of space rather than its forward beckoning. The naves of Bamberg and of Naumburg are both constructed with a severe lack of ornamentation that seems to owe as much to the simplicity of Speyer as to the influence of Cistercian Burgundian architecture.[23] This severity increases the tension between the east and west choirs, as though one were made to feel through the drama of spatial tension the continuing pulls and counter-pulls of the Investiture Contest.

Yet another imperial tradition, that of building high western towers for Romanesque abbey and cathedral churches, may lie behind the German liking for concentrating the emphasis of the west front on a single high tower as at Freiburg and Ulm or else on a massive cliff-like screen as at Strasbourg. This was a tradition that continued long after the townspeople, as at Strasbourg and Ulm, had shaken off both ecclesiastical and direct imperial control and had taken the rebuilding or building of their great churches into their own hands. It was also a tradition that allowed the easier assimilation of French Gothic influence, so that the west façade of Strasbourg rises from its triple sculptured portals to a central rose bordered by frameworks of skeletal tracery derived from the Rayonnant style but with a clean vertical emphasis that was to be one of the hallmarks of later German Gothic.

There were attempts in the early thirteenth century to introduce the four-storey elevation of Laon, as at Limburg an der Lahn and in the choir of Magdeburg Cathedral, but these did not set a style.[24] The French high Gothic style of Rheims and Amiens reached the Rhine in the rebuilding of

the nave and south transept of Strasbourg between 1240 and 1275, not long after the completion of the massive late Romanesque choir and crossing in 1225.[25] It is a giant framework, like its French predecessors, for stained glass, much of which remains, though given a particularly German flavour by the windows of the north aisle of the nave which are filled with nineteen full-length portraits of the Holy Roman Emperors, taking the role in style and position of the prophets of the Old Testament and facing in the south aisle windows of the life and passion of Christ. The love of vertical emphases is seen at its most dramatic in the choir of Cologne Cathedral, its vaults, at 150 ft (50 m), higher than any cathedral except Beauvais. Begun in 1248 and consecrated in 1352, it is a phenomenal achievement with its double ambulatory, its corona of seven chapels, and its neck-breaking upper vista of high clerestory windows coming down into a range of glazed triforium windows[26] (fig. 41).

It was, however, the earlier Elisabethkirche at Marburg, the first German Gothic hall church, that set the style for originality in spatial effects.[27] By raising the aisle roofs to the same height as the central nave, the need to play games with galleries, triforia, and clerestories was abolished, with the added gains of spatial unity and greater light. It had another advantage, in stressing verticality without requiring excessive and dangerous height. It was a model that could nevertheless be expanded to a gigantic size, as at Ulm (though there is a central clerestory in the Minster) and the Stefansdom in Vienna, or kept to a more intimate scale as in the numerous city churches of the Empire. Its strong vertical emphasis led to another abolition, that of the capital—or at least its diminution—so that the eye could travel swiftly to the *Sondergotik* vaulting, those elaborate patterns of clean-cut ribs that, as at Schwäbisch-Gmünd (fig. 40), seem an ultimate triumph of the dream of the later Gothic masters to lighten the mind by the contemplation of stone seemingly floating in the air without visible means of suspension or support.

The story of the range of Gothic space in the north is one of an increasing skill in capturing and playing with light. As we turn south we meet the ancient and justified fear of the sun, but we can also interpret the desire for cool as a reflection of the coolness of thought attained by the founders and great thinkers of the mendicant orders in the thirteenth and fourteenth centuries in Italy and Spain. In churches such as the Dominican Santa Maria Novella and the Franciscan Santa Croce, both in Florence, the architects would seem to have striven for a simplicity as extreme as that of the Cistercians, but by widening the bays of the arcades they introduced a feeling of grand spaciousness.[28] This extension of spatial effect was not followed up in the manner of the north, which was to dissolve the exterior walls into windows, but it was used in combination with the old-established Italian tradition of enriching the wall space with many-coloured marbles, mosaics, and paintings. Thus, at Orvieto, the exterior design of banded black and white marble is used in the interior on the immensely high and widely spaced piers of the nave that march without interruption to the combined transepts and apse, the walls of which are coated from top to bottom in frescoes with little interruption from the slim windows.

It is the use of a much wider range of building materials, many unfam-

145 Florence. The grand and simple interior of Santa Maria Novella, built from about 1246.

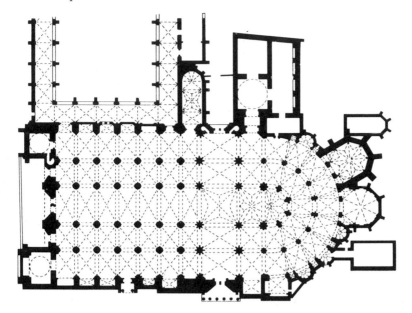

iliar to northern eyes, that gives to Italian Gothic so much of its variety and zest, as in the use of marble tracery in the Campo Santo at Pisa or in the transept galleries at Lucca. Most prodigal of all is the prospect that greets the eye on one's ascent to the roof of Milan Cathedral, where one is dazzled by a snow-white piazza bordered by a crowd of pinnacled statues surmounting the buttresses, with, as its focus, the temple-like lantern topped by the statue of the Madonnina.[29]

Plan of Toledo Cathedral.

Spain was far readier at an earlier date to learn from Northern France. The cathedral of León, built from about 1250 onwards, has been called a pure example of the *rayonnant* style.[30] Scattered over the area of the Iberian peninsula are the constructions of Toledo, Segovia, and Seville, each revealing a desire to express the horizontal expansion of space. For hundreds of years the Spanish national character had been formed by the desire to conquer what the Moors had taken from them. When, in the same year, they finally drove the Moors from Granada and discovered the New World, they perhaps opened up a path of adventure for possessors of the particular combination of skills and objectives that had originated and maintained the Gothic, so that the desire for thrilling, dangerous occupations was filled through the conquest of the space of unknown lands rather than of architectural space—though the Conquistadores took masons with them and the earliest churches of the New World were built with Gothic vaulting.[31]

In earlier chapters I have spoken of the part played by the Gothic style in releasing and expressing emotions and in reconciling dualisms and conflicts, such as those between the pagan past and Christian doctrine and practices. The resolution of those dualisms must derive from a greater unifying principle, one that is beyond the act of synthesis and yet brings it about. The clearest evidence of that unifying principle is the new language of space created by the Gothic masters. Without that newness of spatial effect there would have been no context for the brilliant new essays in sculpture, painting and stained glass to be manifested. These change with fashion and different kinds of patron just as do the details, linearity, and disposal of internal volumes by which the spatial effects will vary with the dominance of different styles over the period. There is one effect, though, one that strikes the deepest emotional response in us, that remains a constant in the finest buildings over a period of four hundred years, and that is

146 Freiburg-im-
Breisgau. The lantern and
spire of the Minster,
c. 1280–1330.

146 Freiburg-im-Breisgau. The lantern and spire of the Minster, *c.* 1280–1330.

the sense of soaring spirituality that is given both by the interiors and the exterior profiles. The sculpture of King's College Chapel may be largely heraldic[32] and therefore secular but the inspiration of its shafts and fan vaulting is from the same inner source as the choir of St-Denis. The two spires of Chartres and the single spires of Salisbury, Freiburg-im-Breisgau and Strasbourg point in the same direction, with the same yearning. These great buildings were designed to express through carefully calculated spatial effects the totality of man; they tell us, in the words of Aquinas, 'all men are one Man'.[33] They derive from the highest states of consciousness of which men are capable and they are designed to alter and expand the awareness of everyone who sees and enters them.

CHAPTER 10

The Prentice Pillar

The Prentice pillar stands in the Lady chapel or retrochoir of Rosslyn Chapel, a chantry church built for the Sinclair princes of Orkney from 1446 onwards.[1] The chapel is near their castle of Rosslyn, in the country south of Edinburgh, and it is placed on the edge of a bluff so that its lower church is set into the side of the cliff. The chapel itself is one of the few remains from one of the most splendid periods of Scottish history, when, under the Stewart Kings James II and James III, their tiny population, possessed by a fuller sense of national identity, produced the outburst of creative talent that is best known through the poems of Henryson and Dunbar.

Only the choir up to the start of the crossing was completed. Massive buttresses dominate the exterior, extending over the low aisles, their size made necessary by one of the more unusual features of the chapel. This is its high pointed barrel vault, carved throughout its length with stars, paterae, and rosettes. This gives an ancient and even archaic feeling to the interior, even though the deep windows of the clerestory proclaim its Gothic spirit. A similar archaic feeling attaches to the transverse vaults of the aisles with their successions of foliaged lintels, set so that they provide a vista of carved stone beams stretching down to the double ambulatory of the retrochoir. This is a rectangular projection to the same height as the aisles, but with crocketed pendants hanging from its vaults and leafy branches of stone thrusting out from the walls around the windows. Set behind the piers of the choir are three elaborately carved pillars: that set in the place of honour to the south is called the Prentice pillar because of the legend associated with its making. This story, it must be said, was first recorded in the seventeenth century and it is told of other churches, notably at Rouen and Gloucester.[2]

The founder of the chapel had given the master mason a model of a pillar of exquisite workmanship. The master mason, feeling his powers were inadequate to the task without a sight of the original, went to Rome (or wherever the original was to be found: the story is curiously vague on this point) so that he could learn how to make it. In his absence his apprentice had a dream in which he made and finished the pillar. He obeyed the dream and built the pillar. His master returned, eager to start work, and found the pillar already in place. In his fury he picked up a mallet and struck the apprentice dead on the forehead. The only contemporary reference that might apply to the story is that the chapel had to be reconsecrated a year after its first consecration, a rite that would only be performed when a serious crime had been committed within a church. There are three corbel heads in the western angles of the choir said to represent the apprentice with an open wound on his forehead, his sorrowing mother, and the scowling master. Whether they are contemporary with the rest of the building or not is hard to say. There is, however, a symbolical interpretation of the story which is this: when the apprentice achieves his masterwork, he dies as an apprentice because he is self-evidently a master.[3]

It is not surprising that the pillar should attract legends. It is vital, beautiful and strange. Around its base are eight winged dragons from whose mouths issue ropes that swirl widdershins round the fluting of the pillar, turning into bands of foliage that rise to a richly foliaged capital. On one side the capital is carved with Isaac bound for sacrifice and the lamb caught in the thicket. The vegetation extends above this capital into the two vaulting ribs and the two lintels which the pillar supports. One of the lintels is carved in Latin with the words of the contest of the three youths to state what is the strongest thing in the world and thereby win the favour of King Darius: one youth said that wine was the strongest, the second said the King was the strongest, but the third youth, Zerubbabel, a Jew of the Exile, said, 'Women are strongest but above all things Truth beareth away the victory.'[4] Zerubbabel won the contest and, when asked by Darius to state his reward, he requested to be allowed to return to Jerusalem and rebuild the Temple.

Whatever links may be made between the symbolism of the parts of the pillar and its meaning as a whole, it is an extraordinary creation, intended to arouse wonder and thought. It stresses and resolves polarities: between the cthonic world of the dragons, each one with his tail linked round the head of the one following, at its base and the world of sacrifice and transformation at its top; between the upward striving of the bands of foliage and the movement of the fluting dropping like a shower of grace; between the pagan world of the dragons and the Judaeo-Christian imagery of the stories of Abraham and Zerubbabel. The pillar may represent at once the Christian tree of life and the Norse world tree Yggdrasil whose roots were gnawed by a dragon. This was the tree on which Wotan (or Odin) hung for nine days and nights 'sacrificing myself to myself' to win wisdom for mankind. This Norse legend may have been incorporated here because of the Orcadian associations of the chapel's founder. The same idea of sacrifice is found in the spiritual interpretations of the sacrifice of Isaac which signified the sacrifice of Christ for mankind, the sacrifice necessary in a life devoted to Christ, and the surrender of the soul to its Father.[5] The story of Zerubbabel, which must have been one dear to the hearts of masons, brings together several themes: renewal through the rebuilding of the Temple, the church as a symbol of the Heavenly Jerusalem, and the glorification of woman as Truth or Sapientia. All these are but associations evoked by the pillar, which is not a textbook but a work of art in stone, with a marvellous variety in the plastic

147   Rosslyn. Dragons round the base of the Prentice pillar. Cords (or roots) from their mouths are transformed into the four swathes of vegetation that spiral the pillar.

148 *Left*   Rosslyn. A Green Man on one of the pendants decorating the vault of the retrochoir.

qualities of its carving from the smooth muscular bodies of the dragons to the imbrications of its splayed foliage. The origins of the wonder it arouses lie in some profound experience of the sculptor, whose best expression of it was in the form of a pillar.

Some three hundred years separate the carving of the Prentice pillar from the beginnings of the Gothic style in St-Denis, Sens, and Chartres, yet it clearly belongs to the tradition established in those great churches. The double ambulatory of which it forms part, though in the square form of the British style, owes its origins to the double ambulatory of St-Denis. In the fifteen years from 1135 to 1150 in which the Gothic style was developed, largely in those three centres, nearly all the important themes that artists and architects were to come back to again and again were first expressed, and they can be seen as a series of constants throughout the period: they include the new deployment of enclosed spaces within a unifying skeletal frame intended to spiritualize the effect of light, the adaptation and synthesis of various Romanesque forms such as the repetition of bays, the ribbed vault, and the incipient flying buttress, the new representation of man as an individual, a change in attitude to Nature shown by the exact delineation of plants and creatures, and the rose window, first seen at St-Denis, as a cosmic symbol. These inventions and discoveries are directly linked to the renewed influence of Christian Neoplatonic mysticism and philosophy, such as the writings of Dionysius the Areopagite and the School of Chartres. They would also seem to reflect a deliberate attempt to incorporate the archetypes of the ancient religions of Northern Europe into a new artistic expression of the truths and doctrines of Christianity, so that the teachings of Christ and the stories of the Old and New Testaments could be portrayed with an immediacy and a sense of modernity reinforced by the psychic energies contained in the native symbolism of the past. Named in scorn as the architecture of barbarians,[6] the Gothic style repudiates the masculine imperialism of Rome and the south and asserts with pride for four hundred years the necessary rights and beauty of the Eternal Feminine.

What kept the style so alive, so adaptable to change, so responsive to new social, intellectual, and contemplative moments? We have considered some of the main constants within the aesthetic language of the style itself.

149   Rosslyn. The Prentice pillar: one of the three elaborately carved piers in the retrochoir of this chapel built from 1456 onwards.

There are, as well, the constant of religious and social needs in medieval society which required the building and adornment of new churches, and the constants within the training and organization of the masons and their associated craftsmen and artists, which ensured continuity of tradition and the maintenance of high standards of execution. The chief constant in the religious context was the unchanging liturgy of the mass. The general agreement in Christendom that this was the central act of worship meant that there was always a need for churches in which it could be celebrated. When, at the Reformation, there was no longer agreement on this point, both sides turned increasingly, and then almost completely, to the revived classicism of the Renaissance for architectural expression of their opposing tenets. Another constant was the universal desire for spectacle and drama: conspicuous expenditure on vestments, liturgical vessels, and shrines was as necessary to prelates and clergy in the fifteenth century as it was to Suger in the twelfth. In the next century, with the secularization of drama, the desire of people for theatrical performance was satisfied in new ways and a series of edicts brought to an abrupt end most of the rites and dances described in Chapter 8.[7] A third constant was the general agreement that it was right and proper to spend a high proportion of surplus income on sacred architecture: it was an urge that satisfied the self-exaltation of the clergy, the ambitions of kings and princes, and the civic and local pride of burghers, gentry and peasants. By the sixteenth century the palace and the villa or country house were taking the funds that rulers, bishops and nobles had formerly devoted to church-building and attracting the architects and artists to their design and decoration.

The steadiness of these religious and social constants throughout all the vicissitudes of medieval history meant not only that there was always a need for trained masons and craftsmen but also that their patrons were generally keen for them to try something new and spectacular. This would apply as much to a Somerset village that wanted its tower to be finer and with buttresses more cunningly designed than that of the next village as to the canons and citizens of Beauvais wanting their cathedral to climb higher than that of Amiens. This pressure from the patrons was paralleled by a particular advantage of the Gothic building style: this was its capacity for organic development and addition, which meant it was always open to innovation. There must have been something in the training and organization of the masons that allowed for fluidity of invention as well as providing the structure that is necessary for continuity of a tradition.

The guild system of training through the stages of apprentice, journeyman, and master would ensure continuity of expertise and the transmission of high standards of craftsmanship. By the thirteenth century the hereditary principle would also be at work: the sons of successful masons would follow their fathers in their trade. They would probably have had the benefit of education in cathedral and church schools, studying Latin and mathematics as part of the Trivium and Quadrivium. Villard de Honnecourt could write in French and Latin, and Latin would probably have been his means of communication with his patrons in Hungary. A master like him with international contacts would have to be literate. The inscription on the tombstone of Pierre de Montreuil calling him *Doctor lathomorum*,[8] doctor of masons, shows by the academic title that as part of the esteem in which he was held, he was thought to be the possessor of a special kind of learning. Children destined by family ties to become masons or architects would have been brought up steeped in the iconography of the sculptures on which their fathers and uncles were working. This aspect of their education could have continued throughout their lives whenever they

150 Lichfield. The sequence of number symbolism in the interior of the nave, built 1265–95, from the three trefoils in the clerestory to the four openings in the tritorium of each bay surmounted by quatrefoils, and a cinquefoil in the lower spandrels.

discussed the theological or liturgical purpose of their creations with their patrons.

Among the subjects that would have been the intellectual food of their lives and work were numerology, the study of proportions, and geometry. Numerology is the study and symbolism of number. Examples of its use can be found throughout the Middle Ages in art and literature. Hugh of St Victor wrote at length on its use.[9] Dante used numerology in all his works from the *Vita Nuova* to the *Commedia*.[10] The composer John Dunstable constructed his music on elaborate numerological patterns. The prophet Joachim of Fiore owed much of his authority to his skill in using number for his predictions.[11] Guillaume Durand used number symbolism in his writings on the symbolism of the different parts of the church.[12] Suger expressly calls the twenty-four columns of his choir at St-Denis the twelve apostles and the twelve prophets[13] and I have already described how a similar use of symbolism can be seen at Sens and in the south tower of Chartres. It should be seen, not as an arid arrangement of dead ciphers, but as a fruitful method of letting the symbolic associations of a desired elevation or plan come together into a natural unity. It was a game played with numbers to bring the computational side of the brain into harmony with the symbolism of its right side, and it is nowadays a pleasant game in going round a Gothic church to let the number symbolism suddenly become apparent and speak to one. An instance where it seems particularly plain to me is the nave of Lichfield, where a symbolism of the creation is developed from the Trinity in the tripartite clerestory windows, each with three trefoils. Creation passes into the number four in the triforium with four openings in each bay and quatrefoils in the tracery. Four is here the number of the Trinity and what it acts upon—the world. From there in the spandrels of the main arcade the power of creation descends through the shafts to cinquefoils, expressing five, the number of man, of love, and the cycles of generation.

There has been a revived interest in some quarters in recent years in the idea that the Gothic masters also employed the number system of *gematria*, the system derived from Cabbalism and ancient Greek practice of relating the symbolism of number to the meanings of words and names. Though we have the evidence of Suger and Durand for the use of numerology in church design, there is no contemporary evidence that *gematria* was employed for this purpose. Attempts have been made to show that the various dimensions of the ground plan of Chartres conform to sums derived from the Greek and Latin titles of the Virgin Mary.[14] The nearest to a convincing demonstration of its use is at King's College Chapel, of which it has been said that its design is founded on the number 26, derived by *gematria* from the Hebrew name of God, giving it 26 clerestory windows, 26 ribs in each pair of vaults, and 26 apertures in each screen to the side-chapels.[15] Such systems, without the backing of contemporary evidence—as with my own example at Lichfield—are always open to the charge that they are an imposed rationalization on a design which was arrived at by a completely different process of solution. We must remember William of Baskerville.

No such doubts attach to the Gothic masters' use of proportions and geometrical construction. Sometimes, as we have seen at Sens, the number symbolism and the proportions of width and height of the parts can be shown to accord. Many masons would have had access, directly or by report, to the *De architectura* of Vitruvius, the Roman architect of the period of Augustus. The writings of Vitruvius and those of Vegetius on fortifications and military engineering were the only classical works connected with building to survive the Dark Ages. Vitruvius taught the masons the importance of moral character in architects and their need to be of wide general education. He also showed them how proportion in building should be related to the nature of man and the universe.

With the translation of Arab works on geometry, computation, and algebra in the twelfth century, such as those by Adelard of Bath, there was a rapid diffusion of mathematical skills. How rapid it was among masons can be demonstrated from one example: when the statues of the west front of Wells were examined in the last century they were found to be marked with Arabic numerals.[16] The latest date at which they could have been marked is 1240. The *earliest* full account, in the west, of the use of Arabic (or, properly, Hindu) numerals is that of Leonardo Fibonacci, written in 1202. Fibonacci also is responsible for the numerical series bearing his name which can be used to relate the logarithmic spiral to the golden section, the most harmonious of all proportions and one used by Gothic architects and sculptors.

The other sets of proportions they used in setting out and planning their elevations range from the simpler forms of 2:1 and $\sqrt{2{:}1}$ to much more complex variations. Yet a further variation is to be found in the use of different modules in their designs by different masons. John James, who has analysed the campaigns of building Chartres between 1194 and 1226 through close study of the mason's marks, the changes in courses of stone and in design, says that there were nine different master masons each with their teams of workers engaged successively on the construction of the cathedral. Nearly all worked to a different basic module.[17]

The development of stone window tracery from Rheims in the early thirteenth century has given us even more obvious signs of their delight in geometric patterns. The west rose of Chartres has been analysed into three separate but overlapping geometric patterns.[18] The architects' designs were drawn up in different ways, incised on stone as on the crypt floor of Bourges or on the aisle roof-slabs at Clermont-Ferrand, cut on plaster boards or traced out on wide planks (called Eastland boards at Rosslyn because they came from the Baltic) or on vellum. The Strasbourg Museum contains magnificent examples of full elevations of the west façade of the cathedral showing different solutions from 1270 onwards, and there remain many more of these parchment drawings in Germany and Austria than elsewhere.[19]

Certain of the methods they employed were revealed in two books. One, by Matthew Roritzer of Regensburg, published in 1486, is concerned with raising a pinnacle from a square.[20] The other is a Spanish book published in 1681, drawing on the work of a famous architect, Rodrigo Gil de Hontañón.[21] Other information comes from the debates beginning in 1392 between the German and French masons and the Italian masons over Milan Cathedral. Part of the debate centred on whether the relationship of width to

153 *Below*   King's College Chapel, Cambridge. The fan vaulting of the choir, 1512–15, by John Wastell.

154 *Below right* Strasbourg. Part of the drawing on parchment by Michael Parler *c.* 1385 for the west rose and upper stages of the west front of the cathedral, now in the Musée de l'oeuvre de Notre-Dame.

the height of the vault should be *ad quadratum*, meaning that the horizontal line should be equal in length to the vertical line, or *ad triangulum*, according to which the vault height was that of the apex of an equilateral triangle raised from the base line of the square.[22] One French master became so exasperated at the refusal of the Italians to submit to the logic of geometry that he burst out with the denunciation *Ars sine scientia nihil!*, which may be translated either in its more modern sense of 'Art without science is nothing' or 'Craft without a knowledge of proportions is empty.' The Italians reversed the sentence to *Scientia sine arte nihil* and continued in their ignorant ways.

Craftsmanship, a knowledge of proportions and geometry, a wide knowledge of the teachings of the Church and its symbolism, to which we can add, on the part of architects entrusted with huge and costly buildings, great administrative and financial abilities—these are all basically techniques. They are necessary for fulfilling inspiration and manifesting it. On their own they lead to dullness, repetition, lack of spirit.

The power of regeneration in the Gothic spirit is such that it could only have found renewal in returning to its source in the soul. We have seen how the canons of Gerona welcomed Guillem Boffill's design for the nave in terms that would have been familiar to Suger.[23] Perhaps by using the casts of mind of certain modern disciplines or professions as analogies we can come closer to defining what it was in the Gothic that produced this power of regeneration.

Modern mathematicians are generally at one with Thierry of Chartres in believing that on mathematics all rational explanations of the universe depend.[24] Like him they also work on the assumption that they are not imposing empirical and useful constructs upon reality but that they are discovering truths already existing in the structure and forms of nature. They are unlike him in this, that their private or personal set of beliefs or unbeliefs is unimportant compared with the Platonic framework within which they work and think. Similarly the Gothic masters were given by the creators of the style a general attitude to nature and to art, founded on the imagery of light. That was the creative paradigm within which they had to work, which was stronger than their personal preferences or beliefs. They could only build and create in the style if they had received the correct wide-ranging education. In this they were like the scientists and musicians of today. No one can hope to, or should presume to, contribute to the findings of science who has not received the rigorous formal education of a modern scientist. The graduate resulting from all the stages of higher education may be a dull and uninventive fellow or an initiator of new and exciting lines of investigation. He forms, however, part of a wide international community which can judge his abilities and which is generally willing to applaud anything of value he contributes, so long as it is expressed within the received context of the current paradigm. He can be tested and judged only by his peers. The masons of the Middle Ages would seem to have founded a comparable community, successful in excluding outsiders without their training, international in their connexions, and encouraging the flowering of talent and genius in their company.

My third analogy is with the profession of the classical musician. The analogy works in two ways; one is the manner in which the profession is supported and the other concerns its spiritual and aesthetic renewal. The hundreds of symphony orchestras in the world are largely supported or kept in being by public money. In utilitarian terms, they are as useless as the cathedrals of the Middle Ages. It may be that, just as many of our ancestors in the sixteenth century not only rejected the practice of building new churches but did their best to destroy them, our children's children will not

155   Barcelona. The choir, 1298–1329, with its immense columns rising up to a ring of rose windows in the clerestory and the steps going down to the shrine of St Eulalia in front of the high altar.

only hear no longer what we hear in Bach, Mozart, Beethoven, and Schubert, but will try to destroy all instruments, all scores, all recordings. They may be so successful that in three hundred years' time a musicologist, who will be one of the revivers of classical music as Pugin and Viollet-le-Duc were among the chief revivers of the Gothic, will come across scores of western music in the records of Peking or Tokyo and will have to reinvent the violin, just as the techniques of Gothic building had to be rediscovered for the revival of the style in the last century. We stand in relation to Mozart and Beethoven as a pious visitor of the fourteenth century did to Chartres. Music, to us now, is as much a necessary food of the soul as Chartres was to the pilgrim then. Our rulers, our civil servants, and our bankers generally agree with us for they have souls needing nourishment as well, and therefore—for a time—we keep our makers of music.

The other point in the analogy with music is that, though our current repertoire extends back to the sixteenth century and in liturgical music even further, partly because of the high level of professional training that the composer must share with the performers of his music, partly because music has become an international language of feeling, there is a power of regeneration within the western tradition of music that can still create new works giving voice to unexpressed emotions, state moods of the past in fresh ways, and change the state of awareness of the performer and the listener. We have an extreme dependence on music today as the one certain means, outside theory, belief, or specialized education, of awakening the powers and emotion of the righthand hemisphere of the brain, that side of our natures that is depressed or extinguished by our systems of education which concentrate on developing the lefthand hemisphere. As a living tradition music is our chief contemporary means of transmitting and experiencing pure emotion. In a similar way, for the Middle Ages, Gothic space was the chief medium of pure emotion, reflecting the insights of mystics and contemplatives as well as the currents of popular devotion and maintaining through silent experience a balance with the words of doctrinal exposition and philosophy. We can see therefore the power of regeneration within the Gothic style, as owed, on the one hand, to the continuity of traditions and skills preserved by the Gothic masters through their professional training and organizations, and on the other hand to an awareness of the need to return to the creative source of the style, which individuals of each generation had to find within themselves and reinterpret in order to revive it.

Where did they find this source of renewal? In certain cases, as with the influence of the Dionysian writings and Neoplatonic ideas on St-Denis and Chartres, and later the influence of the school of Rhineland mystics following Meister Eckhart on the architecture and art of Germany, we can see a direct connexion between the mysticism of a particular time and place and its expression in the form and mood of a building. The few remaining masonic texts[25] give us few hints of the deeper experiences from which such great art derives, and we are forced—as I have frequently done in these pages—to turn to parallels with the writings of Church fathers and theologians.

The Prentice pillar gives us the theme of sacrifice. Sacrifice should be considered in its older sense of making something holy as well as that of renunciation. The medieval mason undertook a life as devoted to a higher spiritual cause as any of the monks and clergy he worked for. His life was devoted to transforming stone, minerals, and wood into holy buildings. Though the material rewards of wealth, position, and esteem could, as we have seen, be considerable, as was remarked earlier, no Gothic cathedral of great size was ever completed. The masters working on these cathedrals must often have known they would not live to see the completion even of the part they had designed and begun. Progress on the spire of Ulm gives an indication of the time scale against which they had to set themselves: because Ulm is made of a mixture of brick and stone, which takes longer to settle than do the materials used separately, fifty years was allowed to elapse between the construction of each stage built in the Middle Ages.[26] The knowledge that their own working lives were only part of a greater work stretching into the future must have affected their attitudes deeply. It would help to explain, for example, those passages in the Strasbourg Constitutions which forbid the destruction of any work by a dead master.[27] It would also emphasize the importance of maintaining the standards of the craft through training and education. Though in one way you know you will never finish a job, in another way, you know it will be finished by the hands, heart, and mind of someone you have taught. The wonderful mythical history of their craft, taking it back to early biblical times, to Euclid in Egypt, and to King Athelstan, preserved among English masons, reveals the strength of the tradition and the conviction of an honourable calling.[28]

Such a sense of tradition must have helped in the many disappointments that must have come their way. Several masters competed for the job of rebuilding the choir of Canterbury. When William of Sens was chosen, several dreams that were centred on the chance of a lifetime never came to fruition. For all the hundreds of great buildings that were built, there must have been thousands of bitter experiences when war, a change of bishop, the rejection of too revolutionary a design, the running out of funds, or plague, meant that great talent never found its opportunity. Just as the young student, musician, or actor today knows there is a thousand to one chance that he or she will spend a life practising the art for which they are trained, so the young mason, though granted every necessary talent, must have known how few would be the great chances of his life.

There is another way in which we can see their life as one of sacrifice. The Gothic architect, sculptor, artist, and painter of stained glass all had to devote their minds to the contemplation and manifestation of symbolic forms and archetypal images. The greatest sacrifice must have been made by those artists and sculptors who came to Abbot Suger and the canons of Chartres in the 1140s, having broken with the traditions of their Romanesque masters and teachers, and about to undertake the transformation of the images by which men and women lived. To achieve the calm of the pillars and light of Suger's ambulatory and the peace of the faces of the column statues of the Royal Portal of Chartres their makers must have undergone, spiritually and aesthetically, the experience of Doomsday. The Judgment portals of the late Romanesque and the early Gothic are not solely illustrations of the Apocalypse created for religious teaching: they are fitting emblems of events in the soul of western man of the twelfth century, of which the artists were the keenest witnesses and portrayers. Presiding over many of these scenes sits Christ on the great throne in Revelation who says 'I will make all things new.'[29] It was the archetypes that were made new, most notably as we have seen that of the Virgin Mother.

There is only one contemporary piece of evidence that lets in light on the sufferings endured by these artists in making manifest the new. This is the inscription carved round the base of the pulpit of Pisa Cathedral by Giovanni Pisano. On his pulpit at Pistoia, finished in 1306, he had boasted of his gifts, even exalting himself above his father. At Pisa, where his pulpit received severe criticism, there is an upper inscription, conventional in its praises, saying of Giovanni that there are many sculptors but only to him remain praise and honour, and ending with the prayer: 'Christ have mercy on him to whom such gifts are given. Amen.' In the lower inscription, though, he speaks directly:

> Giovanni has encircled here the rivers and the parts of the earth.
> Attempting much, freely learning, and preparing all with great labour,
> he now proclaims: I have not taken enough care. Though I have
> achieved much, I have been more condemned. Yet with an indifferent
> heart and a calm mind I bear the penalty. That I may avert hostility,
> from this pulpit, mitigate my sorrow . . . join tears to these verses . . .[30]

For the rest, the joys and the sorrows of the personal lives of the masons and artists have gone into the mood and the psychological richness of the churches to which they devoted their lives. They were fortunate in their tradition: the ideal cathedral to which their work aspired is an image of the totality of man in the universe. All their fears, neuroses, jokes, loves, observations of people and nature, all their finest feelings and thoughts could be devoted to that capacious and inexhaustible image, so that a great cathedral such as Strasbourg can be seen as the contribution of the countless small lives of its creators, its priests, and the citizens who thronged there, offered up and contained within the greater context of divine love.

It may seem an extraordinary conclusion to reach, in seeking for the source and maintaining power of Gothic civilization, to say that it comes from love: the love of humanity that produced the new representation of man, the love of nature that redeemed the pagan past of Europe and allowed it to take its place in the context of Christian art, the love that most especially flows from womankind and that found its universal expression in the Virgin as Queen of Heaven, the love of God that appears in the equivalence between the mystic way and the journeyings through Gothic space, and the love of their craft and their art that was the continuing inspiration of the Gothic masters. It fits, however, with Frankl's words, already quoted, on Gothic culture as the realization of the spirit of the New Testament.[31]

It is an art that can give us immediate understanding of what St Paul meant when he bowed on his knees 'to the Father of our Lord Jesus Christ' and asked:

> That Christ may dwell in your hearts by faith: that
> ye being rooted and grounded in love,
> May be able to comprehend with all saints what is
> the breadth, and length, and depth, and height;
> And to know the love of Christ, which passeth knowledge,
> that ye might be filled with all the fullness of God.[32]

Such a feeling is given by the choir of Barcelona, with its sense of many levels conveyed by the great fall of steps that descends before the high altar to the shrine of the martyr St Eulalia, and the counter-rhythm of the steps rising gently to a rounded stage from which in a broad semicircle the massive, high piers soar up to the keys of the vaulting, formed by bosses containing carvings of the Virgin and of Christ. You stand before the high altar and you feel space fall from you, stretch out from you, climb above you, hang over you as a palpable image of the pleroma of God and you feel that subtle feeling of gladness, of being humbled, of inner stillness, of true knowledge, for which our language has no single name.

That in so many churches of so many lands we can experience this special effect of space is owed to the best of many lives preserved in the works of a corporate art, an art that only exerted its vast influence in renewing European civilization because it was so attractive, so stimulating that it drew towards itself a surplus wealth that would otherwise have been

156   Pisa. The pulpit in the cathedral by Giovanni Pisano. The inscription referred to in the text runs round the base.

157   Rievaulx. The ruined thirteenth-century choir of this famous Cistercian Yorkshire abbey.

devoted to war. To these devoted lives is owed the fact that most people in North-Western Europe today live within a few tens of miles of one of the great cathedrals or churches which remain the souls of their cities, which give intensity and heightened emotion to the landscapes they dominate, and which speak to earth of other higher worlds. Those many lives of their makers have been absorbed into the presences of the cathedrals so that they are like huge living beings, instinct with individuality and authority. Such is the love they inspire they are constantly worked on, renewed and restored, but they cannot last for ever. The sight of holes the size of fists in the glass of Canterbury, the scattered fragments of carvings fallen to the parvis from the high façade of Amiens, the burnt-out south transept of York, all remind us that, whether because of pollution or natural catastrophes, such as strikes of lightning or war, they will one day, like the generations buried within them, be 'entombed and inurned in the sepulchres of mortality'. The sight of the wholly new towns that surround so many cathedrals of France and Germany, at Beauvais, Rheims, Cologne and Freiburg, for example, is a chilling sign of how close a major part of the cultural heritage of Europe came to total destruction. The bronze doors of the Johanneskirche in Magdeburg portray the night in 1944 when all five of the great churches along the Elbe went up in flames. All are now restored except for the Johanneskirche which is left as a memorial. The doors bear this inscription:

> Wer aber aus der Vergangenheit
> nichts gelernt hat und weiter
> Hass und Zwietracht sät
>   den klagen wir an!

> We mourn the man who has learnt nothing from the past
> and who sows further hatred and division.

The great art of the Gothic masters lives under the same shadow as modern man: the threat of destruction so complete that, should any of them survive as ruins as beautiful and as haunting as those of Rievaulx and St-Jean des Vignes at Soissons, the men and women who also survive will be sunk into a barbarism so absolute that in their struggle to live there will be no learning to preserve their history, no time to contemplate the message of their remaining fragments. Yet to help in the avoidance of such disaster, these great buildings, the greatest works of art achieved by our western civilization, can still challenge us with the transformation of hatred and barbarism into love and civilization brought about by our ancestors, saying to us, 'We were made the images of man for our time in his wholeness, in his beauty, in the identity of his true self with his creator. What image of man will you construct that will be the vocation of a new civilization, bringing harmony to the dualism of materialism and the needs of the soul, transforming fear and hatred into love, and returning the spontaneity of joy to art?'

200

Notes

Abbreviations

P.L. *Patrologia Latina* ed. J-P. Migne, Paris.

R.S. Rolls Series.

S.T. St Thomas Aquinas, *Summa theologiae*, Latin text and translation, London and New York, 1964.

Introduction

1. See White (1968) p. 63.

2. The phrase is Jacques Maritain's. See Maritain (1974) especially Chapters 3 and 4 and also Bede Griffiths's development of the same thought, in Griffiths (1983) pp. 163–5.

Chapter 1
The Beginnings

1. The expression appears in several of Cicero's works. For his influence on John of Salisbury see Liebeschütz (1950).

2. Lynn White Jr says 'Whatever its specific abuses, technology is a profoundly spiritual form of thought and of action.' See White (1968) p. 148.

3. These words are from the description of the vision in which the Apostle Bartholomew appeared to Rahere and commanded him to build the priory church. With modernized spelling they are taken from the English translation *c*. 1400 of the original Book of Foundation *c*. 1180. See Moore (1923) p. 5.

4. Neoplatonic ideas had been studied at St-Denis and Chartres since the tenth century. See Duby (1976) pp. 31–3 for the importance of the Carolingian cathedral schools in maintaining learning and education.

5. See Harvey (1972) p. 74 for the significance of Barbastro.

6. See Frankl (1960) pp. 84–5 and 846–7 for the text of the expertise of the masons.

7. See Anderson (1980) Chapter 1 and its notes for numerous examples.

8. *Milton* Book I, p. 413, Nonesuch edn.

9. Velleius Paterculus (1967) pp. 40–1.

10. *Ibid.* pp. 42–3.

11. *Ibid.* pp. 44–5.

12. See the discussion of religion, art, philosophy and science as the major forms of knowledge and their dependence on one another in Ouspensky (1982) pp. 193–4. See Bohm (1983) pp. 1–26 for a discussion of the *opposite* effect of fragmentation on our world view and on society.

13. Frankl (1960) p. 234.

14. John 14: 10.

15. John 14: 16–17.

16. Translation by Editors of the Shrine of Wisdom (see Dionysius (1935) p. 49). The passage may be found in the Latin version by Eriugena in *P.L.* 122, cols. 1065–6.

17. St John Cassian, *Collationes IX*, cap. 31, *P.L.* 49, cols. 807–8.

18. From the canzone *Le dolci rime d'amor*, lines 38–9.

19. See White (1968) p. 65.

20. See Stranks (1973) p. 32.

21. For the antiquity of these patterns and their association with the Goddess or Goddesses of prehistory, see Gimbutas (1982) and Dames (1976 and 1977).

22. See Dames (1976) pp. 149–51.

23. Heer (1974) p. 404.

24. See Anderson (1980), Chapter 17, especially pp. 295–301.

25. Raoul Glaber describing the rush to build new churches after the year 1000, *P.L.* 142 col. 651.

26. The phrase from the *Bhagavadgita* that came to Robert Oppenheimer's mind on seeing the first atomic explosion. See Jungk (1958) p. 198.

27. See Gimpel (1961) p. 5.

28. The indictment is against the guiding philosophy, not against individual scientists. The consequences may be seen as another effect of the fragmentation described by David Bohm (see *n.* 12 above).

29. Quoted in de Bruyne (1946) Vol. II, p. 411.

30. Bernardus Sylvester, tr. Winthrop Wetherbee (1973) p. 90.

31. See Maier (1910) for a survey of Gerhaert's career and works.

Chapter 2 St-Denis, Sens and Chartres

1. For Suger's career see E. Panofsky's introduction in Suger (1979) pp. 1–37.

2. Translation by E. Panofsky in Suger (1979) pp. 47 and 49.

3. Translation by E. Panofsky in Suger (1979) pp. 63 and 65.

4. Bony (1983) pp. 32–43.

5. Suger (1979) pp. 104–5.

6. See Bony (1983) pp. 57–9 for the design and influence of St Martin-des-Champs.

7. Von Simson (1956) pp. 121–2.

8. Gage (1982) p. 46.

9. Bony (1983) pp. 94–5.

10. Tr. by E. Panofsky in Suger (1979) pp. 50–1.

11. *Ibid.* pp. 114–15.

12. See his letter to his friend William of St Thiery, *Apologia ad Guillelmum, Sancti Theodorici Remensi abbatem, P.L.* 182 cols. 914–16.

13. Ernst Levy, 'On the proportions of the South Tower of Chartres Cathedral' in von Simson (1956) pp. 235–61.

14. For these accounts see Frankl (1960) pp. 207–10.

15. *Ibid.*

Chapter 3 The Pointed Arch: people, patrons and masons

1. See Bony (1983) p. 17 for a summary of the transmission of the pointed arch from Islamic Africa to Christian Europe.

2. See White (1962) especially Chapter II 'The Agricultural Revolution of the Early Middle Ages' pp. 39–78.

3. Suger (1974) pp. 94–7.

4. See Forsyth (1972) for an account of the distribution and origins of the figure of the Black Virgin.

5. Martinet (n.d.) p. 2.

6. See Gervase ed. Stubbs (1879) p. 27, tr. in Harvey (1972) p. 214. See also Ayrton (1969) pp. 30–2 for a discussion of the tools used by sculptors.

7. Duby (1976) pp. 183–8.

8. Quoted from Jung (1933) pp. 191–2.

9. Harvey (1972) p. 172.

Chapter 4 Technology and the Spirit

1. See Auerbach (1961) pp. 174–5.

2. *Ibid.* p. 26.

3. See Crombie (1953).

4. See White (1968) pp. 83–7.

5. Gimpel (1979) pp. 69–70.

6. See Mortet (1911) pp. 159–60 and Harvey (1972) p. 22.

7. See Dimock ed. (1860) and tr. in Harvey (1972) pp. 236–9.

8. Gimpel (1979) p. 15.

9. Suger (1979) pp. 108–9.

10. See the account of the consecration of a church in Durand (1859) pp. 39–49, and also Chambers (1903) Vol II p. 3.

11. Quoted in Heer (1974) p. 371.

12. Bony (1983) p. 470.

13. Branner (1960) pp. 16–17 and 163.

14. Anderson (1970) p. 126.

15. See Liebeschütz (1950) for an account of John of Salisbury's period in Paris.

16. See Campbell (1976) pp. 3–9.

17. See Taylor (1963) and Seznec (1972).

18. Suger (1979) pp. 78–9.

19. See Crosby *et al.* (1981) especially the carvings illustrated pp. 54–8.

20. See Gervase ed. Stubbs (1874) p. 6 and tr. in Harvey (1972) p. 210.

21. Bony (1983) p. 159.

22. See Gervase ed. Stubbs (1879) p. 21 and tr. in Harvey (1972) p. 212.

23. Dimock ed. (1860).

24. Ruskin (1898) Vol I p. 17.

25. See 'Architettura degli Ordini Mendicanti in Umbria—problemi di rilievo' by Alessandro Curuni in the exhibition catalogue *Francesco d'Assisi: chiese e conventi* (1982).

26. Duby (1976) pp. 121–33.

27. Such as Benno of Osnabrück, Bishop Gundolf who designed the White Tower or the Bishop of Mende who built the siege weapons for the destruction of Montségur.

28. See Harvey (1972) p. 33 *seq.*

29. *On the Sublime* IX 2.

30. See the account in von Simson (1956) pp. 159–82.

Chapter 5 A New Image of Man

1. See the instructions of Pope Gregory the Great to Mellitus in Bede, tr. Sherley-Price (1955) pp. 86–7.

2. See *n.* 12 to Chapter 2 above.

3. In, for example, his sermons on the Song of Songs.

4. See Ephesians I:21; 3:10; 6:12 and Colossians 1:16; 2:15–20.

5. See, for example, the descriptions of the dances for the dead and churchyard dances in Backman (1952) pp. 131–54.

6. Heer (1974) p. 377. See also Sheridan and Ross (1975) p. 107 for examples of Romanesque columns at Millstatt, Austria, where human faces stare out of what appear to be large peepholes cut into the decoration of the columns.

7. See *Germania* 10 and, for the savage punishments, Frazer (1917) *The Magic Art and the Evolution of Kings*, Part I of *The Golden Bough*, p. 9.

8. As in the fragment of the Magdalen weeping over the feet of Christ in the church of Toller Fratrum, Dorset.

9. See the discussion in von Simson (1956) pp. 150–1.

10. *Ibid.* pp. 151–2.

11. *De gemma animae*, CXXXI *P.L.* 172 col. 586.

12. Suger (1979) pp. 104–5.

13. See Katzenellenbogen (1964) p. 40.

14. *Ibid.* pp. 27–36.

15. Dunlop (1982) pp. 29–32.

16. See Katzenellenbogen (1964) pp. 43–4.

17. Revelation 20:11; 21:5.

18. *Metalogicon* III 4. See *Opera omnia* ed. Giles (1848) Vol. V p. 131.

19. See de Lubac (1954–64) for the fullest account of the history of the fourfold interpretation of scripture.

20. Mâle (1913) pp. 170–1 and Suger (1979) figs. 14 and 16.

21. *De arca Noe morali*, *P.L.* 176 cols 62–9 and 617–19.

22. See Auerbach (1959) pp. 11–76.

23. See Webb (1956) pp. 81–2.

24. This suggestion is cogently expressed in an unpublished paper 'Hugh of Saint Victor and the West Front of Wells' (1984) by Patrick Mitchell.

25. See, for example, the passages on the relationship between the individual consciousness and the universal consciousness in both Christian and Hindu thought in Griffiths (1983) pp. 91–4.

26. *De vulgari eloquentia*, I IV 4, ed. Aristide Marigo, 3rd edn, Florence 1957.

27. The horsemen we now see at Strasbourg are all of the nineteenth century: only three were actually erected in the Middle Ages and these were destroyed at the time of the Revolution. See Klein-Ehrminger (1980) p. 63.

28. The original statue is now in the Kulturhistorisches Museum, Magdeburg.

Chapter 6 The World of the Green Man

1. See the monograph on the Green Man by Kathleen Basford (1978) and also Sheridan and Ross (1975) pp. 31–43.

2. See plate 15 in Basford (1978).

3. See Sheridan and Ross (1975) pp. 44–5.

4. Hrabanus Maurus, *Allegoriae in sacram scripturam*, *P.L.* 112 col. 1037.

5. See Hahnloser (1935) plates 10 and 43.

6. Sir James Frazer records country rites in Germany and Bohemia in which young men, dressed in leaves like the English Mayday figure, Jack o' the Green, underwent a symbolic decapitation. See Frazer (1900) Vol. II pp. 61 *seq.*

7. Basford (1978) pp. 14–15 and plate 23a and b.

8. Volpiano was described as *super regula*, for the asceticism he imposed on his monks which went far beyond the Rule of St Benedict. See Duby (1976) pp. 81–2.

9. See the interesting discussion of Wotan in Begg (1984).

10. *Aeneid* VI 304.

11. Basford (1978) pp. 1–2.

12. See Behling (1964) pp. 55–64.

13. *Ibid.* pp. 64–82.

14. Another use of trees and vegetation as the setting for redemption is in Dante's description of the Earthly Paradise in *Purgatorio*.

15. See Panofsky (1924) and Behling (1964) pp. 90 *seq.*

16. Behling (1964) plate XCVIIa and p. 86.

17. *P.L.* 196 col. 1433–4. See also Mâle (1972) p. 30.

18. See Behling (1964) pp. 37–43 and pp. 120–7.

19. This is similar to what Nicolaus Pevsner says in his remarkable essay (Pevsner, 1945, pp. 66–7): 'The inexhaustible delight in live form that can be touched with worshipping fingers and felt with all senses is ennobled—consciously in the philosophy of Thomas, the science of Albert, and the romance of Wolfram, unconsciously in the carving of the buttercups and thorn leaves and maple leaves of Southwell—by the conviction that so much beauty can exist only because God is in every man and beast, in every herb and stone.'

20 *Ibid.* for a description of the Southwell leaves and the artistic and philosophical background.

21. Sheridan and Ross (1975) p. 71.

22. Mâle (1972) pp. 33–4.

23. Sheridan and Ross (1975) pp. 50–68.

24. *Ibid.* p. 15.

25. See Chapter 1 *n.* 13.

Chapter 7 The Angelic Orders and the Eternal Feminine

1. The sculptor has been given this name from a tomb by his hand in St Erminold, Regensburg.

2. They were originally placed in the choir and only later removed to their present position.

3. These were the Middle Danube and Tisza civilizations, fifth and early fourth millennia BC. See Gimbutas (1982) pp. 27–9.

4. *De contemptu mundi* ed. Hoskier (1929). The translation is taken from S. M. Jackson, *The Source of 'Jerusalem the Golden'* Chicago (1919) pp. 139–40.

5. Thus the new cathedral in Florence was dedicated to the Virgin, not to St Reparata, the patroness of the demolished cathedral.

6. Such as those brought together by Jacobus de Voragine in the *Legenda Aurea*.

7. See the account of the sheela-na-gig in Andersen (1977).

8. Sheridan and Ross (1979) pp. 54 and 64.

9. *Ibid.* p. 66 and see also Andersen (1977).

10. See Begg (1984) for a view of the part played by the old gods and goddesses as current archetypes.

11. See Forsyth (1972).

12. Song of Solomon 6:10.

13. See the account of the Sibyls and their importance as a theme in the work of Giovanni Pisano in Ayrton (1969) pp. 126–31.

14. Suger, ed. Panofsky (1979) p. 121.

15. See Rosenberg (1967).

16. Numerous commentaries on the *Celestial Hierarchies* were written in the course of the Middle Ages, a work started by John Scotus Eriugena and complemented, amongst others, by Hugh of St Victor, St Thomas Aquinas, and Dean Colet.

17. *S.T.* 1a. 79.8.

18. *Convivio* II. v. 18, ed. G. Busnelli and G. Vandelli, 2nd edn Vol. I (1954), Vol. II (1964) Florence.

19. *De caelesti hierarchia* XII, *P.L.* 122, col 1060.

20. See Rosenberg (1967) pp. 142–3. There is a delightful portrayal of the nine orders in the roof carvings of the chancel of the church of St Eia at St Ives in Cornwall.

21. Lewis (1964) pp. 74–5.

22. *Purgatorio* XI 10–12.

23. Wisdom of Solomon 2:8–9.

24. See Gombert (1978) pp. 11–14.

25. See the excellent account of Mont Saint-Michel in Froidevaux (1969).

26. Dunbar (1929) p. 466.

27. Cowen (1979) pp. 33 *seq.*

28. *Ibid.* fig. 25.

29. *Paradiso* XXIX 16–18.

30. Julian of Norwich (1901) pp. 31–2.

Chapter 8 The Drama of the Gothic

1. *Epistolae Roberti Grosseteste episcopi quondam Lincolniensis* (R.S. 25) ed. H. R. Luard 1861 pp. 4–5. The passage is translated in Harvey (1972) pp. 23–4.

2. Mortet and Deschamps (1929) pp. 203–4.

3. This is how the style was described in the description of the rebuilding of the collegiate church of St Peter, Wimpfen-im-Tal, near Heidelberg, by a French architect from 1268 to 1278, Mortet and Deschamps (1929) p. 296.

4. The decline in France from the late thirteenth century has been forcefully described by Jean Gimpel. See Gimpel (1979) pp. 181–214.

5. Primrose (1913) pp. 38–9.

6. Ruskin (1894) p. 92.

7. Ayrton (1969) pp. 88–9.

8. *Ibid.* p. 123.

9. For the maze or labyrinth at Chartres see James (1982) pp. 86–7.

10. The inscription is given in Lazzarini (1982) p. 10.

11. Backman (1952) p. 67.

12. Chambers (1903) Vol. I, p. 129.

13. Backman (1952) pp. 56–7.

14. Watts, Sheldon J. (1984) pp. 72–3.

15. Backman (1952) pp. 64–6.

16. Chambers (1903) Vol. I pp. 274–333.

17. Dunlop (1983) pp. 54–5.

18. Chambers (1903) Vol. I p. 287.

19. Backman (1952) p. 75.

20. Chambers (1903) Vol. II p. 66.

Chapter 9 Gothic Space

1. See Stone (1955) p. 93.

2. Panofsky (1957).

3. See Foster (1959) p. 52.

4. Henderson (1967) pp. 181–2.

5. See Ruskin (1898) Vol. II p. 178 and pp. 199–200.

6. Bony (1983) p. 32.

7. *Ibid.* pp. 32–43.

8. *Ibid.* pp. 49–52.

9. See Dunlop (1982) pp. 15–16.

10. Bony (1983) pp. 103–11.

11. *Ibid.* pp. 141–7.

12. *Ibid.* pp. 137, 141, 149, and Dunlop (1982) pp. 67–71.

13. Bony (1983) pp. 180–3.

14. Viollet-le-Duc restored some of these oculi in the transepts in the course of his restoration work.

15. Bony (1983) pp. 126–9.

16. *Ibid.* pp. 212–13.

17. *De vanitate mundi, P.L.* 176 col. 705.

18. Bony (1983) p. 271.

19. An effect pointed out to me by Clive Hicks.

20. Bony (1983) p. 161.

21. Dimock ed. (1860).

22. Heer (1974) pp. 382–3.

23. Frankl (1962) p. 121 sees Norman influence in the nave of Bamberg as well.

24. See Frankl (1962) p. 117 and Bony (1983) pp. 315–16.

25. Frankl (1962) p. 106.

26. The architect Gerhard had made a close study of many French cathedrals and was deeply influenced by Amiens. See Frankl (1962) pp. 135–8.

27. See Leppin (1983) and, for the influence of Marburg on later churches, Harvey (1950) p. 89 and pp. 112–14 and Frankl (1962) pp. 154–9.

28. Frankl (1962) pp. 144–5.

29. Nearly everything one sees from the roof of Milan cathedral is of a later date, largely nineteenth century. Only one buttress with its pinnacles and statues was completed in the fifteenth century, enough to act as a model for an approximate completion of the original design.

30. Bony (1983) pp. 415–16.

31. See Harvey (1950) pp. 105–6 and plates 151–7.

32. See Saltmarsh (1970).

33. *S.T.* 1a2ae. 81.1.

Chapter 10 The Prentice Pillar

1. See the account of Rosslyn by Christopher Wilson in McWilliam (1978) pp. 409–17 and also Rosslyn (n.d.).

2. Jones (1950) pp. 320–1.

3. *Ibid.*

4. I Esdras 3:12.

5. Dunbar (1929) p. 21.

6. Henderson (1967) pp. 178–81.

7. Not all though. The Easter dance at Sens was performed up to the

French Revolution and the choirboys of Seville still sing and dance before the high altar at Eastertime.

8. Du Colombier (1973) p. 65.

9. *Exegetica* XV *P.L.* 175, cols. 22–3. See also Hopper (1938).

10. See Anderson (1980) especially Chapters 8 and 9.

11. See Hopper (1938) pp. 109–10 and Reeves (1976).

12. In Book I (on the parts of a church and its consecration) of the *Rationale Divinorum Officiorum*, Durand (1859) pp. 11–63.

13. Suger (1979) pp. 104–5.

14. James (1982) pp. 106–8.

15. Pennick (1979) pp. 136–8.

16. Dearmer (1903) p. 32.

17. See James (1982).

18. Cowen (1979) pp. 122–3.

19. See Chapter IV 'Methods: drawings, models and moulds' in Harvey (1972).

20. *Ibid.* pp. 103 and 125.

21. *Ibid.* pp. 30 and 108.

22. See Frankl (1960) pp. 62–83.

23. See Chapter I pp. 12–13.

24. See Von Simson (1956) pp. 27–9.

25. See the medieval English texts in Knoop, Jones and Hamer (1938).

26. Frankl (1962) p. 169.

27. Frankl (1960) pp. 110–58 on masons' guilds and stonemasons' lodges.

28. See Knoop, Jones and Hamer (1938) pp. 105–8.

29. See Chapter 5 *n.* 17.

30. The text of the inscriptions is given in Ayrton (1969) p. 160.

31. Frankl (1960) p. 234.

32. Ephesians 3: 17–19.

Bibliography

Andersen, Jørgen (1977) *The Witch on the Wall; Medieval Erotic Sculpture in the British Isles.* Copenhagen & London.

Anderson, William (1970) *Castles of Europe from Charlemagne to the Reformation:* London & New York.

—— and Hicks, Clive (1978) *Cathedrals in Britain and Ireland.* London & New York.

—— (1980) *Dante the Maker.* London & Boston.

—— (1983) *Holy Places of the British Isles* with photographs by Clive Hicks. London.

Arieti, Silvano (1976) *Creativity: The Magic Synthesis.* New York.

Aubert, Marcel (1952) *La Cathédrale de Chartres.* Paris & Grenoble.

Auerbach, Erich (1953) *Mimesis: the representation of reality in Western literature.* Princeton.

—— (1959) *Scenes from the Drama of European Literature,* tr. R. Manheim *et al.* New York.

—— (1961) *Dante, Poet of the Secular World,* tr. R. Manheim. Chicago.

Ayrton, Michael (1969) *Giovanni Pisano: Sculptor.* Introduction by Henry Moore, photographs by Ilario Bessi. London.

Backman, E. Louis (1952) *Religious Dances in the Christian Church and in Popular Medicine,* tr. E. Classen. London.

Basford, Kathleen (1978) *The Green Man.* Ipswich.

Bäuml, Franz H. (1969) *Medieval Civilization in Germany 800–1273.* London & New York.

Bede, the Venerable (1955) *A History of the English Church and People,* tr. Leo Sherley-Price. Harmondsworth.

Begg, Ean (1984) *Myth and Today's Consciousness.* London.

Behling, Lottlisa (1964) *Die Pflanzenwelt der mittelalterlichen Kathedralen.* Cologne.

Bernard of Cluny (1929) *De contemptu mundi,* ed. H. C. Hoskier. London.

Bernardus Sylvester (1876) *De mundi universitate,* ed. C. S. Barach and W. J. Wröbel. Innsbruck.

—— *Ibid.* (1973) tr. Winthrop Wetherbee, under the alternative title *Cosmographia.* London & New York.

Bohm, David (1980, 1983 paperback) *Wholeness and the Implicate Order.* London.

Bony, Jean (1983) *French Gothic Architecture of the 12th and 13th Centuries.* Berkeley, L.A.

Bosanquet, B. (1912) *The Principle of Individuality and Value.* London.

Branner, Robert (1960) *Burgundian Gothic Architecture.* London.

Bruyne, Edgar de (1946) *Etudes d'ésthetique mediévale.* 3 vols. Bruges.

Campbell, Joseph (1976) *The Masks of God; Creative Mythology.* Harmondsworth.

Cardini, Franco *et al.* (1982) *Francesco d'Assisi: storia e arte.* Milan.

Chambers, Sir E. K. (1903) *The Mediaeval Stage,* 2 vols. Oxford.

Conant, Kenneth John (1959) *Carolingian and Romanesque Architecture: 800–1200.* Harmondsworth.

Cowen, Painton (1979) *Rose Windows.* London.

Crombie, A. C. (1953) *Robert Grosseteste and the Origins of Experimental Science 1100–1170.* Oxford.

—— (1956) *From Augustine to Galileo: the History of Science, AD 400–1650.* London.

Crosby, Sumner McKnight, Hayward, Jane, Little, Charles

T., and Wixom, William D. (1981) *The Royal Abbey of Saint-Denis in the Time of Abbot Suger (1122–1151)* (Metropolitan Museum of Art catalogue). New York.

Dames, Michael (1976) *The Silbury Treasure.* London.

—— (1977) *The Avebury Cycle.* London.

Dearmer, Percy (1903) *The Cathedral Church of Wells.* London.

Delaporte, Y. (1978) *L'Art du vitrail aux XIIe et XIIIe siècles: technique-inspiration.* Chartres.

Demaray, John G. (1974) *The Invention of Dante's Commedia.* New Haven, Conn., & London.

Dimock, J. F. (ed.) (1860) *Metrical Life of St Hugh, Bishop of Lincoln.*

Dionysius, the Areopagite (1920) *The Divine Names and the Mystical Theology,* tr. C. E. Rolt. London.

Deulofeu, A. (1978) *L'Empordà: bressol de l'art romànic,* 4th edn. Barcelona.

Duby, Georges (1976) *Le Temps des cathédrales: l'art et la société 980–1420,* new edition. Paris.

Du Colombier, Pierre (1973) *Les Chantiers des Cathédrales: ouvriers-architectes-sculpteurs,* 2nd edn. Paris.

Dunbar, H. Flanders (1929) *Symbolism in Medieval Thought and Its Consummation in the Divine Comedy.* New Haven, Conn.

Dunlop, Ian (1982) *The Cathedrals' Crusade.* London.

Durand, Georges (1977) *Description abrégée de la cathédrale d'Amiens.* Amiens.

Durand, Guillaume (1859) *Rationale Divinorum Officiorum,* ed. G. Dura. Naples.

—— (1843) *The symbolism of Churches and Church Ornament: a translation of the first book of the 'Rationale Divinorum Officiorum',* tr. the Rev. J. M. Neale and the Rev. B. Webb. Leeds, London & Cambridge.

Eckhart, Meister (1941) *Meister Eckhart,* tr. Raymond B. Blakney. New York

Ellis Davidson, H. R. (1964) *Gods and Myths of Northern Europe.* Harmondsworth.

Erlande-Brandenburg, Alain (1976) *L'Eglise abbatiale de Saint-Denis,* 2 vols. Paris.

Eschapasse, Maurice (1967) *La Cathédrale de Reims.* Paris.

Forsyth, Ilene H. (1972) *The Throne of Wisdom: Wood Sculptures of the Madonna in Romanesque France.* Princeton.

Foster, Kenelm (1959) *The Life of St Thomas Aquinas: Biographical Documents.* London.

Francesco d'Assisi: chiese e conventi (1982) (catalogue of the exhibition for the eighth centenary of the birth of St Francis). Milan.

Frankl, Paul (1960) *The Gothic: Literary Sources and Interpretations through Eight Centuries.* Princeton.

—— (1962) *Gothic Architecture,* tr. Dieter Pevsner. Harmondsworth.

Frazer, Sir James (1900–20) *The Golden Bough,* 12 vols. London.

Froidevaux, Yves-Marie (1969) *Le Mont Saint-Michel.* Paris.

Gage, John (1982) 'Gothic Glass: Two Aspects of a Dionysian Aesthetic'. *Art History* **5** no. 1 pp. 36–58.

Gardner, Arthur (n.d.) *Lincoln Angels* 3rd edn. Lincoln.

Gervase of Canterbury (1879) *The Historical Works of Gervase of Canterbury* Vol. I, R.S. 73 i, ed. W. Stubbs. London.

Gimbutas, Marija (1982) *The Goddesses and Gods of Old Europe 6500–3500 BC: Myths and Cult Images,* 2nd edn. London.

Gimpel, Jean (1961) *The Cathedral Builders,* tr. Carl F. Barnes. London & New York.

—— (1977, paperback 1979) *The Medieval Machine: The*

Industrial Revolution of the Middle Ages. London.

Gombert, Hermann (1978) *Das Münster zu Freiburg im Breisgau.* Munich & Zurich.

Griffiths, Bede (1976, paperback 1978) *Return to the Centre.* London.

—— (1982, paperback 1983) *The Marriage of East and West.* London.

Grivot, Denis, and Zarnecki, George (1961) *Gislebertus: Sculptor of Autun.* London.

Hahnloser, Hans R. (1935) *Villard de Honnecourt: Kritische Gesamtausgabe des Bauhüttenbuches ms. fr 19093 der Parisen Nationalbibliotek.* Vienna.

Harvey, John (1950) *The Gothic World 1100–1600: A Survey of Architecture and Art.* London.

—— (1971) *The Master Builders: Architecture in the Middle Ages.* London.

—— (1972) *The Mediaeval Architect.* London.

Heer, Frederick (1962, paperback 1974) *The Medieval World: Europe 1100–1350,* tr. Janet Sondheimer. London.

Henderson, George (1967) *Gothic.* Harmondsworth.

Hopper, Vincent Foster (1938, repr. 1969) *Medieval Number Symbolism: Its Sources, Meaning, and Influence on Thought and Expression.* New York.

James, John (1982) *Chartres: the Masons who Built a Legend.* London & Boston.

Jones, Bernard E. (1950) *Freemasons' Guide and Compendium.* London.

Julian of Norwich, Dame (1901) *Revelations of Divine Love.* London.

Jung, C. G. (1933) *Modern Man in Search of a Soul,* tr. W. S. Dell and Cary F. Baynes. London.

Jungk, Robert (1958) *Brighter than a Thousand Suns,* tr. James Cleugh. London.

Katzenellenbogen, Adolf (1959) *The Sculptural Programs of Chartres Cathedral.* Baltimore.

Klein-Ehrminger, Madeleine (1980) *Cathédrale: Notre-Dame de Strasbourg.* Lyons.

Knoop, Douglas, Jones, G. P. and Hamer, Douglas (1938) *The Two Earliest Masonic Mss.* Manchester.

Kraus, Henry (1979) *Gold was the Mortar: the Economics of Cathedral Building.* London & Boston.

Kline, Morris (1964) *Mathematics in Western Culture.* New York.

Lazzarini, Pietro (1982) *Il Duomo di Lucca.* Lucca.

Leppin, Eberhurd (1983) *Die Elisabethkirche in Marburg.* Marburg.

Lewis, C. S. (1964) *The Discarded Image: An Introduction to Medieval and Renaissance Literature.* Cambridge.

Liebeschütz, Hans (1950) *Mediaeval Humanism in the Life and Writings of John of Salisbury.* London.

Lubac, Henri de (1959–64) *Exégèse médiévale: les quatre sens de l'écriture,* 4 vols. Paris.

McWilliam, Colin (1978) *Lothian except Edinburgh* (The medieval churches by Christopher Wilson). Harmondsworth.

Maier, August Richard (1910) *Niclaus Gerhaert von Leiden: ein niederländer Plastiker des 15 Jahrhunderts. Sein Werk am Oberrhein und in Osterreich.* Strasbourg.

Mâle, Emile (1913) *Religious Art in France: XIIIth century,* tr. Dora Nussey. London.

Maritain, Jacques (1930) *Art and Scholasticism,* tr. J. F. Scanlan. London.

—— (1942) *St Thomas Aquinas: Angel of the Schools.* London.

—— (1974) *Creative Intuition in Art and Poetry.* London.

Martinet, Suzanne (n.d.) *La Cathédrale de Laon.* Paris.

Miller, Malcolm (1980) *Chartres Cathedral: The Medieval Stained Glass and Sculpture.* London.

Moore, Sir Norman, ed. (1923) *The Book of the Foundation of St Bartholomew's Church in London* E.E.T.S. Vol. 163.

Mortet, Victor (1911) *Recueil des textes relatifs à l'histoire de l'architecture & à la condition des architectes en France au moyen uge, XIe XIIe.* Paris.

—— and Deschamps, P. (1929) (Vol. II of above, covering the twelfth and thirteenth centuries).

Moreau, Abel (n.d.) *La Cathédrale de Sens.* Paris.

Ouspensky, P. D. (1982) *Tertium Organum,* tr. the author and E. Kadloubovsky. London.

Panofsky, Erwin (1924) *Die deutsche Plastik des elften bis dreizehnten Jahrhunderts,* 2 vols. Munich.

—— (1957) *Gothic Architecture and Scholasticism.* New York & London.

Pennick, Nigel (1979) *The Ancient Science of Geomancy: Man in Harmony with the Earth.* London.

Pevsner, Sir Nikolaus (1945) *The Leaves of Southwell.* London & New York.

Primrose, The Rev. James (1913) *Mediaeval Glasgow.* Glasgow.

Reeves, Marjorie (1976) *Joachim of Fiore and the Prophetic Future.* London.

Rosenberg, Alfons (1967) *Engel und Dämonen: Gestaltwandel eines Urbildes.* Munich.

Ross, Anne, see Sheridan, Ronald

Rosslyn, Earl of (n.d.) *Rosslyn, its Chapel, Castle and Scenic Lore.* Kirkcaldy.

Ruskin, John (1898) *The Stones of Venice,* 3 vols. London.

Saltmarsh, John (1970) *Carving in King's Chapel.* Cambridge.

Seznec, Jean (1972) *The Survival of the Pagan Gods: the Mythological Tradition and its Place in Renaissance Humanism and Art,* tr. Barbara F. Sessions. Princeton.

Sheridan, Ronald, and Ross, Anne (1975) *Grotesques and Gargoyles: in the Medieval Church.* Newton Abbot.

von Simson, Otto (1956) *The Gothic Cathedral: the Origins of Gothic Architecture & the Medieval Concept of Order* with an appendix *On the Proportions of the South Tower of Chartres Cathedral* by Ernst Levy. London.

Stone, Lawrence (1955) *Sculpture in Britain: The Middle Ages.* Harmondsworth.

Stranks, C. J. (1973) *This Sumptuous Church: The Story of Durham Cathedral.* London.

Suger (1929) *Vie de Louis le Gros,* ed. and tr. H. Waquet. Paris.

—— (1979) *Abbot Suger on the Abbey Church of St-Denis and its art treasures,* tr., ed. and annotated by Erwin Panofsky, 2nd edn by Gerda Panofsky-Soergel. Princeton.

Swaan, Wim (1969) *The Gothic Cathedral,* with an introduction by Christopher Brooke. London.

Taylor, Henry Osborn (1963) *The Classical Heritage of the Middle Ages.* New York.

Velleius Paterculus (1967) *Res gestae divi Augusti,* ed. and tr. Frederick W. Shipley. London & Cambridge, Mass.

Warner, Marina (1976) *Alone of all her Sex: the Myth and the Cult of the Virgin Mary.* London.

Watts, Alan (1954, paperback 1983) *Myth and Ritual in Christianity.* London.

Watts, Sheldon J. (1984) *A Social History of Western Europe 1450–1720: Tensions and Solidarities among Rural People.* London.

Webb, Geoffrey (1956) *Architecture in Britain: The Middle Ages.* Harmondsworth.

White Jr., Lynn (1962) *Medieval Technology and Social Change.* Oxford.

—— (1968) *Dynamo and Virgin Reconsidered.* Cambridge, Mass.

Wiener, Claude (1981) *Pontigny.* Paris.

Worringer, Wilhelm (1927) *Form in Gothic,* tr. Herbert Read. London.

Index

Aachen, 152
Aberdeen Cathedral, 55
Adam, portrayals of, *73, 74, 78*, 101
Adam of St Victor, 127
Adelard of Bath, 190
Aigues Mortes, 65
Alan of Walsingham, 162
Albertus Magnus, 116
Albi, *124*, 148, 154
Albigensians, 48, 57, 85, 148
Amiens Cathedral, 41, 48, 50, 67, 177, 186, 199; west front and exterior, *2, 119*; interior, *22, 95*, 155, 172, 174; labyrinth, 156; sculpture, *28, 73, 94*, 96–7, 101, *116*, 140, 155, 159
Angels: in the writings of Dionysius the Areopagite, 17, 28, 131, 133; in Romanesque sculpture, *105*, 132; in Gothic sculpture and art, *108, 109, 110*, 125, 134–5, 140
Angers, 66
Angoulême, 66
Annunciation, the, *109, 114, 115*, 125, 135
Anselm, St, 48
Anthony of Egypt, St, 17
Arabic numerals, use of, 190
Arch, pointed, 12, 21, 39–41, 66
Archetypes, 4, 11, 41, 82, 108, 109, 123, 129, 195
Architects and master masons, 10, 12, 15, 50–2, 57, 67–8, 82–3, 157, 159–60, 167, 169, 180–2, 186, 193–6, 199; education and training, 12, 51, 186, 189, 190, 193; organization, 51–2; standing in society, 50–2
Arnolfo da Cambio, 154
Arthurian Legends, 68, 128
Assisi: Basilica of San Francesco, *56*, 77, 79, 148; Santa Chiara, 77
Augustine, St, 16, 70
Autun Cathedral, 20, *21, 29*, 40, 47, 69, 88, 94, *105*
Auxerre Cathedral, *120, 121, 122*, 148; sculpture, *97, 100*, 121, 126, 131; Easter dance, 156
Avignon, Palace of the Popes, *44*, 65

Bamberg Cathedral, 95, 96, 102, 177; Annunciation, *76*, 103, 135; Green Man, *79*, 103, 109; Rider of, *77*, 103
Barbastro, siege of, 12
Barcelona: Cathedral, 150, 155, *155*, 196; shipyards, 65
Bath Abbey, 152
Beauce, Jean (Texier) de, *14*, 34, 35, 152
Beauvais: Cathedral, *9*, 20, 67, 144, 152, 157, 178, 186, 199; St Etienne, 140
Becket, St Thomas à, 70, 73, *158*
Benedict of Nursia, St, 17, 63, 65
Bernard of Chartres, 95, 137
Bernard of Clairvaux, St, 25, 31, 67,

86, 87, 113, 127
Bernard of Cluny, 126–7
Beverley Minster, 59, 118, 155, 176
Blake, William, 13 quoted
Blanche of Castile, Queen of France, 82, *118*, 144
Boethius, 130
Boffill, Guillem, 12, 13, 23, 193
Bolsena, miracle of, 77, 79
Bony, Jean, 172
Bourges Cathedral, 67, 148, 172 (plan); exterior, *141*, 172; interior, *136*, 172–3; sculpture, *111, 112*, 128, 137
Boxley, Rood of, 159
Bridlington, 128
Bruges, Notre-Dame, 79
Brussels, St Gudule, 79
Building methods and techniques, 55, 56–9, 62, 148
Burgos Cathedral, 81, 82, *121*, 155

Caen stone, 58, 70, 170
Cambrai, 70
Cambridge, King's College Chapel, *153*, 177, 181, 190
Campbell, Joseph, 67
Canterbury Cathedral, 45, 70–3, 76, 82, 95, 154, 195; choir, *48*, 70, 73; nave, 76, 159; Bell Harry tower, *128*, 159; cloisters, *39*; glass, 95, *152*, 199
Capetian monarchy and the Gothic style, 15–16, 22, 70, 82, 93, 134
Carcassonne, 148
Carlisle, 177
Castel del Monte, 76
Castles, 9, 65
Caudebec, 152
Chambiges, Martin, 144
Charles IV, Emperor, 150, 152
Chartres Cathedral, 12, 13, 21, 24, 33 (plan), 34–7, 65, 67, 83, 96, 97, 102, 127, 129, 148, 154, 171–4, 184, 194; west front and exterior, *5, 140*, 171–4; towers, *5, 16*, 33, 34–7, *181*; north transept, *10*, 24, *99*, 101, *113*, 159–60; south transept, *11*, 24; Royal Portal, *18*, 33, 35, 48, 57, *61, 65, 66*, 67, 69, 89–94, 96; column statues, *61, 65, 66*, 89–94; glass and rose windows, *32*, 37, *87*, 113, *118*, 142, 191; interior, *19, 32*, 33, 54, 171–4; fire of 1194, 37, 83; labyrinth, 156
Chartres, School of, 11, 23, 40, 48, 67, 93, 184
Château Gaillard, 65
Chauvigny, *62, 63*
Chelles, Jean de, 50
Chester Cathedral choirstalls, 155
Chichester Cathedral, *51*, 76, 176
Christmas festivals and rites, 156–7
Churches and cathedrals: design and symbolism of, 23–4, 29, 57, 157–8;

169–74, 175–81; consecration of, 62
Cicero, 9
Cimabue, Giovanni, 77
Cistercians, 25, 31, 62–3, 65, 76, 83
City life, rebirth of, 10, 45
Civilization: source and purpose of, 9, 22, 23, 83; based on harmony of religion, art, science, and philosophy, 16, 22; sudden appearance of, 15; and individual inspiration, 14–16; and Christianity, 16–17, 57, 85; and the image of Man, 85, 96–7
Clermont-Ferrand, 191
Clonfert, 120
Cluny, *8*, 13, 18–20, 63, 69, 170
Cologne Cathedral, 102, 118, 147, 152, 199; choir, *61*, 62, 178; sculpture, 107, 135, 159
Consciousness: states of higher consciousness and art, 22, 69, 103, 180–1; and will, 9; collective, 50, 54, 69
Coucy, 65
Coutances Cathedral, 79, 160, *130*, 162
Creativity, 10, 12–14, 16, 68–9
Cult of the carts, 36–7

Dagobert, King, 25, 62
Dante Alighieri, 17, 55, 102, 132–4, 142, 155, 189
Denis, St, 25, 28, 103
Dijon: Chartreuse de Champmol, *110, 126*, 152; St Bénigne Abbey (now cathedral), 108, 167; Musée Archéologique, *81, 84*, 108; Notre-Dame, *26*
Dionysius the Areopagite, 11, 16–17, 28, 69, 102, 103, 131, 132–4, 184
Dome, as cosmic and imperial symbol, 16, 39, 167
Dominic, St, 77
d'Orbais, Jean, *15*
Dublin, Christchurch Cathedral, *50*, 73, 76
Duby, Georges, 48
Dunbar, William, 182
Dunblane, *24*, 41
Dunfermline Abbey, 21
Durand, Guillaume, 189, 190
Durham Cathedral, 13, 20–1, *35*, 43, 127, 157, 174

Easter dances and rites, 156, 157
Eckhart, Meister, 62, 194
Edward I of England, King, 152–3
Edward II of England, King, 153
Ekkehard, Margrave (see Naumburg)
Eleanor of Aquitaine, Queen, 30
Eleutherius, St, 25
Elgin, 176
Elias of Dereham, 54
Elisabeth of Hungary, St, *57*, 79–80
Ely Cathedral, *14, 131*, 162, 170, 174

England, architecture in, 70–76, 150, 152, 176–8; Anglo-Norman, 28, 170, 171, 174; Early English, 113; Decorated, 150; Perpendicular, 150
Erfurt Cathedral, 155
Eriugena, John Scotus, 11, 28, 69
Erminoldmeister, *114*, *115*, 125
Erwin, Master, *33*, 51, 80
Etampes, 90
Euclid, 93, 195
Eulalia, St, *192*, 196
Europe, North-Western: impact of Christianity on, 9, 10, 43, 57; and Gothic style, 21, 39–40, 55; expansion of, 43
Evreux, 170
Exeter Cathedral, 62, 109, *143*, 177

Farleigh, Richard, *51*
Festival of the Fools, 156–7
Fibonacci, Leonardo, 190
Figura, 96
Florence, 146, 155; Duomo, 154; Santa Maria Novella, *145*, 179; Santa Croce, 179
Fontenay, 31, 63
Fossanova, 76
Fountains, 65
Fourfold interpretation of scripture, 96
France, architectural styles in: Early Gothic, 13, 15–16, 25–31, 33–7, 57–8, 65, 169–71; High Gothic, 66–7, 171–4 of France; Rayonnant, *38*, 80, 177, 180; Flamboyant, 144
Francis of Assisi, St, 55, 77, 133
Frankl, Paul, quoted, 16, 122, 196
Frederick I (Barbarossa), Emperor, *165*
Frederick II Hohenstaufen, Emperor, 76, 149
Freiburg-im-Breisgau Minster, 59, 199; tower, *129*, *131*, *146*, 160, 181; Easter sepulchre, *86*, 112; sculpture, *71*, *74*, 101, *106*, *107*, 128, 135–6

Gelnhausen, 113
Gematria, number system, 190
Geometry, applied, 189–90, 191, 193
Gerhaerts, Nicolaus, *1*, 24
Gerhard, *61*
Germany, architectural styles in, 76, 79–81, 148, 150, 152, 177–8; Hall churches, 80, 176; Sondergotik, 150–1
Gerona Cathedral, *4*, 10–12, 13 (plan), 23, 193; Tapestry of Creation, *3*, 10–11
Gervase of Canterbury, 45, 70, 73
Gil de Hontañón, Rodrigo, 191
Gimpel, Jean, 57
Giotto di Bondone, 77
Gislebertus, *46*, 88, *132*
Glasgow Cathedral, 152, 159
Gloucester Cathedral, 153, 182
Goddess, the Great, 21, 43, 88, 119, 125
Gothic architecture and art: stylistic and technical features of, 15, 16, 21, 28–30, 39–41, 45, 65, 169–74, 176–81; realism and expressiveness of, 17, 85, 169; and conscience, 22; and the expression of happiness, 22–3, 55, 102–3;

spread of the style, 70–82; inner resources of the Masters of, 69, 82–3, 94, 194; spatial effects of, 163, 167, 168, 169, 184
Gothic civilization, 10; reconciles dualisms between Christianity and paganism, 10, 67–9, 87–8; origins of, 11, 12, 13, 15; appeal of, 16; ideal of man, 13, 15, 16, 55, 82, 85ff.; compared with contemporary science, 22, 193; achievement of its makers, 55, 57, 163; as the source of Western technological supremacy, 55, 56, 65; and scholastic philosophy, 40–1, 48, 66, 67, 163, 169; discovery of individual soul, 85, 96; compared with the tradition of classical music, 194
Green Man, the, 21, 103, 105–13, 115, 119, 121, 123; derived from Celtic, classical and Nordic gods, 68, 105, 121
Grosseteste, Robert, Bishop of Lincoln, 55, 145

Harvey, John, 51
Heer, Friedrich, 88
Henry of Blois, Bishop of Winchester, 69
Henry I of England, King, 10
Henry II of England, King, 66, 70
Henry III of England, King, 76, 81, 149
Henry VII, Emperor, 155–6
Henry VIII of England, King, 158
Henryson, Robert, 131
Hildegarde of Bingen, 116
Honorius of Autun, 89
Hrabanus Maurus, 105
Hugh of Avalon (Great St Hugh), 76
Hugh of Cluny, St, 20, 47
Hugh of St Victor, 96, 101, 173, 189
Hugo von Wettin, Bishop of Naumburg, 115
Hugues de Doignes, 23
Hurle, William, 162

Incarnation, Doctrine of the, 57, 85
Inspiration, 22, 35, 69
Ireland, architecture in, 76
Islam, architectural and intellectual influences of, 11, 12, 21, 40, 59, 129
Italy, Gothic style in, 76–7, 79, 178–80
Ivo de Ragheton, 177

Jacopo de Almannia, 77, *78*
James, John, 191
James II of Scotland, King, 182
James III of Scotland, King, 182
Jerusalem, 41, 65; image of Heavenly J., 158, 183
Joachim of Fiore, 189
John Cassian, St, 21 quoted
John of Salisbury, 66, 95
Joy, William, *153*
Juan de Colonia, *147*
Judaism, 11, 131
Julian of Norwich, Dame, 144
Jung, Carl G., 48, 50

Killaloe, 41, *25*
Kilpeck, *85*, 109, 119, 128; Sheela-na-gig at, *102*, 128

Kirkstall, 65
Kirkwall, 21
Krak des Chevaliers, 41

Labours of the Year, *28*, 43
Landshut, St Martin, *144*
Laon Cathedral, 43–4, 54, 66, 101, 177; towers, *27*, 44; interior, *46*, 66, 170–2; rose windows, 142
Laon, school of, 11, 40, 48
Las Huelgas, Cistercian Convent, 81
La Tène Celts, 105
Le Mans, *23*, 66, 94
León Cathedral, 81, 82, *101*, *134*, *142*, 180
Leoninus, 24
Lessay, 170
Lèves, Geoffroy de, Bishop of Chartres, 59–60
Levy, Ernst, 35
Lewis, C. S., quoted, 133
Lichfield, *150*, 190
Liège, St Trond, 57
Light, philosophy and symbolism of, 12–13, 15, 17, 27, 28, 29–30, 55, 160, 178, 184, 193
Lille, 157
Limburg-an-der-Lahn, 79, 177
Lincoln Cathedral, 58, 76, 144, 155, 176; exterior, 123, 157; pulpitum, 118, 154; Angel choir, *99*, *102*, 123; sculptures, *98*, 113; rose windows, 144
Llandaff, 76
Lock, Adam, 72
Longinus, 83
Louis VII of France, King, 30
Louis VIII of France, King, 82, 144
Louis IX of France, King (St Louis), 22, 25, 80, 82, *102*, 144, 149, 150
Louis the Pious, Emperor, 28
Lucca, 156, 180
Luzarches, Robert de, *9*, 41

Magdeburg Cathedral, 79, 103, 177; Johanneskirche, 199
Mainz, 115
Maitani, Lorenzo, *75*, 135
Manichaeism, 88, 126
Mantes, 142
Marburg, Elisabethkirche, *57*, *60*, 80, *88*, 109, 112–13, 154, 178
Mary, the Blessed Virgin: and the Eternal Feminine, 10, 43, 67, 93, 123, 125–7, 129, 140, 142, 144, 195, 196; shrines and relics of, 37, 83, 127, 176; portrayals of, *26*, *37*, *38*, 38, 43, *101*, 109, 113, 115, 196
Mason, Robert, *51*
Mass, the, 154, 168, 170, 186
Maulbronn, 76
Milan Cathedral, 152, 154, 180, 191
Moissac, 47
Mont St-Michel, 55, *117*, 137; Abbot of, 37
Montereau, Pierre de, 39
Music, 24, 194; and proportion, 31–2, 35–6, 100
Mysticism, 17, 87, 184

Naumburg Cathedral, 96, 177; pulpitum leaf and figure sculptures, *90*, *91*, 113, 115–16,

Naumburg Cathedral – *contd.*
154, 155; sculptures of Uta and
Ekkehard, *103, 104,* 129–30
Neoplatonism, 11, 13, 16, 23, 35, 48,
93, 113, 117, 132–3, 184, 194
Nicholas of Ely, *51, 53,* 54
Normandy, dukes of, 25; conquest of,
148
Norwich Cathedral, *38,* 62, *82,* 134,
154, 157, 170, 176
Noyon, *45,* 66, 115
Numerology, 29, 33, 35–6, 155, 162,
172, 189–90

Orvieto, *52,* 77, 79, 135, 144, 179
Oxford, 55

Pagan and prehistoric symbols and
survivals (see also Archetypes;
Green Man; Sheela-na-Gig;
Goddess, the Great), 21, 31, 43,
67–8, 87–8, 103, 108–9, 112, 118–
23, 126, 127–8, 156, 157, 169, 183, 184
Palma Cathedral, 150
Paris, Notre-Dame Cathedral, 30, 57–
8, 66–7, 113, 121; west front, *6;*
exterior and flying buttresses, *47,*
107, 172; interior, *43,* 54, 171; roses,
144; sculpture, *78, 96,* 102, 113
Parler, Michael, *154,* 191
Patrons, bishops and higher clergy as,
45, 47–8, 67, 149, 150
Paul, St, 16, 28, 87, *89,* 196 quoted
Peasants, contribution of to
cathedrals, 43–4
Perotinus, 24
Peterborough, *69,* 100, 170, 174
Philip Augustus of France, King, 79,
148
Philosophy, see Sapienta
Pierre de Montreuil, 186
Pilgrimages, 20, 158–9
Pisa, Baptistery, 155; Cathedral, 155,
156, 167, 195; Campo Santo, 180
Pisano, Giovanni, 131, 154, 155–6,
156, 195–6
Pisano, Nicola, 70, 77, 155
Pistoia, Sant'Andrea Church, 155
Plato, 11, 15, 16, 85
Poitiers, 66
Pontigny, *42,* 65
Prague, 118

Rahere, 10
Regensburg Cathedral, 118, 125, 131;
Annunciation sculptures, *114, 115,*
125
Rheims Cathedral, 67, 113, 177, 191,
199; west front, *7, 31,* 47, 48, 57;
exterior, *108,* 134, 157; interior,
174; sculptures, 70, *75, 89,* 94, 96,
102, *109,* 113–14, 118, 121;
labyrinth, 50, 156; rose windows,
144
Rheims, St-Rémi Abbey, 65
Rhineland art, 62
Richard the Lion-Heart, King of
England, 65, 148
Riemenschneider, Tilman, 159

Rievaulx, *157,* 199
Rochester, 94
Rognvald, Earl, 21
Romanesque architecture and art, 21,
57, 87–8, 118; in Burgundy, 18–20,
27, 63, 69; Anglo-Norman, 28, 170,
171, 174
Romanesque civilization, 9; and
monasticism, 18
Rome, St Peter's, 20, 167
Roritzer, Matthew, 191
Rose windows, 140, 142, 144
Ross, Dr Anne, 120 quoted
Rosslyn Chapel, *148,* 182–4, 191;
Prentice pillar, *147, 149*
Rouen Cathedral, *58,* 79, 148, 150, 157,
182
Rouen, St Ouen Church, *123,* 150
Rouen, St Maclou, 152
Ruskin, John, 77, 154, 167, 169
Rusticus, St, 25

St Bartholomew the Great,
Foundation Book of, 10
St-Benigne, see Dijon
St Davids Cathedral, 159
St-Denis, Abbey of (see also Suger,
Abbot): history and prestige of, 25,
26, 44; part played in origins of
Gothic, 11, 13, 69; west front, *12,*
25, 26; narthex, *20,* 25, 26; crypt,
13, 25; choir, 25, 28–31, 169–70;
nave and transepts, *20,* 25, 149
St Martin-des-Champs, Paris, 29, 169
St Sophia, Istanbul, 39, 167
Salisbury, *34, 36,* 54, 159, 176–7, 181
San Galgano, 76
Sanglier, Henri le, Archbishop of
Sens, 31
Santiago de Compostela, 157, 159
Sapientia, 93, 131, 183
Schwäbisch-Gmünd, *40,* 62, 178
Scotland, architecture in, 21, 41, 152,
182
Segovia, *125,* 180
Senlis, *17,* 48, 170
Sens, 12, 13, *15,* 31, 33, 36, 59, 65, 102,
113, 144, 152, 172, 184, 190
Seville, 180
Sheela-na-gig, 128–9
Sherborne Abbey, 152
Siena Cathedral, 146, 154, 155, 162
Silvanus, 108
Simon of Thirsk, 123–4
Simson, Otto von, 30
Sluter, Claus, *126,* 152
Soissons Cathedral, 66, 171
Soissons, St-Jean des Vignes, 199
Southwell, *92, 93, 94,* 113, 116–18, 154
Spain, Gothic style in, 81–2, 150, 178
Speyer Cathedral, 57, 177
Spoleto, 65
Strasbourg Cathedral, 80, 196; west
front and spire, *33,* 152, 181;
interior, 177–8; glass, *135,* 178;
sculpture, *68,* 80, *80,* 95–6, 135;
Masons' Lodge, 51, 195; Museum,
154, 191
Suger, Abbot of St-Denis, 13, 15, 25,

62, 69, 89, 93, 159, 193; as a patron,
25, 26–31, 43, 53, 69, 96, 113, 131;
works quoted, 27, 28, 30–1, 62, 131
Sully, Maurice de, Bishop of Paris, 66
Sylvester, Bernardus, 23
Syrlin, Jörg, 155

Tacitus, 88
Tauler, Johannes, 62
Technology, 9, 22; and medieval
inventions, 43, 45; and the
cathedrals, 65
Templar Order, 148; and churches,
167
Thierry of Chartres, 93, 193
Thomas Aquinas, St, 132, 163, 181
Toledo Cathedral, 82, *138,* 180 (plan)
Toscanella, 105
Tournai, 70, 79
Tours, *151,* 152
Trier, 109
Troyes, 152

Ulm Minster, *83,* 131, 152, 155, 177,
178, 195
Uta, Margravine of Meissen, see
Naumburg

Valenciennes, 70
Vaults, ribbed, 21, 62; construction of,
62; domical, 66
Vegetation, Romanesque and Gothic
portrayals of, 68, 69–70, 105–19,
184
Vegetius, 190
Velleius Paterculus, 14, 16
Venice, 77; Ca' d'Oro, *52;* Doge's
Palace, *55;* St Mark's Cathedral,
133, *133,* 167
Vercelli, San Andrea Church, *54,* 76
Vézelay, 20, *30,* 47, *64,* 69, 94, 129
Vienna, Stefansdom, 178
Villard d'Honnecourt, 186
Viollet-le-Duc, *6,* 194
Virgil, 109 quoted
Vitruvius, 190
Volpiano, Guillaume, 108

Walsingham, 127
Walter of Coventry, *73*
Wastell, John, *128,* 191
Wells Cathedral, 73–4; west front, *70,*
100–1, 152–3; interior, *49,* 73–4,
127, 153; chapterhouse, 176
Werve, Claus van, *110*
Westminster Abbey, 102, 135, 144,
177; Henry VII Chapel, 177
William of Sens, 45, *48,* 62, 70, 73, 76,
82, 176, 195
William the Englishman, 73
Winchester Cathedral, 157, 174
Windsor, St George's Chapel, 177
Witney, Thomas, *127*
Worcester Cathedral, 176
Worms Cathedral, 21, 103, 177
Wynford, William, 174

Yeveley, Henry, *39,* 48, 76, 159
York: St Mary's Abbey, 94; Minster,
154, 176, 177